MAKING SENSE OF SOMALI HISTORY

(Volume One)

Adonis & Abbey Publishers Ltd
St James House
13 Kensington Square,
London, W8 5HD
United Kingdom

Website: http://www.adonis-abbey.com
E-mail Address: editor@adonis-abbey.com

Nigeria:
Suites C4 & C5 J-Plus Plaza
Asokoro, Abuja, Nigeria
Tel: +234 (0) 7058078841/08052035034

British Library Cataloguing-in-Publication Data
A catalogue record for this book is available from the British Library

ISBN: 978-1-909112-79-7

MAKING SENSE OF SOMALI HISTORY

(Volume One)

Abdurahman Abdullahi
(Baadiyow)

TABLE OF CONTENTS

TABLE OF PICTURES

TABLE OF MAPS

TABLE OF FIGURES

DEDICATION

For my parents, Moallim Abdullahi and Zainab Afrah, my wife Muhubo Haji Iman, and our seven offspring for their endless support, care, patience and love;

For the educated Somali generation who have learned in a very hostile and difficult environment, and who are now mature and require a deep understanding of their history to repair their injured dignity;

For the compatriots striving to rebuild a better Somalia on the principles of common citizenship, rule of law, and commitment to the Islamic faith;

For all those who seek to understand the history of the current political conditions in Somalia.

ACKNOWLEDGEMENT

Publishing this book was made possible by the sponsorship of the Institute for Somali Studies (ISOS) to commemorate 20th anniversary of the opening Mogadishu University on 22 September, 1997. The views and historical interpretations expressed in this book are those of the author and do not necessarily reflect the official policy or position of ISOS. These interpretations are always subject to change, revision, and rethinking at any time.

ISOS is a research center affiliated to Mogadishu University which aims at research and analysis on Somali affairs in the Horn of Africa, and in the Diaspora. It focuses mainly on issues which are critical to the recovery and rebuilding of Somalia. ISOS conducts and coordinates researches, workshops, conferences, discussions, and dialogues; and disseminates findings, reports, and analysis through publications and events. ISOS publishes annually in print and online forms "*Somali Studies: A peer-reviewed academic journal for Somali Studies*", a multidisciplinary academic journal specialized in Somali studies.

Contact: isos@mu.edu.so   +252 1 858118
http://www.isos.so

PREFACE

The expression "to make sense of history" often comes with various meanings, which include; understanding, awareness, feeling, consciousness, judgement, and interpretation. My own intention with this book, "Making Sense of Somali History," is to foster conscious understanding and critical examination of Somali history through a variety of themes. In reconstructing Somali history and examining events that occurred in different times and spaces, my objective is to capture the Somali perspective through emphasis on human agency and its interaction with incurred ideas, institutions, and material production. This means to discover what worked for Somalia and what was accepted by the Somali society as useful and had a sustained influence on it. This also means to uncover what was borrowed from other nations and remained foreign, incompatible and inadaptable to Somali society and culture, and was ultimately changed or dismantled altogether. In undertaking this project, I consulted various literatures on Somali history in Somali, English and Arabic languages, and I was convinced of the critical need to rewrite our history through a thematic approach, which is what the reader will find in the two volumes constituting "Making Sense of Somali History."

The first volume deals with major historical periods before the collapse of the Somali state and besides introductory chapter, examines four themes: Somalia's ancient and medieval history, the role of Sufi orders and colonialism in reshaping Somali society, the rise and fall of Somali nationalism, and theoretical framework and perspectives of the Somali state collapse. The second volume deals with the aftermath of the Somali state collapse and examines four themes critical to this period of transition: the changing role of Somali women in culture and society, the re-shaping of the traditional clan elders; the shifting role of Islamism and reconciling the state and society; and the reconfiguration of the Somali national identity. These eight chapters, equally divided in these two volumes are part of a project aimed at providing a comprehensive perspective on Somali history, one reconstructed with a view to encompass all elements of society. It is based on the state-society model, which includes the role played by Islam and women in the historical studies. The old model, based on the dichotomous equation of state versus clan (Qaran iyo Qabiil), became obsolete and inadequate in part because it had failed to account for the roles of Islam and women in its attempt at historical construction. Historical themes in these two volumes recognize continuity and change in the dialectical process of making history, without exclusion of the possibilities of cyclical rise and fall of the state.

This book attempts to interpret history with human agency in mind, including the role and responsibility of our leadership in making and breaking the Somali states. Somali people made their history through interaction with the geography and ecology, with colonialism and decolonization, with regional political dynamics and super-power rivalry of the Cold War. My hope is that this book offers a brief thematic overview of Somali history to university students and the general public. Most importantly, it is meant to aid the new generations of Somalis, especially those aspiring to political leadership, to make sense of their own history and the prevailing issues and events that have shaped the Horn of Africa.

These two volumes are a serious attempt to transform, through the understanding of history, the prevailing political culture of Somali elites, frequently driven by personal interest, which is promoted through primordial attachment combined with nationalistic and Islamic rhetoric. At present, the predatory elite culture of the past—the very culture that caused the breakdown of the state—cyclically reincarnates into the fabric of the polity, undermining any hope for effective state recovery and legitimate state-society relations. I hope that by drawing lessons from the difficult and precarious Somali history, the people of Somalia will be able to rebuild their nation and their state in innovative ways, overcoming bad governance and misuse of the traditions: Islam and clan factors. I hope that Somalia will once again be a shining example of democracy, peace and prosperity.

Finally, some of the sections of the book may look repetitive, but for the sake of covering each chapter independently, some of these duplications are indispensable and justified. It is also justified from the Islamic point of view as evidenced in the Qur'an where narrations of the same stories are repeated many times to emphasize its importance and also to elucidate lessons relevant to various historical conditions. All chapters, except the first and second ones, are developed from the published papers in the different journals or as book chapters.

Abdurahman M. Abdullahi (Baadiyow)
Mogadishu, Somalia, 15th April, 2017

CHAPTER ONE

INTRODUCTION: MAKING SENSE OF SOMALI HISTORY

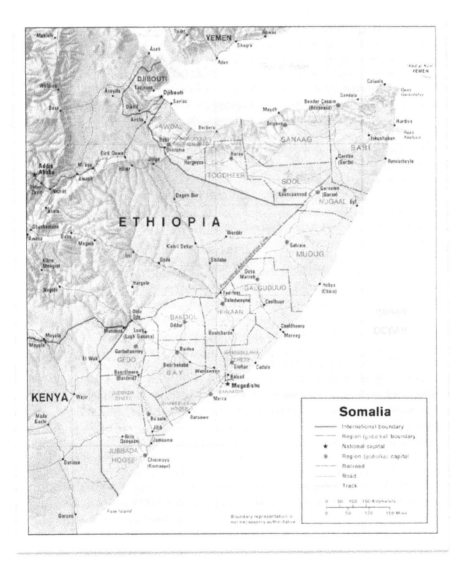

Map1. Political Map of Somali Federal Republic

> *"Allah changes not the condition of a people until they change what is related to their own conduct and behaviour" (The Qur'an, 13 :11)*

> *"The most effective way to destroy people is to deny and obliterate their own understanding of their history"* - *George Orwell*

The Somali people have passed through historical crossroads in recovering their state which collapsed almost three decades ago. The elite power struggle, which turned into a civil war fought in the name of clans, and at times in the name of Islam, protracted Somali agony and crushed national pride. However, with the awakening of a new generation raised during the civil war, as displaced refugees in the Diaspora and humiliated from the loss of their statehood, nostalgia for the re-emergence of Somali nationalism has grown. The emerging Somali nationalists despite sharing many characteristics with the fallen nationalists were tasked with recovering and resurrecting the postcolonial state of the Somali Republic, which fell in 1991. Moreover, the emerging nationalists are now more conscious of the culture of their society and have recognized the social realities of clans and Islam, with the objective of reconciling them with the Somali state. This conception marks a total paradigm shift from the vision of the old Somali nationalists who, having accepted modernization theory, attempted to diminish the role of tradition: clan and Islam. Therefore, the groundwork for the emergence of a more mature and experienced Somali nationalism is mounting.

In the vision of the resurgent nationalists, there are no longer any urgent programs of eradicating clannism, though there is acquiescence and adaptation in the belief that diminishing clannism requires long time socio-economic development and the nurturing of universal ideas. With respect to the Greater Somalia project, these resurgent nationalists are well aware of what binds all Somalis in the Horn of Africa and their extension in the Diaspora together: a common language and faith, and shared aspirations and destiny. Moreover, emotional attachment is alive, and a sense of collective belonging within all Somalis will remain forever. However, the conception of Greater Somalia, as was projected by the old nationalists, has experienced considerable changes in the transition from a project of political unity to a project of cultural and economic integration. This transition was gradual because of the failure of the old project in the test of history. In a new era of globalization and building larger economic and political blocks, in which all countries in Africa are eager to unite, there is not much room for the old conception of a Greater Somalia. Also, there is not enough room for those working to divide an already-divided nation in advocating for a separate entity, justified only on the basis of historical colonial division of the Somali nation.

Hence, nurturing resurgent generation of nationalists demands an objective historical reconstruction, and deconstruction of the dead ideas that failed to withstand the test of history. This is because the new generation desperately needs to make sense of their history in an objective way. This reconstruction has to shed a light on what went wrong with Somalia in order to be corrected, with the successful elements continued and developed further. Moreover, the new historical reconstruction should be aware that the fall of the Somali state was not simply the fault of political actors and outside enemies, but behind these politicians were academicians who misinterpreted history, provided wrong state-building concepts, and inculcated ideologies that deconstructed the very idea of Somaliness. Some of those claiming academic credentials have even justified and participated the internecine conflicts and civil wars. Therefore, Somali historiography requires critical review and bold investigation to sift the knowledge production that deepened and justified the division of the Somali society. This great task is what this brief thematic history of Somalia attempts to initiate and modestly undertakes in order to make sense of Somali history. Making sense of history is vital in developing a sense of connectedness to the homeland, to understand past challenges and crises, to preserve collective memory, and revive the conception of historical nationhood. At the beginning of this introduction, there are a number of important questions to briefly go through in order to set the stage of the topic. These questions are: what is the meaning of history? Who are historians? What is the definition and role of historiography? And what is the meaning of the philosophy of history? Understanding these conceptions helps to grasp the idea and the general theme of the book.

The word "history" entered the English language from the French terminology of *histoire*, the Latin word *historia*, and the Greek construction of *historie*.[1] The original Greek etymology is related to the verbs "to see" and "to know", and consequently to inquiry and knowledge. The

---

[1]   http://www.etymonline.com/index.php?term=history (accessed on February 6, 2017)

meaning of "history" was the same as the word "story" until the sixteenth century, and was signified any narrative of the past, whether fictional or factual. Since then, the two words took distinctive characters, and the word "story" drifted to connote only fictional narratives, either imaginary or fantasy, while the word "history" stood for factual, coherent narratives of the past. It engages events as a particular product of their time and space. Therefore, the study of "history" is the study of facts as perceived about the past. Gradually, the meaning of word "history" took the final shape and was restricted mainly to three correlated inferences. Firstly, narratives of all human past, or the recorded past of human civilizations. The construction of such narratives uses historical evidence such as folk tales, memories, artefacts, and written materials. As such, events that happened before written record are often termed "prehistory."[2] This term implies that where there is no record, there is no history. However, this term was rejected as pejorative, though an alternative term was not coined since it excludes 99.8 percent of the total existence of humanity.[3] Secondly, it also signifies what historians write in the form of narratives about the past as they observe, analyze, and revise the records and interpretations of their predecessors. Thirdly, the capitalized term "History", is also an academic subject which examines and analyses a sequence of past events and determines patterns of causes and effects. What is more, history is the human laboratory, the result of which offers an evidential base for pondering and an analysis of how societies functioned, factors that shaped history, and the changes that happened through the years. Furthermore, it offers insights into the human experience in time and space, enabling us to draw lessons from past mistakes and successes, as well as to avoid and discard, or emulate and develop further, respectively. This is very important because the present is the product of the past, which also furnishes the groundwork for the future.

The second conception that demands comprehension is to understand who historians are and what historians do to produce history. Historians are the engineers of history who relentlessly pursue the lives of our predecessors in order to understand the circumstances under which they toiled, the calamitous events that affected them, in addition to

---

[2]   S.J. De laet (ed.), *History of Humanity: Prehistory and the beginning of Civilization*, Vol.1, first edition (Routledge, 1994), 94-95.

[3]   Ibid..94.

their joys, grief, beliefs, and views of the world. Then, they mould these source materials to construct a historical narrative in an organized fashion. Like engineers who build houses, bridges, or any structure that uses raw or manufactured materials to mould different forms of structures and shapes, historians build history from the raw materials termed as "primary sources", and manufactured materials termed as "secondary sources."[4] History deals with a huge field of study and is divided into subfields to establish more focused academic fields. Even though such subdivision does not have a clearly demarcated borderline, according to the University of Kentucky, there are six types of history: political, diplomatic, social, cultural, economic, and intellectual.[5] Historians mostly focus on the political history such as the history of civilizations, the rise and fall of empires, and different types of governments. This is true and relevant regarding the history of human civilizations, as well as the particular historical experiences of a particular nation. History, being a subjective interpretation of the historians on the one hand and its basis of factual records on the other, offers fascinating dialogue and debates among historians. However, historians are individuals whose interests are to research, study, and construct the history of human activities to achieve a profound understanding with high objectivity. Moreover, they strive to be objective and critical in their work to avoid errors while deciphering historical facts. Needless to say, all human events are not fully recorded, and as one looks back in time, the available recorded historical sources become scarce, until no history point is reached. Obviously, historians cannot know everything and cannot find all of the sources that relate to the topics of their historical writings. Therefore, historians select from the available sources what they consider important and relevant, and at times recreate parts of the past, or in other words, "invent" and fill in the gaps, albeit with creative imaginations based on little or no evidence.

Moreover, most historians do not present all of the existing facts, but rather choose those facts that support their worldview and their school of thought while belittling or disregarding as insignificant facts they deem

---

[4] An Introduction to Historical Sources. Available from
    http://archives.govt.nz/exhibitions/currentexhibitions/chch/downloads/RHS-201-
    Introduction-to-Historical-Sources.pdf (accessed on February 7, 2017)

[5] See types of History by fields, produced by the University of Kentucky. Available
    from http://www.uky.edu/~dolph/HIS316/handouts/types.html (accessed on
    February, 2017).

irrelevant. At times, they amplify what suits their societies and beliefs, and disparage what they consider adversaries as irrelevant. This is the way some of those claiming to be historians lose their objectivities and become what are termed "conscientious historians."[6] These types of historians deliberately misrepresent and manipulate historical evidence to support their political views. That is why history is the subjective process of recreating past occurrences interpreted in accordance with various perspectives based on different theories concerning human behaviour. Thus, historians are mostly involved not only in discovering what happened in the past, but they are also engaged in the battle of ideologies and conflicts of beliefs; thus, required objectivity often becomes a victim and very rare in that sense.

The third concept to be addressed here is defining historiography. Historiography is simply defined as the study of the history of historical writing, or the body of historical literature, which means the methods of historians in developing history, and any corpus of historical work on a particular subject and their changing interpretations.[7] Different from the historical studies, historiography does not study the events of the past but delves into the interpretations of those events in the works of individual historians.[8] Historiographic studies are extremely crucial for colonized nations, which, as part of their liberation, require revisiting and discovering of various historical interpretations in the production of historical narratives of their countries. As such, they have to sift and analyze historical literature produced by colonial anthropologists and amateur historians. In the Somali context, it is very important to examine produced historical literature in the postcolonial period, some of which were written in the spirit of the official state narratives or biased clan-centric sprit. The postcolonial period is characterized with the growing battle of ideologies, liberalism versus socialism and emerging Islamism, which offered various interpretations for the historical events. Thus, historiographic studies discover various perspectives used in the historical analysis and find out contentious interpretations, historical

---

[6] William H. McNeill, Mythistory, or Truth, Myth, History and Historians. Available from https://www2.southeastern.edu/Academics/Faculty/jbell/mcneill.pdf (accessed on February 7, 2017).

[7] Conal Furay and Michael Salevouris, *The Methods and Skills of History: A Practical Guide* (Harlan Davidson Incorporated, 1988), 223. Moreover, consult, Tej Ram Sharma, *Historiography: A History of Historical Writing* (Concept Publishing Company, 2005).

[8] Fury and Salevouris, The Methods, 223.

gaps, and missing or less addressed issues in the particular historical event. Common questions of the historiographical studies include reliability of the sources, credibility of the authors, authenticity or corruption of the texts, various interpretations, and historical metanarratives. The historiography of any specific topic covers how historians have studied that topic, what sources are used, and the theoretical approaches pursued.[9] Historiography is studied by topics such as the historiography of Africa, the historiography of modern development of Islam, the historiography of the Somali state collapse, and so on.

Brief Notes on the Somali Historiography

Modern Somali historiography is dominated by Orientalist and anthropological perspectives that focus on primordialism and the static nature of the traditional structures. This perspective confers a superseding influence of clan factor over all other aspects. Scholars of this perspective belong to the modernization school, which focuses on the transition from tradition to modernity. The metanarrative of modernization theory is founded on the belief that traditional societies can be brought to development with the assistance of the developed countries in the same path taken by more developed Western countries. This theory essentializes the demise of tradition, which means Islam and clan in the Somali case.

Being the dominant paradigm in the 1950s and 1960s, most leaders of nationalist movements in postcolonial states followed modernization theory, including Somali nationalists. This pattern of scholarship is evident in the writings of the Orientalist Richard Burton and the

---

[9] Patrick Manning, "African and World Historiography." The Journal of African History / Volume 54 / Issue 03 / November 2013, 319 – 330. Also, see Bathwel A. Ogot, "African Historiography: From Colonial Historiography to UNISCO's General History of Africa." Available from http://rjh.ub.rug.nl/index.php/groniek/article/viewFile/16429/13919 (accessed on February 7, 2017). Also, Lidwien Kapteijns, "The Disintegration of Somalia: A Historiographical Essay." Bildhaan: An International Journal of Somali Studies, Vol. 1, 2008.

anthropologists I. M. Lewis and Enrico Cerulli. It has been passed on to their disciples Berhard Helander, Virginia Lulling, and Said Samatar. Edwad Said and other postcolonial scholars criticized the Orientalist method, ideology, and discourses. According to Said, the Orientalist paradigm allowed European scholars to represent the Oriental World as inferior and backward, irrational and wild, as opposed to a Western Europe that was superior and progressive, rational and civil—the opposite of the Oriental Other. Somali nationalists were influenced by the theory of modernization and adopted nationalistic programs and policies of eradicating tradition of clannism. Moreover, the military regime adopted aggressive policy of eliminating clannism *"Dabar-goynta Qabyaaladda."* Furthermore, Islam was dealt with as part of social culture, not as the comprehensive guide for all aspects of Muslim life.

Nonetheless, the plethora of literature produced by the proponents of this perspective has been criticized for the limitations of its scope and flaws in its interpretations, as well as for its lack of "historical specificity in the use of key concepts."[10] Hence, the other competing perspective challenged assumptions of the modernization perspective and adopted a critical perspective claiming to sustain specificity and historicity of the interpretation of their object of analysis. Scholars who proposed transformationist perspective were informed by the Marxist traditions. Prominent among these scholars are Lidwien Kapteijns, Ahmed Samatar, and Abdi Samatar. Ahmed Samatar and Abdi Samatar later changed their argument to a more comprehensive perspective founded on analyzing traditional Somali society within triangular model comprising clan attachment (*tol*), traditional law (*heer*), and Islamic Sharia. Ahmed Samatar further suggests the need for a successful synthesis of Somali kinship, Islamic teaching, and secular political theory.[11] According to this perspective, the internal dynamics and interactions between the elements of this model (clan, Heer, and Islam) are dialectically bound, and to be reconciled with the pervasive modernity represented by the state and its globalized context. However, Ahmed Samatar further recognizes that "the challenge of transition is the challenge of synthesis," and the

---

[10] Abdi I. Samatar, "Destruction of State and Society in Somalia: Beyond the Tribal Convention," The Journal of the Modern AfricanStudies30 (1992): 625-641.

[11] Ahmed Samatar, "The Curse of Allah: Civic Disembowelment and the Collapse of the State in Somalia" in Ahmed Samatar (ed.), *The Somali Challenge: From Catastrophe to Renewal?* (Lynne Rienner, 1994), 138

beginning of the "alteration of attitude and direction, to be followed by resolute assumption of the burdens of building necessary organizations and institutions."[12]

After the collapse of the state, a revisionist tendency had emerged in which the two perspectives cited above are criticized for accepting the constructed myths and utilizing the official narratives that contributed to the conceptualization of the old Somalia. Scholars who adopt this new perspective set out to demystify the conventional image of Somaliness as one constructed by idealist Somali nationalists, colonial historiographers, and post-colonial hegemonic clan interests. Moreover, they criticize constructed history as chauvinistic history, focusing on northern pastoralists to the exclusion of the southern agrarian population of Somalia. With this in mind, the revisionists have re-examined conventional national symbols and myths such as racial homogeneity, linguistic unity, and common historical experience. Prominent scholars in this group include Mohamed Mukhtar, Ali Jumale, Abdi Kusow, Hassan Mahaddala, and Catherine Besteman. The major themes of their perspective can be traced in two recent works comprising the collected papers entitled *The Invention of Somalia,* edited by Professor Ali Jumale Ahmed, and *Putting the Cart before the Horse,* edited by Professor Abdi Kusow. The revisionist scholars express regional disparities, clannishness of historical interpretations, and grievances about the one-sidedness of the northern nomadic bias of the Somali studies. However, according to the critique of Edward Alpers, revisionist historians fall into the same paradigm they seek to replace in the development of "a southern and agro-pastoral paradigm that is at least as frightened with regional ethnocentrism."[13] They create historical binary of nomadic north versus agro-pastoral south, which augments divisiveness of Somali society.

The fourth emerging perspective of historical analysis was spearheaded by this author. This perspective criticizes the above three perspectives for their neglect and exclusion of women and Islam in their historical research and analysis. This perspective began with the studies

---

12   Ahmed Samatar's view on the role of Islam in the reconstruction of Somali State, refer to footnote 104, Ibid., where he refers MA thesis of this author. Abdurahman Abdullahi, Tribalism, Nationalism and Islam: The Crisis of Political Loyalties in Somalia. MA thesis submitted to the Institute of the Islamic Studies, McGill University, 1992.

13   Edward Elper, "On Critique of the Somali Invention" in Ali Jumale (edt.), *The Invention of Somalia* (The Red Sea Press, 1995), 223-232.

of the crisis regarding political loyalties of tribalism, nationalism, and Islam, which most Somalis claim to adhere to.[14] The multi-level loyalties that create inner-conflict within individuals, societies and the whole nation, demand prudent ways of reconciling and synthesizing. It argues that Islam and women were missing components of the colonial and postcolonial Somali historiography.[15] Hence, this comprehensive perspective suggests to reconsider the dichotomous clan versus state scholarship (*Qabiil iyo Qaran*), and to enlarge the scope to a society versus state (*Bulsho iyo Qaran*) approach. In this case, while the nature of the state as the product of colonialism is concurred, structural change of the state can be easily adopted. However, the nature of society should be seen as transformed, which is essentially not clan-centric as anthropological perspective ponders. Moreover, within clan dynamics, it should be considered that patriarchal dominance that traditionally marginalized women in the decision-making process within society had changed significantly after the collapse of the state. Furthermore, the Islamic movement, which had evolved considerably after the collapse of the state, should also be accounted for in the comprehensive historical analysis.[16] This perspective argues that any success of Somali nation-

---

[14] Abdullahi, Tribalism, Nationalism and Islam.

[15] Somali Women's study is growing and new historiography is appearing. See, Lidwien Kapteijns, "Women and Crisis of Communal Identity: The Cultural Construction of Gender in Somali History," in *The Somali Challenge: From Catastrophe to Renewal?* ed. Ahmed Samatar (Colorado: Lynne Reinner Publishers, 1994), 212, Mohamed Haji Ingiriis, 'Sisters; was this what we struggled for?': The Gendered Rivalry in Power and Politics. Journal of International Women's Studies Vol. 16, No. 2 January 2015, 382; Christine Choi Ahmed. "Finely Etched Chattel: The Invention of Somali Women" in *The Invention of Somalia*, edited by Jumale Ahmed. (Lawrenceville: The Red Sea Press,1995); Judith Garner, and Judy Al-Bushra, *Somalia: The Untold Story, the War Though the Eyes of Somali Women* (London: Pluto Press, 2004). Kapteijns, Lidwien, and Maryan Omar Ali. *Women's voices in a man's world: women and the pastoral tradition in Northern Somali Orature, c.1899-1980* (Portsmouth, NH: Heinemann, 1999); Hamdi Mohamed, *Gender and the Politics of Nation Building: (Re) Constructing Somali Women's History* (Lambert Academic Publishing, 2014). There also a number of MA and PhD theses.

[16] Abdurahman Abdullahi, *The Islamic Movement in Somalia: A Case Study of Islah Movement (1950-2000)* (Adonis & Abbey, 2015). Also, Abdurahman Abdullahi, *Recovering the Somali State: Islam, Islamism and Transitional Justice* (Adonis & Abbey, 2016). The whole idea behind this perspective began with the MA thesis, Abdullahi,

building depends on the reconciliation between nationalism and Islam on one hand, and accommodating clan attachments on the other. In achieving this goal, this author had suggested what he termed as MEGA reconciliation, or in other words, "Reconciling the State and Society", which in principle concurs with the idea of the "triangular synthesis", lately suggested by Ahmed Samatar with more developed and nuanced way.[17]

Brief Notes on the Philosophy of History

The philosophy of history provides conceptualization behind drivers of history, such as the role of Allah (God), the human agency, and the role of material circumstances. It begins with determining what is the proper unit for the study of the human past, the individual subject, *polis* ("city"), sovereign territory, a civilization, culture, or the whole of the human species.[18] Then, it pursues the discovery of "any broad patterns that can be discerned through a study of history, and what factors, if any, determine the course of history, and the goal, destination, and driving force of history."[19] The philosophy of history is different from historiography and the history of philosophy. Historiography is concerned with the methods and development of history, while the history of philosophy is the study of the development of philosophical ideas through time. Generally, there are three main views of history in the Western tradition. These are cyclical, providential, and deterministic views.[20] The initial conception of the cyclical view was produced by the Greeks, and asserts that history has no beginning, no end, and no goal, but only repeats itself in a circular motion, just as the four seasons of spring, summer, autumn, and winter occur year after year. This view asserts that history has no meaning and that there is no God or purpose

---

Tribalism, Nationalism and Islam.

[17] Abdurahman Abdullahi (Baadiyow) and Ibrahim Farah, Reconciling the State and Society in Somalia. Available form
https://www.scribd.com/document/15327358/Reconciling-the-State-and-Society-in-Somalia (accessed on February 20, 2017).

[18] http://www.newworldencyclopedia.org/entry/Philosophy_of_history
[19] Ibid.

[20] For descriptions and analysis of approaches for writing history, the philosophy of history and historiography, consult, Andrew Szanajda, *Making Sense in History: Historical Writing in Practice* (Bitngduck Press LLC, 2007).

behind occurrences. The cyclical view was later developed in China and in the Islamic world by Ibn-Khaldun, and was applied in the rise and the fall of empires and states.[21] In the West, the cyclical view was used to explain the rise and fall of the empires, conceiving the human past as a series of repetitive rises and falls.[22]

The second philosophical view is the providential view of history (the Christian view of history), which asserts, contrary to the cyclical view, that history has a starting point and progresses in a straight line toward a specific goal. In this view, history is completely guided by God and everything is determined in advance and that humankind is unable to do anything about it; he is not more than a tool moved by God.[23] This view was reversed in the Western philosophical tradition in considering the human being, rather than God's providence, as the main driver of history. This view was put forth at the beginning of the secular view of history and the emergence of secular deterministic theories of history.[24] For instance, Hegel argued that history is a constant process of dialectic conflict, with each thesis encountering an opposing idea or antithetical incident which produces synthesis. In contrast to Hegel, who advocated a spiritual view of history and asserted that it is the idea that drives history, Karl Marx asserted that it is material forces that drive history, and presented his theory of "historical materialism."[25] In all three views, everything in the world happens irrespective or independently of individual's free will and the idea of the free human individual who can choose and carry moral burdens disappears.[26]

Having seen some glimpses of the Western viewpoint of the philosophy of history, let us now turn to the Islamic view. The Islamic

---

[21] Ibn Khaldun, *An Arab Philosophy of History: Selections from the Prolegomena of Ibn Khaldun of Tunis (1332-1406)* (Darwin Press, 1987).

[22] Shigeru Nakayama, "The Chinese "Cyclic" View of History versus Japanese "Progress," in *The Idea of Progress* (ed.) by Jurgen Mittelstrass, Peter McLauphlin, Arnold Burgen (Berlin: Walter de Gruyter &Co., 1977), 65-76.

[23] C.A. Patrides, *The Grand Design of God: The Literary Form of the Christian View of History* (Routledge Library Edition, 2016).

[24] G. W. F. Hegel, and Leo Rauch, *Introduction to The Philosophy of History: With Selections from The Philosophy of Right* (Hackett Publishing, 1988).

[25] T. Borodulina, *On Historical Materialism* (Progress Publishers in the Union of Soviet Socialist Republics, 1972).

[26] A concise narration of the Western and Eastern Philosophy of History excluding Islamic philosophy, refer to David Bebbington, *Patterns in History: A Christian Perspective on Historical Thought* (England: Inter-Varsity Press, 1979).

philosophy of history is founded on the belief that Allah gave humans the autonomy and mind to judge rationally. He also gave them messages sent through the prophets that offer them general guidelines in all aspects of their life. He made them *khalifat Allah* ("successor to God") to administer the universe according to his general guidelines and urged them to use their intellect to discover his natural laws. He gave the humans freedom of choice, and liberty to obey the prophets of Allah and accept His guidance or to reject and deviate from it. Thus, humans are responsible for their deeds and actions in this world and are accountable in the hereafter since they have been given intellect and freedom of choice. The Qur'an repeatedly refers to the rise and the fall of nations and urges humans to learn from the lessons of bygone nations.[27] The main causes of the decline and destruction of the civilizations are related to the deviation from Allah's moral guidance at the personal and social levels. Islam includes a providential element in its conceptualization of history, but is not fatalistic, and does not negate the role of ideas and economic factors as drivers of history.[28] What Islam refuses in its historical conception is excluding the role and responsibility of the humans or just pointing the finger to Allah's grand design without human responsibility.[29] Hence, according to this view of history, whatever happened to the Somalis during their long history, they bear its responsibility, particularly their leaders and simply censuring external factors is inconsistency with the Islamic view of history. There are many verses in the Qur'an which capture bluntly Islamic conception of history. For example, "Whatever misfortune happens to you, is because of the things your hands have wrought, and for many (of them) he grants

---

[27] See the Qur'anic verse "There was certainly in their stories a lesson for those of understanding. Never was the Qur'an a narration invented, but a confirmation of what was before it and a detailed explanation of all things and guidance and mercy for a people who believe." (12:111).

[28] The *American Heritage Dictionary* defines fatalism as "The doctrine that all events are predetermined by fate and are therefore unalterable." In opposition to fatalism stands determinism which says that every event has a cause that necessarily precipitates the event. In both concepts of fatalism and determinism, there is no human free will.

[29] Zaid Ahmed, "Muslim Philosophy of History", in edited by Aviezer Tucker,*A Companion to the Philosophy of History and Historiography* (Published Online, 2009), 437-445.

forgiveness" (The Qur'an 4:30). Moreover, another Qur'anic verse clarifies whatever happens in this world is because of our deeds whether it is bad or good. "Corruption has spread on land and sea on account of what people's hands have wrought" (The Qur'an, 30:41). Furthermore, other Qur'anic verse even clarifies more directly stating "We have shown the path to humans, and they are free to choose the right path and be thankful or to choose the path of ingratitude" (The Qur'an, 76:3)

Organization of the Book

This book is the first of a series of books aimed at producing an overview of Somali history in a comprehensive perspective. This ambitious project and the books produced are designed to answer major historical questions, using accessible language while combining both thematic and chronological approaches. The first book consists of five chapters, some of which were previously partially published as academic papers in various academic journals or as book chapters. These papers were revised, modified, and enlarged to suit the thematic historical reconstruction of Somalia. As the title of the book implies, the sense of Somali history delves into the deep history of the Somali peninsula, the ancient history, the medieval period, the role of Sufi orders, the impact of colonialism, the rise and the fall of Somali nationalism, and the collapse of the Somali state. It addresses Somali history in thematic form until the collapse of the state. Some sections of the book, particularly the historical backgrounds, may seem repetitive, but for the sake of covering each topic independently, some of these duplications are indispensable and justified. These chapters offer a panoramic overview and are not intended to give a deep historical analysis; rather, they provide further reading material for those interested for a deeper scholarship. The forthcoming second book of this series will discuss the events following the collapse of the state, and will focus on the reconfiguration of the state and society in four major spheres, which comprise the reconfiguration of the role of Somali women, the changing role of traditional elders, the reconfiguration of the national identity, and the way for ward of how to reconcile the state and society in order to rebuild viable and stable Somali state. Finally, general conclusions will be drawn and recommendations will be provided. So far, this introductory chapter provided definitions of some important conceptions indispensable for the study of history. These conceptions include the meaning of history, historians and their role, defining historiography with notes of Somali historiographic studies, and the philosophy of history clarifying the difference between Western philosophy of history and Islamic philosophy of history. Grasping meaning of these conceptions are essential to understanding the idea and the general themes of this book. Following paragraphs will briefly introduce the other four chapters of this volume.

The second chapter of this book constructs the history of the Somali peninsula from ancient times to the medieval period. It offers a deep historical awareness in depicting the Somalian peninsula as a kernel of ancient civilizations and developed independent states in the medieval Islamic period. However, the balk of the general historiography of the Somali Peninsula presents a picture as if its history began with the colonial period, while its rich ancient and medieval Islamic history have been given less attention.[30] This shortcoming diminishes a sense of pride and historical awareness of the Somalis and reduces the value and importance of the rich and unique human civilizations that flourished once upon a time in this region. A sense of history is vital to developing a sense of connectedness to the homeland and to understand past challenges and crises, to preserve collective memory, and revive the conception of historical nationhood. Therefore, this chapter aims to make an overview of the less-addressed historical period of the people of the Somali Peninsula, and to reconstruct, in a concise manner, its ancient and medieval Islamic history. The literature review covers the ancient and medieval Islamic civilizations and emergence of Muslim sultanates in the Somali territory. The chapter forms a conclusion on the major historical themes of the period under study and puts forth contested narratives that require further attention and research.

The third chapter of this book explores early reconfiguration of the Somali society done by the Sufi orders and colonialism. It looks at the period that begins in the pre-colonial era, which is divided into three major phases interactively overlap each other. The first phase explores the social impact of the revival of Islam embodied in the role of the Sufi orders. The second phase investigates the incursion of multiple

---

[30] Recently, professor Muhammad Shamsaddin Megalommatis developed a study course on "History of pre-Islamic Somalia". Available from https://www.academia.edu/23220147/HISTORY_OF_PRE-ISLAMIC_SOMALI A_-_COURSE_DESCRIPTION_Muhammad_Shamsaddin_Megalommatis. (accessed on January 17, 2017).

colonialism in the Somali Peninsula, which provoked Somali resistance in the form of sporadic and organized militant, and peaceful resistances. In the process of interaction with the colonial administrations, Somali people have learned about modern warfare, material production techniques, and modern approaches to politics. The third phase explores the impact of colonialism on the education sector and the production of westernized elites. During this phase, political clannism was developed with the introduction of the political parties. Moreover, in this phase, a bifurcation of the elites into Islamists, non-Islamists and westernized was observed, and the growing tension began between modernity and tradition.[31] This state of affairs triggered conflict among the elites and politicized clans, thus prompting an Islamic awakening. At this point, state-society relation drastically deteriorated, succumbing to disastrous implications that finally collapsed the Somali state in 1991.

The fourth chapter of this book produces the history of the rise of Somali nationalism and the causes of its fall, examining two nationalist projects: curbing clannism and pursuing Greater Somalia. It also examines state policies in the civilian and military periods with their moderate and radical approaches in pursuing nationalist goals. The political consciousness and the institutional expression of nationalism were delayed in the Somali Italian colony during the Fascist era (1923-41), in which all socio-political activism was banned. However, this situation was changed after the defeat of Italy in WWII in the Horn of Africa in 1941. The British Military Administration (BMA), who took over the administration of Somali territories, granted freedom of speech and association.[32] Thus, the process of Somali liberation from colonialism began with the emergence of the first nationalist movement,

---

[31] The categorization of the elites into Islamists, non-Islamists, and Westernized is in accordance with the Qur'anic categorization of the Muslims as the following Qur'anic verse bluntly shows. "Then We have given the Book for inheritance to such of Our Servants as We have chosen: but there are among them some who wrong their own souls; some who follow a middle course; and some who are, by Allah's leave, foremost in good deeds; that is the highest Grace." (The Qur'an, 35:32). This categorization avoids generalizing Muslim elites who are not Islamic activists as secularists. Some westernized elites may claim to be secular which is also debatable.

[32] Robert Patman, *The Soviet Union in the Horn of Africa: The Diplomacy of Intervention and Disengagement* (Cambridge: Cambridge University Press, 1990),34. Also, Cedric Barnes, "The Somali Youth League, Ethiopian Somalis and the Greater Somalia Idea, 1946-48." Journal of Eastern African Studies Vol. 1, No. 2, 277-291, 2007, 80.

the Somali Youth Club on 15 May 1943. The rise of Somali nationalism and the process of state-building was a long process and its fall did not occur abruptly, but rather went though different stages of ups and downs. These two processes were intermittent and cross-cutting until the final fall, the breakdown of order and the collapse of the state. This chapter explores the history of the rise and the fall of Somali nationalism and its nation-state by traveling through historical stations of the emergence and formation of the nationalist elites. Moreover, it examines performance of the nationalist elite in the process of the state-building in dealing with the political clannism and the Greater Somalia project. The final section of the chapter comprises the conclusion section.

The fifth chapter of this book explores the Somali state collapse and offers theoretical background and historiography of the state collapse. This subject matter had been attracting immense academic interest for about last three decades. However, the bulk of these studies have focused on the topics of practical relevance in formulating options of intervention for the international community, such as descriptions of human suffering and agony as consequences of state collapse, civil wars, piracy, and extremism in the name of Islam and terrorism. Therefore, major themes of the works presented initially focused on the situational analysis of the civil war and humanitarian disaster, the coping mechanisms of the Somalis both inside Somalia and in the Diaspora, international humanitarian intervention, and recently, international terrorism and security issues.[33] Moreover, global studies on state collapse were growing throughout academic circles and Somalia was exposed as an emblem of a classic example of state collapse.[34] However, most of the produced works are in the form of articles and occasional academic papers.[35] Obviously, these writings look at the Somali state failure and

---

[33] Somalia is projected as a safe haven for terrorist groups after the events of 9/11, with a number of institutions closed, and groups identified as having terrorist links.

[34] Examples of this could be Harvard University's "Failed State Project" of the Failed States under the auspices of the World Peace Foundation and "Failed State Project" at Perdue University. These two projects have produced considerable literature and research papers on this topic.

[35] Terrence Lyons and Ahmed Samatar, *Somalia: State Collapse, Multilateral intervention, and Strategies for Political Reconstruction* (Washington: The Brooking Institution Occasional Paper, 1995); Ahmed Samatar (ed.), *The Somali Challenge: From Catastrophe to Renewal?(Lynne Rienner Publishers, 1994;* Hussein M. Adam, "Somalia: A Terrible Beauty Being Born?" In I. William Zartman (ed.), *Collapsed States: The Disintegration and Restoration of Legitimate Authority* (London: Lynne Reinne, 1995); Walter S. Clarke,

collapse from different theoretical perspectives, and most of the time, a comprehensive picture of the causes of the collapse is not drawn. Moreover, the analysis of the most researchers has focused on the operational and proximate causes, leaving the genesis of the state collapse as marginal. Filling this lacuna, this chapter intends to investigate, sift, and regroup the perspectives of the various academic fields into major themes to identify main factors and to build a comprehensive picture that contributed to the collapse of the Somali state. To do so, firstly, an overview of the rise and fall of the Somali state is recaptured. Secondly, theories of state capabilities, conflicts and impacts are briefly produced. Thirdly, major academic perspectives of the Somali state collapse are recollected, analyzed, and classified into genesis, operational, and proximate causes. Finally, conclusions will be drawn and recommendations are offered.

In conclusion, in reconstructing Somali history and examining the events that occurred in different times and spaces, this book emphasizes Somali agency and its interaction with the incurred ideas, institutions, and material production. This entails discovering what worked well for the Somalis, accepted by society, and believed its usefulness to sufficiently remain intact and sustained. Conversely, to uncover what was borrowed from other nations, considered alien, incompliant, and inadaptable to the societal culture and norms that have fallen apart and vanquished. While doing that, we should not shed tears or be nostalgic about what caused the agony of the people and ultimately failed the test of the historical experiment undertaken by the late Somali nationalists. This doesn't mean, however, to demean the noble cause of the founders of Somali nationalism, the fathers of the nation, or to put all of the subsequent nationalists in one basket. Rather, what we are concerned is to uncover the policies and actions, as well as their consequences during the colonial and postcolonial periods and their cumulative effect that caused the collapse of the state after 30 years. Finally, the imagination and production of Somali history should be grounded on the deep understanding of the two pillars of Somaliness: Islam and clan, and how

---

"Somalia: Can a Collapsed State Reconstitute itself?" In Robert I. Rotberg (ed.), *State Failure and State Weakness in a Time of Terror* (Washington: Brooking Institution Press, 2000); Brons, Maria, "The Civil War in Somalia: Its Genesis and Dynamics" Current African Issues, *(11*, Uppsala, Nordiska Africainstitutet, 1991); Virginia Luling, "Come back Somalia? Questioning a Collapsed State" Third World Quarterly, 18:2 (1997), 287-302.

to reconcile them with the modern state. Singling out clan factor, as has been the focus in the previous historiographical studies, and aggrandizing its divisive role is misleading. Also, disregarding Islam and its integrative role, or merely looking at it as useless societal culture in the state-building or as a threat in building modern state, is indeed, existential threat to our people. In particular, Somalia has crossed the threshold of dominated secular views after the collapse of the state and emergence of the various Islamic organizations, actively operating in all sectors. Currently, Islam and its promoters stand firm as the most organized and motivated group in Somalia, with widespread societal networks and supporters.

Further Readings

Ahmed, Zaid. "Muslim Philosophy of History", in edited by Aviezer Tucker, A Companion to the Philosophy of History and Historiography. Published Online, 2009), 437- 445.

Bebbington, David. Patterns in History: A Christian Perspective on Historical Thought. England: Inter-Varsity Press, 1979.

Hegel, G. W. F. and Rauch, Leo. Introduction to The Philosophy of History: With Selections from The Philosophy of Right. Hackett Publishing, 1988.

Sharma, Tej Ram. Historiography: A History of Historical Writing. Concept Publishing Company, 2005.

Szanajda, Andrew. Making Sense in History: Historical Writing in Practice. Bitngduck Press LLC, 2007.

CHAPTER TWO

THE HISTORY OF THE SOMALI PENINSULA: FROM ANCIENT TIMES TO THE MEDIEVAL ISLAMIC PERIOD

Map2. Somali people's territory in the Somali Peninsula

Have they not travelled in the earth and seen how was the end of those before them? They were stronger than these in power (The Qur'an, 30:9)

Until lions have their historians, tales of the hunt, Shall always glorify the hunters   - Chinua Achebe

History is the study of past events using the sources of what is written, what is said, and what is physically preserved. It is also a subjective process of recreating past occurrences and is a matter of perspective. It gives people a sense of identity, prevents them from repeating previous mistakes, and makes them aware of their roots, as well as those of different cultures, peoples, and countries. History can be studied at different levels, such as national, regional, and global, but these entire levels exhibit that humankind is not isolated from each other in the past and present, and are interdependent. Historians, specifically Western historians, divided historical studies into four periods. The first period is called Prehistory, which begins at the first appearance of human beings on earth and continues until the development of writing systems. The prehistoric era is also subdivided and named according to tool-making technologies, such as Stone Age, Bronze Age, and Iron Age.[1] Archeology is the subject matter and the only source for the study of this period. The second period is called Ancient History (3600 BC-500 AD) which begins with the first records in writing and ends after the fall of several big empires, including the Western Roman Empire (285-476 AD), the Han Dynasty in China (206 BC–220 AD), and the Gupta Empire in India (320- 550 AD). The third period is called Medieval History (500-1500 AD), which begins with the fall of the aforementioned empires and ends with the invention of the printing press (1440), the discovery of America (1492), and the Ottoman Empire's conquest of Constantinople (1453). The fourth period is called Modern History (1500-present) which begins from the end of the medieval period up until today. Each period is sub-divided into phases with specific common characteristics although each phase generally lacks clearly demarcated lines and tends to overlap one another. Evidently, the Western historical narrative has been portrayed as the universal history, which rightly conforms to the theory of power relations and the production of history.

---

[1]   Grahame Clark, *World Prehistory: A New Outline* (Cambridge University Press, 1971)

To sift through what is generally shared from what is distinct and specific in the history of humankind, it is evident that the first two periods, Prehistory and Ancient History, could be considered to a certain degree as the general history of all humankind, with some differences in the different continents and regions. For example, while some regions are still in the prehistoric period, others may be in the ancient or even in the medieval period. So, we should consider historical periods merely as a general trend of human history. With respect to the third and fourth periods, the trends in the human history substantively diverged, and its universality became dubious. For instance, the Dark Ages or the Medieval period in the European history (500-1500 AD) was a period of intellectual darkness and barbarity in Europe, whereas most of this period marked as the golden period for the Islamic civilization.[2] Islamic civilization produced great scientific, philosophic, and artistic culture, while at the same time it assimilated scientific knowledge of other civilizations such as Greece, Persia, and China, and transferred later to Europe.[3] Therefore, from now on, we will use the terms "European Medieval History" and "Islamic Medieval History" to illustrate commonality in the time and difference in the developmental stage. Moreover, modern European history, which is characterized by iconic periods such as the Renaissance (1400-1700),[4] the Industrial Revolution (1760-1840),[5] colonization (16-mid 20) centuries,[6] and the age of technological advancement, was totally different from the conditions of

---

[2] On Islamic civilization in the Dark Ages of Europe, refer to Roger Savory, *Introduction to Islamic Civilization* (Cambridge University Press, May 28, 1976); International Institute of Islamic Thought, *The Essence of Islamic Civilization: Volume 21 of occasional papers* (International Institute of Islamic Thought, 2013); and Gustave Le Bon, *The world of Islamic civilization* (Tudor Publication Co., 1974).

[3] Masoumeh Banitalebi, Kamaruzaman Yusoff and Mohd Roslan Mohd Nor, "The Impact of Islamic Civilization and Culture in Europe During the Crusades." World Journal of Islamic History and Civilization, 2 (3): 182-187, 2012.

[4] The Renaissance was a period in European History in (14-17) centuries, considered as the cultural bridge between the Middle ages and Modern History. It started in Italy and spread to the rest of Europe.

[5] The IndustrialRevolution was the transition from hand production to the use machines such as chemical manufacturing, Iron production, excessive use of water power, stream power, and rise of factory system. Textile was the icon of the Industrial Revolution with mass production using modern technology.

[6] Jurgen Osterhammel, *Colonialism: A Theoretical Overview* (M. Wiener, 1997).

the colonized countries. This period was, for instance, a time of decadence in the Islamic civilization, and an era of colonialism and nation-state formation in the nineteenth century. Thus, this period could be called, in the Somali context, the "Pre-colonial, Colonial and Post-Colonial Periods."

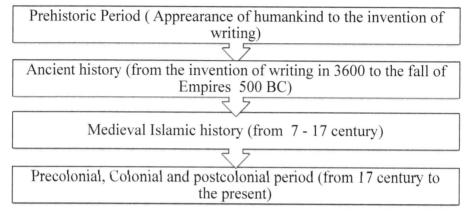

Fig.1. The universal historical periods tuned to Somalia

Hence, in the case of Somalia, being part of Islamic civilization, the third period of its history begins with the introduction of Islam in the Somali Peninsula in the seventh century and ends with the collapse of the Muslim states of Ajuran and Adal sultanates in the seventeenth century. The fourth period could be considered as the era of decadence, as symbolized in the pre-colonial era of fragmented states followed by reconfiguration of the society through colonialism and the postcolonial state. The pre-colonial phase begins with the fall of Islamic sultanates in the Somali Peninsula and the establishment of clan-based emirates until colonial incursion in 1880s. It was followed by the colonial era from 1880s to 1960, in which Somalia experienced multiple colonialism with its rancour and hostility. Finally, the postcolonial phase begins from 1960 and continues until the current time, which is characterized by the rise and fall of the state and its subsequent catastrophic implications. Having laid the frame of Somali history, we will turn now to pen an overview of the ancient and Islamic medieval period of a history of the people of the Somali peninsula, who are often thought of as "the people without history". Herein, we exhibit that colonized people have their own historical trajectory in parallel that of European history.[7]

The Somali peninsula is located on the strategic trade route connecting Africa, Asia, and Europe. It is the cradle of the human race and the kernel of ancient civilizations. The Cushitic speaking people to whom the Somalis belong have dwelled in this region as indigenous people for the past 7000 years. This evidence challenges the previous hypothesis on the origins of the Somali people, which asserts that the Somalis migrated either from the southern Ethiopian highlands in the first century AD, or from the south Arabian Peninsula after the tenth century AD. These two hypothesizes imply that Somalis are newcomers in the territory they occupy today, and that they have dislodged other people in the early centuries. However, historical evidence shows that the Somali Peninsula was the nexus of the global economy and its people traded various commodities such as frankincense, myrrh, and spices, with ancient Egyptians,[8] Phoenicians,[9] Mycenaeans,[10] and Babylonians.[11] These commodities were produced and exported from the Land of Punt, which situated in the North-eastern of Somali Peninsula. Moreover, other trading cities had flourished along the Indian Ocean littorals, as *the Periplus of the Erythraean Sea* reported in the first century AD.

In the medieval Islamic period that began in the seventh century, the Islamization of the Somali society was at pace and intensified in the successive centuries, thereby enhancing its historic ties with the Arabian

---

[7] Eric Wolf challenges the long-held anthropological notion that non-European cultures and peoples were isolated and static entities before the advent of European colonialism and imperialism. See Eric Wolf and Thomas Eriksen, *Europe and the People without History* (Berkeley: University of California Press, 2010).

[8] Ancient Egyptian civilization flourished along Nile River valley and consisted of succession of 30 dynasties spanning three millennia from 3100 to 332 BC.

[9] Phoenician civilization situated on the East Mediterranean coastal part of the Fertile Crescent on the coastline of what is now Lebanon, Palatine, Syria, and south west Turkey. This civilization spread across the Mediterranean region between 1500 BC and 300 BC.

[10] Mycenaean civilization was the last phase of the Bronze Age in Ancient Greece (1600–1100 BC) and represented the first advanced civilization in mainland Greece.

[11] Babylonian civilization was founded as ancient Akkadian-speaking state and cultural area based in central-southern Mesopotamia (present Iraq). The state emerged in 1894 BC and was dissolved in 539 BC. Babylon greatly expanded during the reign of Hummurabi in the first half of the 18th century BC.

Peninsula. Locally, Somalis became part of the Muslim Sultanates of Ifat and Adal in the thirteenth century and played a significant role in the push-pull wars with the Abyssinian Empire in the highlands. In addition, the Ajuran Imamate, the largest state in pre-colonial Somalia, had emerged in the fourteenth century and extended its authority to most of the southern Somalia until the seventeenth century. The Ajuran Imamate is credited for repulsing the Oromo invasion from the west of Somali-inhabited territory, as well as the Portuguese foray from the Indian Ocean. Moreover, the Ajuran Imamate undertook an assertive plan of spreading Islam throughout East Africa. Both Adal sultanate and Ajuran Imamate were weakened in the seventeenth century and were replaced by fragmented, clan-centric states until colonial powers seized the opportunity and dominated the Somali Peninsula.

The general historiography of the Somali Peninsula presents a picture as if its history began with the colonial period, while its rich ancient and medieval Islamic history have been given less attention.[12] This shortcoming diminishes some sense of pride and historical awareness of the Somalis and reduces the value and importance of rich and unique human civilizations that flourished once upon a time in this region. A sense of history is vital to developing a sense of connectedness in order to understand past challenges and crises, to preserve collective memory, and revive the conception of historical nationhood. Therefore, this chapter aims to make an overview of the less-addressed historical period of the people of the Somali Peninsula, and to reconstruct, in a concise manner, its ancient and medieval Islamic history. The literature review covers the ancient and medieval Islamic civilizations and the emergence of Muslim sultanates in the Somali territory. This chapter forms a conclusion on the major historical themes of the period under study and puts forth contested narratives that require further research.

---

[12] Recently, professor Muhammad Shamsaddin Megalommatis developed a study course on "History of pre-Islamic Somalia". Available from https://www.academia.edu/23220147/HISTORY_OF_PRE-ISLAMIC_SOMALIA_-_COURSE_DESCRIPTION_Muhammad_Shamsaddin_Megalommatis. (accessed on January 17, 2017).

Literature Review

Historical studies often begin with a literature review in order to get an idea of what previous scholars have written about a particular topic under investigation. In doing so, this author found that academic studies on the ancient history of the people of the Somali Peninsula are very limited to the extent that it presents an enormous historical gap and an intellectual black hole. Therefore, this chapter relies on bits and pieces of general historical literature, scattered articles, and archeological works. The first written work, which describes commercial links and cities on the littorals of the Indian Ocean, is the *The Periplus of the Erythraean Sea,* a travelogue written by a Greek traveler in the first century AD.[13] The other important document to be consulted is the PhD thesis of Mohamed Nuuh, titled "History in the Horn of Africa, 1000 BC - 1500 AD, which offers a comprehensive ancient and medieval history of the people in the Somali Peninsula until the end of the European medieval period.[14] Other less studied historical sources are archeological work carried mainly by visiting European researchers. The first archeological work on Somalia was published by the Italian scholar Poalo Graziosi in 1940.[15] It was seconded by the British archaeologist Desmond Clark, who published his classical work on the Prehistoric cultures of the Horn of Africa in 1954.[16] Other scholars who contributed to the Somali archeological research include British scholar Chittick H. N, who led an expedition mission to the town of Hafun, the ancient trading port of Opone mentioned in the Perilpus of Erythraean Sea. Chitttick published his first work on Somali archeology in 1969.[17] In addition to that,

---

[13]   Huntingford, *The Periplus of the Erythraean Sea. (*Ashgate Publishing, 1980).

[14]   Mohamed Nuuh Ali, "History in the Horn of Africa, 1000 BC. - 1500 AD: Aspects of Social and Economic Change Between the Rift Valley and the Indian Ocean." A PhD thesis submitted to the University of California, LA, 1975.

[15]   Paolo Graziosi, "L'Eta della Pietra in Somalia: Risultati di una missione di ricerche paletnologiche nella Somalia italiana in 1935 (Universitá degli studi di Firenze. Firenze: Sansoni, *1940).*

[16]   Desmond Clark published his classical work on the Prehistoric cultures of the Horn of Africa. See also, Sune Jonsson, "An Archeological site file in Somalia." Proceedings of the Second International Congress of Somali Studies, University of Hamburg, August 1-6, 1983. Available from http://dspace-roma3.caspur.it/bitstream/2307/2879/1/02_JONSSON%20S._An%20Archeologic al%20Site%20File%20of%20Somalia.pdf (accessed on December 16, 2016).

[17]   Chittick H. N, "An archaeological reconnaissance of the southern Somali coast",

archaeologist Brandt S.A. also published a number of archeological papers on the ancient civilization of Somali peninsula.[18]

Alas, after the collapse of the Somali state in 1991, archeological work came to a complete halt, and National Archives, Museums and the National Academy of Culture, were vandalized. In the misery of conflict and civil war, Somalia lost its valuable artefacts and national heritage, which still requires relocation and repatriation. Recently, Somaliland Department of Antiquity initiated some archeological work that includes mapping the archeological sites. Somali archeologist Sada Mire's paper "Mapping the Archaeology of Somaliland: Religion, Art, Script, Time, Urbanism, Trade and Empire" includes more than 100 new and previously unpublished sites. Sada Mire concludes her research that "The region [Somali Peninsula] had vast Cushitic; pre-Christian and pre-Islamic Empires that at times formed part of the Himyarite and Sabaean cultures of Southern Arabia, the Aksumite Empire and early Islamic Empires of the Horn of Africa."[19]

The literature on the Somali history in the Medieval Islamic period increased in the academia with a number of academic works published. Among these works, four scholarly books stand out of the crowd. The first comprehensive historical book was authored by Ali Abdirahman Hersi.[20] This work is a seminal piece of research dealing with less addressed issues in the Somali history. It digs deep into the history of the Somali Peninsula in the ancient era and its trade links with the rest of the ancient world. The focus of the book is the emigration of Arabs in the medieval period to the Somali peninsula, in addition to their enterprises and massive conversion of the Somalis to Islam. Moreover, the book further explores the emergence of Muslim sultanates in northern Somalia, the rise of the Ajuran Imamate in the southern Somalia, and their interaction with the Portuguese and Turkish powers. Furthermore, the book delves into the colonial incursion of the nineteenth and

---

Azania, 4.

[18] Brandt S.A., "The Importance of Somalia for understanding African and World prehistory", *Proceedings of the First International Congress of Somali Studies in 1992.*

[19] Sada Mire, "Mapping the Archaeology of Somaliland: Religion, Art, Script, Time, Urbanism, Trade, and Empire" (2015) 32:111–136, 111.

[20] Ali Abdirahman Hersi, *The Arab Factor in Somali History: The Origins and Development of Arab Enterprises and Cultural Influence in the Somali Peninsula* (Los Angeles: University of California, 1977).

twentieth centuries, its impact, and subsequent strengthened cultural ties between Somalia and the Arab world.

The second work was authored by Scott S. Reese andtraces the history of the "Banaderi" community, their migration to Somalia in the medieval Islamic era, and their habitat in the cities of Mogadishu, Merca, and Barawe.[21] It is an excellent history that draws substantially on oral collection of the historical data and contributes to the study of history of the Somali minorities. The third work was authored by Virginia Luling, and provides detailed descriptions of the Geledi city-state and the adjacent clans dwelling in and around Afgoye since the late seventeenth century.[22] Luling, besides the good background section, reconstructs social fabric at the larger regional level and investigates the ways in which traditional relationships and cultural features reshape themselves in new and modern contexts. Written in a clear and accessible style, this is an excellent and up-to-date introduction to the ethnography of Somalia. The fourth work was authored by Lee Cassanelli, which reconstructs and interprets certain aspects of Somali history in the pre-colonial period and offers an excellent background section on the medieval Islamic period.[23] It explores the history of southern Somalia from the sixteenth to the nineteenth centuries. This book studies nomadic ethno-history and oral history. The author approached the study of Somalia's pastoral history from the regional perspective. The author is one of the leading western scholars on Somalia, and his research is considered a good basis for the study of the pre-colonial history of Somalia.

Other complementary literature includes Mohamed Mukhtar's paper, which offers historical background on the introduction of Islam to Somalia, which also examines the claims of some Somali clans to originate from Arab descendants putting forth a counter narrative.[24] Moreover, the "*Futuh al-Habasha*" (The Conquest of Abyssinia) authored by Shiba ad-Din Ahmed, offers a detailed description of the military

---

[21] Scott S. Reese, "Patricians of the Banadir: Islamic Learning, Commercial and Somali Urban Identity in the 19th Century." A PhD Thesis submitted to the University of Pennsylvania, 1996.

[22] Virginia Luling, *The Somali Sultanate: Geledi city-state over 150 years* (Transaction Publishers, 1990).

[23] Lee Cassanelli, The *Shaping of Somali Society: Reconstructing the history of the Pastoral People, 1600-1900* (Philadelphia: University of Pennsylvania Press, 1982)

[24] Mohamed Mukhtar, "Islam in Somali History.: Fact and fictions" in the edited book by Ali Jumale titled *The Invention of Somalia.* (Lawrenceville: The Red Sea Press, 1995)

campaign of Imam Ahmed Ibrahim "Gurey" and his encounter with the Abyssinian Empire.[25] This book documents Somali clans who participated in the campaign and their crucial role in the Jihad. The recent Ph.D. thesis by Avishai Ben-Dror provides history of the city of Harar within the context of the medieval history wars between Abyssinian Empire and Muslim sultanates.[26] It particularly focuses on the Egyptian rule of the historic Islamic city of Harar (1875-1884) and its impact.

The Ancient History of the Somali Peninsula

The land inhabited by the Somali people is situated in the Horn of Africa, jutting out into the Indian Ocean to form the Somali Peninsula. The Horn of the African region is believed to be the cradle of the humanity, as archeological discoveries of 1967 in the Ethiopian Omo River had attested.[27] At the bank of this river, the oldest known fossil of modern human skulls was discovered, dating back to approximately 195,000 years ago.[28] The first team of archeologists led by Richard Leaky had unearthed modern human fossils consisting of two skulls and one partial skeleton in the Omo Basin in Ethiopia, which was estimated earlier time to date back to approximately 130,000 years ago.[29] However, another team of scientists from the Australian National University revisited the site in 2005 and came across additional fragments of the fossilized skull that matched those of the original skulls. The new findings were dated approximately 195,000 years old, using modern radiocarbon dating, making them the oldest modern human remains so far discovered. These human remains were deposited in Addis Ababa

---

[25] Shiba ad-Din Ahmed, *Futuh Al-Habasha: The Conquest of Abyssinia* (Tsehai Publishers, 2003)

[26] Avishai Ben-Dror, "The Egyptian Hikimdāriya of Harar and its Hinterland" – Historical Aspects, 1875-1887." A PhD Thesis submitted to the School of *History*, Tel Aviv University, 2008. Available from http://humanities1.tau.ac.il/history-school/files/Ben-Dror.EN.pdf (accessed on December 3, 2016)

[27] Philip Briggs, *Somaliland with Addis Ababa with East Ethiopia* (Bradt Travel Guides, 2012), 4

[28] Hillary Mayell, "Oldest Human Fossils Identified." National Geographic news, February 16, 2005. Available from http://news.nationalgeographic.com/news/2005/02/0216_050216_omo.html (accessed on December 22, 2016).

[29] Alice Roberts, *The Incredible Human Journey* (Bloomsbury Paperbacks, 2010).

Museum to witness that the Horn of African region is the cradle of mankind.[30]

Further, in the northeastern Horn of Africa, nowadays known as Somali peninsula inhabited by the Somalis, the oldest indication of human habitation during the Stone Age was evidenced with the discovery of "Acheulean stone blades and flint tools discovered in the vicinity of Hargeisa and in the caves along the Golis escarpment", dating back to roughly 12,000-40,000 years.[31] Moreover, Heyward Seton-Karr (1859–1938), a game hunter and adventure traveler associated with the British Royal Geographical Society, discovered stone hand axes at Jalelo on the slopes of a hill between the port of Berbera and Hargeisa in 1896, which dates back to 40,000 years. The Somalian prehistoric hand axes were placed in the British and the Australian Museums.[32]

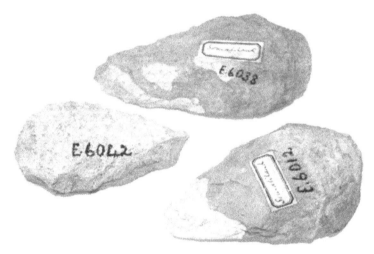

Picture 1. Stone hand axes from Somalia

More evidence of prehistoric human habitation of the Somali territory was discovered at Laas Geel complex, located about 50 km north of Hargeysa. As Ahmed Ali Ilmi puts it,

---

30 Ibid.
31 Philip Briggs, Somaliland with Addis, 4.
32 See brief report and pictures of the Australian Museum, available from http://australianmuseum.net.au/hand-axes-from-somalia-and-our-african-origin(accessed on December, 2016).

The Lass Geel cave paintings depict images of cows, local inhabitants dressed in what appear to be ceremonial robes, and a few dogs in what also appear to be ceremonial robes. The humans have their hands in the air in what is considered a worshiping posture. The cave walls are also covered in old hieroglyphic scripture. Somalis have known of the existence of the caves for centuries and have regarded them as historical sites, hence, the Somali name for the caves. Yet, the Western world only found out about these sites in 2003 when a French team of archaeologists was searching the caves in the area.[33]

In this archeological site, rock art of wild animals is estimated to date back to 5,000 years.[34] Paintings at Laas Geel demonstrate early pastoral livestock herding in the Horn of Africa. In particular, the camel is believed to have been domesticated in the Horn of Africa between the third and second millennium BC, and from there spread to Egypt and North Africa.[35]

Additionally, between the towns of Las khorey and Elaayo lays the Karin-Hegane site, which encompasses numerous cave paintings with real and mythical animals estimated to be 2500 years old.[36] Other prehistoric archeological sites discovered in the southern Somalia included cemeteries at Buur Heybe/Buur Ayle and Gogoshiis Qabe (the furnished place), located near the district of Bardale, 60 km southwest of Baidoa, and is estimated to have been used for over 4000 BC.[37] The 14 burials foundedthere date back to the pre-Islamic period and constitute

---

[33] Ahmed Ali Ilmi, "The History of Social Movements in Somalia through the Eyes of Our Elders within a Diasporic Context." A PhD thesis submitted to Graduate Department of Humanities, Social Sciences and Social Justice Education Ontario Institute for Studies in Education, 2014, 24. References to Gutherz, X., Cros, J.-P., & Lesur, J. (2003). The discovery of new rock paintings in the Horn of Africa: The rock shelters of Las Geel, Republic of Somaliland. Journal of African Archaeology, 1(2), 227-236.

[34] Otto Bakano, "Grotto galleries show early Somali life", April 24, 2011, AFP. Retrieved 22 December, 2016.

[35] Michael Hodd, *East African Handbook: Trade &Travel Publications* (Passport Books, 1994)

[36] Ismail Mohamed Ali, *Somalia Today: General Information* (Ministry of Information and National Guidance, Somali Democratic Republic, 1970), 295

[37] Brandt S.A., "Early Holocene Mortuary Practices and Hunter-Gatherer Adaptations in Southern Somalia." *World Archaeology*. 20 (1 (1988), 40-56

the earliest burials in the Horn of Africa containing the earliest definitive grave artefacts.[38]

Archeological studies and discoveries of the ancient civilizations in the Somali inhabited territories are yet to be given serious attention and may reveal new historical evidence. Nonetheless, the above archeological findings challenge early hypothesis on the origins of Somali people from the southern Ethiopian highlands, specifically those from the Omo-Tana region who later migrated into the northern Kenya in 1000 BC.[39] According to this hypothesis based on historic linguistics and ethnographical studies, Somalis migrated north in the first century AD to populate the Horn of Africa.[40] The new findings suggest that "Somalia is a nation with a history that stretches back more than 10 millennia to the beginnings of human civilization."[41] It also suggests that "the ancestral home of the Somalis was the northern part of the Peninsula, with the Peninsula always being inhabited by the Somalis."[42] This finding also cast doubts on the orally constructed origins of Somalis from the Arabian Peninsula pushing Oromo and Bantu further south and westwards, which had already been discredited by the historic linguistic approach. This migratory hypothesis depicts that Somalis were not the original population of the land, but conquered as I. M. Lewis labeled it the "Somali Conquest of the Horn of Africa."[43] The original homeland of the Somalis being the Horn of Africa was established through linguistic studies and archeological discoveries, which conclude that Cushitic language speaking people such as the Oromo, Somalis, Sidamo, and Afar, have been indigenous people in the Northeast Africa for the last 7000 years.[44]

[38] *Abstracts in Anthropology, Volume 19* (Greenwood Press, 1989), 183
[39] David Shiin and Thomass Ofcansky, *Historical dictionary of Ethiopia* (The Scarecrow Press, 2004), 362
[40] Herbert Lewis, "The Origins of Galla and Somali." *The Journal of African History*, vol.7. No.1 (1966), 27-46.
[41] Raphael C. Njoku, *The History of Somalia* (Santa Barbara, CA: Greenwood), 2013, 13
[42] Said M-Shidad, "The Ancient Kingdom of Punt and its Factor in Egyptian History", 2014. Available from http://www.wardheernews.com/wp-content/uploads/2014/04/The-Ancient-Kingdom-of-Punt_Shidad.pdf (accessed on December 2, 2016)
[43] I. M. Lewis, "The Somali Conquest of the Horn of Africa." Journal of African History 5, no.1 (1964): 213-229.
[44] Kevin Shillington (ed.), *Encyclopedia of African History* (Fitzory Dearborn Tylor and Farancis Group, 2005), 331

The Somali Peninsula was always strategic magnet and commercial nexus of the world trade routes in both the past and present times. Its strategic and commercial importance has continued since ancient times when merchants from the Somali Peninsula traded various commodities such as frankincense, myrrh, cinnamon, ebony, ivory, gold, and animal skin with Ancient Egyptians, Phoenicians, Mycenaeans, and Babylonians. These commodities, which were "the most ancient and precious articles of commerce", are still produced and exported from the north-eastern regions of Somalia.[45] Frankincense is "a resin exuded from various spices of boswellia" (Olibanum Indicum; Latin), a very expensive commodity used as a perfume, for medicinal treatments, and as an incense.[46] The frankincense tree grows in arid regions of the Horn of Africa and the Arabian Peninsula. On the other hand, Myrrh, "a gum from the bark of a small tree," is less expensive than Frankincense and used to perfume clothing as incense, and for embalming.[47] The ancient Somali name for their region was "Bunn", a name referenced in texts related to trade with the pharaohs as "Pwenet" or "Pwene" or *Ta netjer* "Land of the Gods" or as Opone by the Greeks.The name was in reverence to the Egyptian Sun God (RA) and both frankincense and myrrh were used for religious purposes and cosmetics. In particular, the Somali Peninsula had special relationship with ancient pharaonic Egypt, with various Egyptian expeditions sent to the Somali Peninsula being recorded since 2480 BC. Punt was associated with Egyptian ancestry in that it came to be seen as their ancient homeland and the land where their Gods emerged from. It seems that the Egyptians initiated direct commercial transaction with the original source of the merchandise in Somalia, which they began during the rule of Mentuhotep III (around 1950 BC) when the officer Hanu organized multiple trips to the Land of Punt. Trade between Egypt and Punt was not one-sided. John Wilson reports how the Egyptians arrived at Punt with "jewelry, tools, and weapons" and returned with "incense trees, ivory, myrrh, and rare woods"[48] However, as time passed, relations between ancient Egypt and the people of the Somali Peninsula strengthened beyond mere commercial connections. For example, there is evidence of cultural links and the movement of people, as recorded in

[45] Hersi, The Arab Factor, quoted from *the Periplus of the Erythraean Sea*, 44.
[46] Ibid., 44.
[47] Ibid.
[48] John A. Wilson, *The Culture of Ancient Egypt* (The University of Chicago Press, 1956), 176.

some ancient Egyptian inscriptions reporting the arrival of immigrants from the land of Punt. This piece of information is supported by related evidence that the son of Khufu, the Pharaoh of the Great Pyramid, employed one of these immigrants in his court.[49] According to Joshua Mark, "Punt was not only a significant partner in trade, however; it was also a source of cultural and religious influence and a land which the Egyptians viewed as their place of origin and blessed by the gods."[50] There is evidence that one of the most popular Egyptian Gods of child-birth, Bes, (known as the Dwarf God) also came from Punt as did others.[51] Moreover, "Hatshepsut's inscriptions claim that her divine mother, Hathor, was from Punt and other inscriptions indicate that Egyptians in the 18th Dynasty considered Punt the origin of their culture."[52] From historic linguistics, it was also discovered that the Somali language shares a number of etymological words with the ancient Egyptian language that has exactly the same meaning.[53]

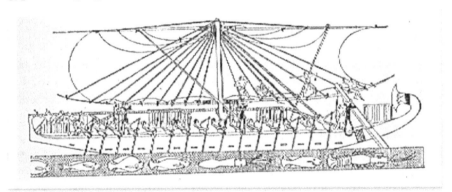

Picture 2. First Egyptian ship bound for Punt.

---

[49] Abdurahman al-Najjar, *Al-Islam fi Al-Somal* (al-Qahira: Madba'at al-Ahram al-Tijariyah, 1973), 53.

[50] Joshua J. Mark, *Punt* in Ancient History Encyclopedia. Available from http://www.ancient.eu/punt/. Accessed on April 10, 2017).

[51] Ibid.

[52] 18th Dynasty ruled Egypt for about 250 years (1570–1544 BC) and its rulers included the famous pharaohs like Ahmose I, Amenhotep I, II, II, and Hatshepsut.

[53] For example, some common words are: Hees (song), Aar (Lion), Shub (pour out), Usha (scepter), neder (divine being), Hibo (gift), Tuf (spite), Webi (river), Kab (shoe), Dab (fire), Hoo (to offer), Awoow (grandfather) and ayeeda (grandmother). This comparative linguistics is from Diriye Abdillahi, "Learn Somali: Somali English Dictionary", 1985.

However, the most authentic piece of historical literature treating the ancient history of Somali Peninsula was in the hierographic diary and arts of the expedition of the fleet that consisted of 5 ships dispatched to the Land of Punt by Queen Hatshepsut of the 18th dynasty in 1478 BC. The history of this expedition was memorialized in the artefacts of the temple of Queen Hatshepsut at Deir el-Bahri, near Luxor in the Valley of the Kings in Egypt, during the reign of the Puntite King Parahu and Queen Ati.[54] Hieroglyphic engravings on Hatshepsut's temple show the following written inscription: 'Sailing on the sea, and making a good start for God's Land. Making landfall safely at the terrain of Punt....". The 31 incense trees brought from the Punt by the expedition was transplanted successfully in Egypt being the first time in recorded history that fauna (plants and trees) was successfully transplanted in another country. The roots of the frankincense trees brought back from Punt by Hatshepsut's expedition in 1493 BC can still be seen outside of her complex at Deir al-Bahri.[55]

A description of a typical man from the Land of Punt is described as "a tall, well-shaped man; his hair is bright, his nose is straight, his beard long and pointed, growing only on his chin; he wears only a loin cloth with a belt in which a dagger is fixed."[56] The people of the Land of Punt were known as warriors who were feared by those who saw them in battle. The ancient Land of Punt originally encompasses the whole region that includes Eritrea, Ethiopia, and Somalia, yet, it is almost undisputable that the site of the Hatshepsut expedition was the tip of the Somali Peninsula.[57] The name "Punt" was well known and was even mentioned in the Bible as "Phut" (Genesis 10:6; cf. 1 Chronicles 1:8), while the ancient Romans called it Cape Aromatica because of the trees that produce aromatic gum resins. Phut is the third son of Ham (one of the sons of Prophet Noah), and in the Bible the name is used for the people who are said to be Ham's descendants.[58] In addition, in the fifth century

---

[54] The history of this journey is well recorded on the walls of Queen Hatshepsut's temple at Deir el-Bahri.

[55] Joshua J. Mark, *Punt* in Ancient History Encyclopedia.

[56] This description is the reading of a scripture of Puntite king Baharu and his wife Atu in the temple of the Queen Hatshepsut at Deir el-Bahri. See https://atlantisjavasea.com/2015/11/14/land-of-punt-is-sumatera/(accesssed on 19 December, 2016)

[57] John A. Wilson, *The Culture of Ancient Egypt* (The University of Chicago Press, 1956), 176.

[58] Sadler, Jr., Rodney "Put". In Katharine Sakenfeld. *The New Interpreter's Dictionary of*

BC, Greek historian Herodotus, known as the Father of History in the Western traditions, refers to a race called the Macrobians who dwelled in the south of Egypt. These people were famous for their longevity (an average of 120 years) due to their diet that mainly comprised meat and milk. They were also, according to Herodotus, the "tallest and handsomest of all men."[59] All descriptions of the people agree with the pastoral Somali figures who are tall, handsome warriors, with a diet predominantly consisting of meat and milk. This point of view was affirmed by the Indian scholar, Mamta Agarwal, who wrote that "these people were none but the inhabitants of Somalia, opposite the Red Sea."[60] Ancient Greek travelers the likes of Strabo, Plinty, Ptolomy, and Cosmos Indicopleustas also visited the Somali Peninsula between the first and fifth centuries AD. These travelers called the Somali people the "Barbaria" and their land as "Barbars."[61] Most likely, the name of "Barbars" was derived from the current town of Berbera in the northern Somali territory.

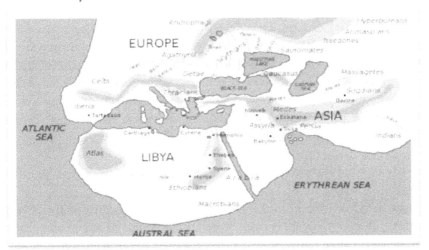

Map 3. Herodotus Map of the World

the Bible (Nashville: Abingdon Press, 2009), 691–92

[59] Herodotus, *the Histories*, 3.20

[60] Mamta Agarwal, "Biography of Herodotus: The Father of History." Available from http://www.historydiscussion.net/biography/biography-of-herodotusthe-father-of-history/1389 (accessed on December 15, 2016)

[61] Abukar Ali, "The Land of the Gods: A Brief Study of Somali Etymology and its Historio-linguistic Potential." Available from http://sayidka.blogspot.co.ke/ (accessed on December 19, 2016).

Finally, several city-states flourished along the littorals of the Indian Ocean of Somali peninsula in the ancient times, such as Opone, Essina, Sarapion, Nokon, Malao, Damo, and Mosylon.[62] The names of these cities and their locations were reported in the *Periplus of the Erythraean Sea*, a travelogue of a Greek explorer dating back to the first century AD.[63] This travelogue is the firsthand description of the region, written by Maris Erythraei, who was familiar with the sea routes of the Red Sea and the Indian Ocean. According to the *Periplus*, trade was flourishing in the region along the coast line of the Indian Ocean. The ancient Indian Ocean cities, as recorded in the *Periplus,* correspond to the modern Somali cities along the littorals of the Indian Ocean.[64] For instance, Sarapion, Nicon, and Opone correspond to Mogadishu, Barawe and Hafun, respectively.[65] Moreover, Somali-Indian trade intensified following the annexation of the Roman Empire in the Nabataean Kingdom in 106 AD.[66] The Nabataeans occupied northern Hejaz and the Negev into the Mediterranean Sea, stretching along the coast of the Red Sea. The Indians traded cinnamon with Somali merchants who re-exported it to the Roman and Greek Empires. The following section begins in the seventh century, which is the onset of the Medieval Islamic period. The six centuries between the first and seventh centuries mark a historical gap in which historic documents and written materials are still absent; as a result, nobody knows what happened to the flourishing cities and civilizations in the Somali peninsula during this period.

The Medieval Islamic Period

The medieval Islamic period in the Somali history begins in the seventh century, during which Islam was introduced to Somalia. Some hagiological sources ponder that Islam reached the northern Somali coast

---

[62] George Wynn Brereton, Huntingford, The Periplus of the Erythraean Sea (Ashgate Publishing, 1980)

[63] Mohamed Jama'a, An Introduction to Somali History from 5000 years B.C Down to the Present Times (s.n; 2d ed., rev. and enl edition,1962)

[64] Opone corresponds that Hafun town, Essina, was somewhere between Barava and Marka; Sarapion was between Mogadishu and Warsheikh; Nikon was near Kismayo; Malao corresponds Berbera; Damo near Cape Guardafui; and Moslyn near Bossaso.

[65] Wilfred H. Schoff, The Periplus of the Erythraean Sea (London, 1912), 60-61

[66] Eric Herbert Warmington, *The Commerce Between the Roman Empire and India* (The University Press, 1928), 54

shortly after the first Muslim migration to Abyssinia before Islam even reached Medina in 624 AD.[67] The first Muslim migration occurred when the Muslim minority in Mecca were persecuted and the Prophet Mohammad (peace be upon him) directed his companions to migrate to Abyssinia, the "land of truth", which was ruled by "a king under whose domain no one will be wronged."[68] As expected, the Abyssinian king of Negus, headquartered in the city of Aksum, whom in the Arabic tradition was named Ashama Ibn Abjar, extended Muslim migrants his full protection and utterly rejected the Quraysh emissary's demand for repatriation to Mecca.[69] The companions enjoyed and lived peacefully in the custody of the Emperor for about 13 years (615-628 AD). During these long years, it is plausible to have some Abyssinian conversion to Islam in a favorable environment of freedom and friendship.[70] However, this proposition remains sheer speculation, since there is no reliable historical evidence that ascertains the occurrence of such conversion.

With respect to the early Somali conversion, it is even hard to accept this fact as accurate, because the distance between Aksum (the seat of Abyssinian Negus) and the town of Zayla, the center of the closest Somali urban territory, is estimated to be more than 1000 km by land and even further by sea. The other possible scenario regarding early Somali conversion to Islam is related to the early Yemeni Muslims who reached Abyssinia during the first migration. It is known that a group of early Yemeni Muslims undertook a voyage across the Red Sea to meet the Prophet after migration to Medina; however, due to strong waves, the group was forced to land on the Western coast of the Red Sea. From

---

[67] Salahadin Eshetu, "King Nagash of Abyssinia." Available from http://dcbun.tripod.com/id17.html (accessed on July 4, 2016).

[68] Ibn Kathir, *Albidaya wa Nihaya*, volume 2 (Arabic), It seems that the people of Mecca were aware of Aksum kingdom as trade partners. Meccans traded with Yemen and Africa through their port of Shyabah (near Jiddah), and the Aksumate port of Adulis (situated about 30 miles south of Mussawa). The distance between the two ports is 660 KM.

[69] Amr bin Aas led a Quraysh delegation to Abyssinia to demand the repatriation of the Muslims to Mecca. Martin Lings, *Muhammad: His Life based on the Earliest Sources* (Inner Traditions, 2006), *81–84*

[70] Ismael Mukhtar, "Milestones in the History of Islam in Eritrea." A paper delivered at the Eritrean Muslim Council's 6th annual convention held in Washington D.C. in July 2008, 2. Available from http://www.muslimpopulation.com/africa/Eritrea/Eritria_Islam_PDF.pdf (accessed on December 20, 2016).

there, they decided to join their Muslim companions in Aksum.[71] The Yemeni Muslims may have reached Zayla after they had returned to Yemen. Regarding the Muslim migrants to Abyssinia, it was reported that some of them had returned earlier to Mecca and participated in the Migration to Medina in 622 AD, and those who remained behind returned later to Medina in 628 AD.

Somali historians are in agreement with the lack of evidence of the early Somali conversion to Islam before Islam reached Medina, as generally preferred and believed. For instance, Professor Said Samatar questioned the possibility of some of the migrants remaining in the region, writing that "might some have remained behind to plant the seed of the new religion in the soil of the Horn?[72] Moreover, Professor Mohamed Mukhtar asserts a "lack of evidence" of early Somali converts to Islam before the Muslim migration to Medina. Furthermore, professor Ali Abdirahman Hersi in his Ph.D Thesis *The Arab Factor in Somali History* considers the introduction of Islam to Zayla in early years of Muslim migration to Abyssinia as "largely conjectural."[73] Nonetheless, historiography on the early reach of Islam in Somalia becomes more problematic considering the fact that the Mosque of the two-Mihrab (*Masjid al-Qiblatayn*) which means the mosque of the two niches, one facing Jerusalem and the other in the direction of Mecca, is located in Zayla.[74] As a matter of fact, the direction of Qibla was changed from Jerusalem to Mecca in 624 AD after two years of Muslim migration to Medina.[75] The story of the Mosque of the two-Mihrab is indeed puzzling and requires comprehensive examination, which may sheds some light in the early history of Islam in Somalia. This undertaking is very crucial to

---

[71] Ibid., 1.

[72] Said Samatar, "Unhappy masses and the challenge of political Islam in the Horn of Africa." Available from http://www.ethiomedia.com/newpress/political_islam.html(accessed on November 24, 2016),

[73] Hersi, The Arab Factor,113

[74] More in-depth research is needed to examine when the mosque was constructed and who constructed and why the mosque has two Qiblas.

[75] The following verse in the Qur'an was revealed when the direction of Qiblah was changed. "Indeed, We see the turning of your face to heaven, so We shall surely turn you to a Qiblah which you shall like; turn then your face towards the Sacred Mosque, and wherever you are, turn your face towards it, and those who have been given the book most surely know that it is the truth from their Lord; and Allah is not at all heedless of what they do" (the Qur'an, 2:144)

avoid mythological hearsay or "idle superstition and uncritical acceptance of historical data", as Ibn Khaldun repeatedly warned against.[76]

The early introduction of Islam in the northern Somalia took place in Zayla and Berbera, and Mogadishu in the southern Somalia, probably as commercial outlets. Professor Mukhtar speculates that the first wave of Muslim migrants was most probably Umani tribes who were defeated and severely persecuted during the Apostasy War (*Hurub al-Riddah*).[77] For them, the easiest escape route and the closest geographic location was Somali Peninsula, which they historically connected through trade. Mukhtar concludes "thus, there is good reason to believe that the earliest wave of Muslim immigrants to the Somali coast occurred as early as the period of Abu Bakar, the first Caliph of Islam."[78] Other pieces of historical evidence show that the early Islamization of Mogadishu may have taken place during the Caliphate of Omar Ibn Khitab (634-644 AD), meaning the first half of the seventh century AD. Moreover, the migration of an Omani group led by brothers Suleiman and Sa'id of Juland settled on the East African Zanj coast in 695 AD. This account is very close to the historical facts witnessed by the inscription on the tombstone of Fatima bint Abdisamad Yaqub, who died in Mogadishu in year 101 of the Islamic calendar.[79] This evidence is strengthened by the records in *Kitab al-Zunuj*, an anonymously authored book discovered by Italian scholar Enrico Gerulli in Somalia, which reveals the presence of Muslims in Mogadishu during the Caliphate Abdulmalik bin Marwan (685-705 AD).[80] According to *Kitab al-Zunuj*, the Caliph dispatched an expedition under the command of Musa ibn Umar al-khath'ami to Mogadishu and Kilwa. He reported to the Caliph that these city-states accepted Islam during the Caliphate of Omar Ibn Khitab (634-644 AD)

---

[76] Ibn Khaldun, Franz Rosenthal, N. J. Dawood (1967), *The Muqaddimah: An Introduction to History.* (Princeton University Press, 1967), 10

[77] Mohamed Mukhtar, Islam in Somali History: Fact and fiction" in *The Invention of Somalia*, edited by Ali Jumale Ahmed. (Lawrenceville: The Red Sea Press, 1995),4.

[78] Ibid., 5. The author quoted from Hassan Ibrahim Hassan, *Intishar al-Islam wa al-Uruba fi ma Yali al-Sahra al-Kubra, Sharq al-Qarra al Ifriqiyyah wa Gharbiha.* (Cairo: Madba'at Lujnat al-Bayan al-Arabi, 1957), 127.

[79] Hersi, *The Arab Factor*, 91. Also, Ahmed duale Jama'a, *The Origins and Development of Mogadishu AD 1000 to 1850: A Study of urban growth along the Banadir coast of southern Somalia* (Repro HSC, Uppsala 1996).

[80] Kitab al-Zunuj was translated to Italian language and was published among various documents collected by Enrico Ceruli. See Enrico Ceruli, *Somalia: scritti vari editi ed inedita, Vol.2* (Roma: Istituto poligrafico dello Stato,1957-1964).

and still honor their allegiance to the Caliphate.[81] Moreover, Mogadishu continued as part of the Caliphate during the reign of Abu-Ja'far al-Mansur as Yahya ibn Umar al-Anzi, a representative of the Caliph in the East African region, reported.[82] However, many East African cities, including Mogadishu rebelled against Harun al-Rashid Caliphate (786-809 AD) and his son, al-Ma'mun (813-833 AD), sent two punitive expeditions to them.[83] It was also reported that a group led by the "Seven Brothers of al-Ahsa," from the Persian Gulf, settled in Mogadishu and Barawe in 920 AD, and other large group from Persia led by Hassan ibn Ali al-Shirazi migrated to East Africa in 1000 AD.[84] These waves of migrations from the Arabian peninsula, Oman and Persia, and later from the subcontinent of India, were spreading Islam and exercising commerce in the littorals of the Indian Ocean of the East Africa.

In the medieval Islamic period, explorers from China, the Arab/Islamic World, and Portugal disembarked on the Somali Peninsula, writing detailed descriptions of its people, cities, and trade linkages with the Asian and Arab states and empires. As African travel specialist, Philip Briggs illustrates, "the earliest medieval description of the Somali region, and arguably the most detailed, was penned by the Chinese explorer and writer Tuan Ch'eng-Sbib in the mid-9th century."[85] Tuan named where he visited as "Po-pa-li" and provided a detailed description of the customs of the inhabitants, which most historians assumed to be the town of Berbera. A similar description of the Somali people was provided by another Chinese writer, Chou Ju-Kua, which dates back to approximately 1225 AD.[86] Another Chinese explorer, Zheng, visited Somali cities such as Mogadishu, Zayla, Merca, and Berbera in 1430. Moreover, Somali Islamic scholar and explorer from Mogadishu called "Imam Said al-Muqdishawi" traveled to China in the 14th century during the Yuan Dynasty (1271-1368 AD). Historical records affirm that Said traveled from Mogadishu and studied in Mecca and Medina for 28 years. He traveled across the Muslim world and visited Bengal and China. He

---

[81] Mukhtar, Islam in Somali History, 3. Hersi, *The Arab Factor*, 86.

[82] Ibid., 4.

[83] Hersi, *The Arab Factor*,112.

[84] Mohamed Mukhtar, *Historical Dictionary of Somalia, New Edition*. (The scarecrow Press, 2003), xxvi

[85] Philip Briggs, *Somaliland with Addis Ababa with East Ethiopia*. (Bradt Travel Guides, 2012), 11.

[86] Ibid.

met Ibn-Battuta on the west coast of India, to whom he is said to have shared accounts of his travels in China, which were most probably included in the Ibn-Battuta chronicles.[87] In the medieval period, the Somali Peninsula exported Giraffes, zebras, horses, exotic animals, ivory, and other goods to the Ming Empire of China (1368–1644 AD) in exchange for ceramics, spices, and muskets.

The Arab/Islamic explorers also provided description of the travel to the Somali peninsula. For example, Arab/Islamic geographer Ibn-Said al-Maghribi (d. 1286) produced a detailed written account on Somalia in the Islamic Medieval period and described that southern Somalia was predominantly populated by Sunni Muslims and called Mogadishu, the city of Islam "Dar *al-Islam*".[88] Moreover, Muhammad al-Idrisi (1100-1166) described the commercial coastal cities of Merca, Barawe, and Mogadishu, as well as the inland commercial routes. Furthermore, Yaqut al-Hamawi (d. 1229 AD) describes Somalis as black to distinguish them from the migrant Asian population, and describes Mogadishu as "predominantly populated by foreigners and not blacks".[89] He also reports the presence of strange animals "not found elsewhere in the world", such as the giraffe, leopard, and rhinoceros. Finally, Ibn Battuta's (1304-1369) visit to Mogadishu in 1331 revealed that the city was at the zenith of prosperity and was "an exceedingly large city" with many rich merchants, which was famous for its high-quality textile fabric that it exported to Egypt. The remarkable description of Mogadishu by Ibn Battuta indicates that the city was highly advanced as a center of trade and Islamic learning. He was puzzled by Somali Sultan Abubakar bin Mohamed and his judicial Islamic system, which he considered to be highly advanced hierarchical system of governance.[90] Ibnu Battuta, in his travelogue, described how he was welcomed in Mogadishu. He noted that,

---

[87] Charles H. Parker & Jerry H. Bentley (ed.), *Between the Middle Ages and modernity: Individual and community in the early Modern World.* (Rowman & Littlefield Publishers Inc., 2007), 160. Also, see Peter Jackson, "Travels of Ibn Battuta", *Journal of the Royal Asiatic Society*, 264.

[88] Mukhtar, Islam in the Somali History, 6

[89] Ibid. Also, Hersi, *The Arab Factor*, 102-103.

[90] David D. Laitin, Said S. Samatar, *Somalia: Nation in Search of a State.* (Westview Press: 1987), 15.

The Qadi took my hand and we came to that house which is near the Shaikh's house. And it was bedded out and set up with what is necessary. Then he came with food from the Shaikh's house. With him was one of his wazirs who was in charge of guests. He said, "*Maulana gives you al-salamu 'alaikum*' [i.e., peace be unto you] and he says to you, "you are most welcome." Then he put down the food and we ate.[91]

Medieval Arab writers like Abu-al-Hassan al-Mas'udi and Yaqut al-Hamawi also visited northern Somali cities such as Zayla and Berbera and described their population as comprising blacks and Arab emigrants, who were not highly visible as compared to Mogadishu.

The city of Zayla, which was the Somali gateway to the Arabian Peninsula, became the capital city of the multi-ethnic Adal Sultanate which flourished from 1415 to 1577 AD. Adal Sultanate succeeded the Sultanate of Ifat, which was later defeated by Emperor Amda Siyon of Abyssinia in 1332.[92] The Muslim-Christian relations were cordial since the early Muslim migration to Abyssinia, and the subsequent centuries. This relation was bolstered with the Prophet's high regard to Abyssinia, relating that "Abyssinia is a land of justice in which nobody is oppressed." Moreover, another Hadith related by Abu Sukainah reported: The Prophet, peace and blessings be upon him, said, "Leave the Abyssinians alone as long as they leave you alone, and leave the Turks alone as long as they leave you alone."[93] Most likely, these prophetic directives and high regard to Abyssinia had spared Ethiopia from Jihad, until their empires initiated Muslim subjugation in the later years.[94] The early historiography of Muslims relates the history of the Abyssinian king converting to Islam and exchanging presents with the Prophet Muhammad (peace be upon him). Also, when the news of the death of the Abyssinian king reached the Prophet, he performed a funeral prayer (*Janaza*) for him in absentia.[95] Such friendly relations

---

[91] Walker, R, *When we ruled: The ancient and medieval history of Black civilisations.* London, U.K: Every Generation Media, 2006, 475.

[92] Ibid., 4.

[93] Sunan Abu Dawud 4302 (authentic) according to As-Suyuti.

[94] The authenticity of this Hadith is questionable but it expresses Muslim sympathy to Abyssinia and directing their Jihad to other directions such as Persians and Byzantine empires.

[95] Abu Huraira reported: The Messenger of Allah, peace and blessings be upon him, told us about the Negus, the ruler of Abyssinia, on the day he died and he said to us,

continued until the sixteenth-century. It was later deteriorated because of the Abyssinian Empire's interest in controlling trade routes, the territory of the Muslims, and growing fear of religious rivalry. Islam has been growing in Abyssinia, and since the ninth century, Muslim sultanates were established. The first sultanate was Makhzumi dynasty (896-1285 AD) headquartered in Shewa, followed by Ifat sultanate (1285-1415 AD) and Adal sultanates (1415-1577 AD) headquartered in Zayla. These Muslim Sultanates controlled trade routes between Christian highland and coastal cities of the Red Sea and the Indian Ocean. They had cordial agreements with the Ethiopian highlanders and shared part of the trade revenues. Lately, these relations soured and they were engaged in economic push-pull wars given religious coloring: Islam versus Christianity.[96] During the war, when cities change hands between Muslim sultanates and the Abyssinian Empire, Muslims lived peacefully with the Christians until the later period of Imam Ahmed Ibrahim's Jihad. Conversely, "when the Abyssinian king Negus Yakuno Amlak (1270-1285) conquered Seylac [Zayla], [he] killed many Muslims and forcibly converted survivors to Christianity and converted mosques to churches."[97]

The most dramatic episode of the wars between the Muslim Sultanate and Abyssinian Empire took place during the reign of Imam Ahmed Ibrahin Al-Gazi (1506–1543) and the Ethiopian Emperor Lebna Dangal "Dawit II" (1501–1540). It seems that Muslims who played subservient role to the Ethiopian Empire for centuries were eager to liberate themselves, refusing to pay tribute and were prepared to avenge for the past wrongs. It is also important to mention the inspiring slogan of war as Islamic Jihad against Christian Abyssinians. This was an indication of the change of power relations between Muslims and Christians in Abyssinia and growing conception from the Muslim side as the war being legitimate against the century's aggressive Christian Abyssinians. The confrontation that began earlier continued during the reign of Emperor Gelawdewos (1521 –1559). The magnitude of the war

---

"Seek forgiveness for your brother." Related in Sahih Bukhari, no.1263, and Sahih Muslim, no. 951.

[96] Nahemia Levtzion and Randall Pouwels, *The History of Islam in Africa.* (Ohio University Press, 2000).

[97] Ben I. Aram, "Somalia's Judeo-Christian Heritage: A Preliminary Survey." *Africa Journal of Evangelical Theology* 22.2 2003, 8, quoted from Bertin, G. Bertin, *Christianity in Somalia.* (Muqdisho: Croce del Sud Cathedral. Manuscript, 1983), 9-10.

was so great that it had attracted the intervention of the two super powers: the Portuguese and Ottoman Empires. These two superpower empires had intervened in the conflict by allying the Abyssinian Christians and the Adal Muslim Sultanate respectively. In this period, the campaign known as the Conquest of Abyssinia (*Futuh al-Habasha*) took place, which started around 1527.[98] Iman Ahmed started his campaign to conquer the Abyssinian Empire and succeeded to conquer more than a half of its territory, thereby inflicting massive devastation on Abyssinian Empire and converted many Christians to Islam. Nevertheless, complete seizure of Abyssinian Empire was thwarted by a timely intervention from the Portuguese, led by Cristovão da Gama, the brother of Vasco Da Gama, the famous Portuguese explorer and the first European to reach India.[99] The Portuguese military expedition included 400 musketeers, as well as a number of artisans and other non-combatants, while Imam Ahmed requested help from the Ottoman Empire and received 700 Turkish troops. The Conquest of Abyssinia remains in the memory of many generations of Ethiopians. "In Ethiopia, the damage which Ahmad Gragn [Imam Ahmed Ibrahim] did has never been forgotten," wrote Paul B. Henze. "Every Christian highlander still hears the tales of Gragn in his childhood. Haile Selassie referred to him in his memoirs, "I have often had villagers in northern Ethiopia point out the sites of towns, forts, churches, and monasteries destroyed by Gragn, as if these catastrophes had occurred only yesterday."[100] The military campaign between the two camps was temporarily halted in 1543, when Imam Ahmed was killed in the battle of Wayna Daga. Nonetheless, the wife of Imam Ahmed Bati Del Wambara repudiated to accept defeat and was highly committed to avenging her husband. As a result, she married his nephew, Nur ibn Mujahid, on the condition that he would avenge Imam Ahmad's death. Thus, the hostilities between the two camps continued under the successor Iman Nur Ibn Mujahid, who reignited the war in

---

[98]   The Chronicle of the Campaign is well Recorded in the Arabic Language Written book. Shihabu Addin Ahmed Bin Abdul-Kadir, *Futuh Al-hanasha: The Conquest of Abyssinia*, Translated by Paul Lester Stenhouse (noo date and place of publishing)

[99]   R.S. Whiteway, *The Portuguese Expedition to Abyssinia in 1441-1543*, 1902. (Nendeln, Liechtenstein: Kraus Reprint, 1967), 42.

[100] Paul B. Henze, *Layers of Time: History of Ethiopia.* (London: Hurst & Company, 2000), 90.

1554 and fulfilling his wife's condition, he avenged for Imam Ahmed by killing Ethiopian Emperor Galawdewos in 1559.[101]

Historiography of the early wars between the Abyssinian Empire and the emerging Muslim Emirates was depicted as though Abyssinia was "a beleaguered fortress in the midst of a sea of Islam."[102] This conception was originally forwarded by J.S. Trimingham, an Orientalist historian who was criticized for the lack of evidence and a counter argument was produced. The contesting narrative was articulated by Travis J. Owens, who wrote "that the Muslim neighbors of the Ethiopian Empire were besieged by Christian Ethiopia throughout the medieval period.[103] Moreover, Travis considered the wars between the two camps as a legitimate Muslim reaction to the expansionist Ethiopia. Expressing his position, he wrote: "the jihads of Imam Gran and Amir Mahfuz before him were reactions to the expansionary policies of the Empire that continually subjugated its neighbors."[104] Furthermore, Tavis concluded his analysis that,

> The Muslim threat of violence rose as the Empire increasingly subjected the Muslim sultanates to violence, taxes and loss of control of trade. The Muslim sultanates were a threat to the Ethiopians not because they wanted to overthrow Christian territory but because they desired to reclaim their own territory, trade routes and independence.[105]

Tavis' narrative was in support of an earlier position of Ethiopian historian Ahmed Hussein, who published a paper in 1992 titled *The Historiography of Islam in Ethiopia* in the *Journal of Islamic Studies*, in which he challenged the Orientalist view of Islam in Ethiopia.[106] Other scholars

---

[101] E. Cerulli, *Documenti Arabi per la Storia dell'Ethiopia*. Memoria della Accademia Nazionale dei Lincei, Vol. 4, No. 2, Rome, 1931.

[102] J. Spencer Trimingham, "The Expansion of Islam," In Islam in Africa, edited by James Kritzeck, and William H. Lewis, (New York: Van Nostrand-Reinhold Company, 1969), 21.

[103] Travis J. Owens, "Beleaguered Muslim Fortress and Ethiopian Imperial Expansion from the 13th to the 16th century." MA Thesis in Security Studies submitted to Naval Postgraduate school, 2008. Available from http://calhoun.nps.edu/bitstream/handle/10945/4031/08Jun_Owens?...(accessed on December, 2016), 1.

[104] Ibid.

[105] Ibid., 40.

[106] Hussein Ahmed, "The Historiography of Islam in Ethiopia," *Journal of Islamic*

who studied the medieval history of this region such as Kapteijns argue that the sixteenth century war between the Christian Empire of Ethiopia and the Muslim Emirates was an indigenous civil war between Ethiopians.[107] This means that the war was not between an indigenous Christian power defending herself from the intrusion of immigrant Muslims.

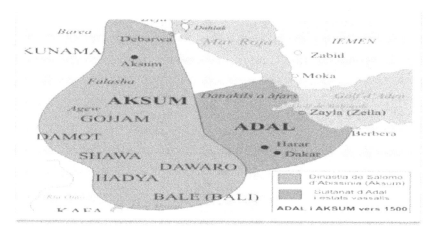

Map 4. The Map of Adal Sultanate

In medieval Europe, Portugal ascended as an imperial power during what was called "the Age of Discovery." The Age of Discovery in the European history is the period between 15th and 18th centuries in which extensive overseas exploration emerged. It paved the way for the rise of European colonialism which marked the arrival of settlers and invaders to enslave, exploit, conquest, and dominate over native populations in Asia and Africa and America. As part of such venture, the Portuguese were the first European explorers to visit Somalia. Portuguese writer and officer Duarte Barbarosa (1480-1521), who participated in the expedition of Ferdinand Magellan, the first circumnavigator of the Earth, noted many ships arriving from India to Mogadishu with clothes and spices to exchange gold, wax, and ivory.[108]   Vasco Da Gama (1460-1524), a

---

Studies, 3 (1992): 15.

[107]   Lidwien Kapteijns, "Ethiopia in the Horn of Africa," in The History of Islam in Africa edited by Nehemia Levtzion, and Randall L. Pouwels, (Athens, Ohio: Ohio University Press, 2000).

[108]   Mensel Longworth Dam (translated and ed.), "The book of Duarte Barbosa: an account of the countries bordering on the Indian Ocean Asian Educational

Portuguese explorer who passed the coast of Mogadishu on January 2, 1499 in his return from his first trip to India, observed that Mogadishu was a large city with houses of four or five stories high, with big palaces in its center and many mosques with cylindrical minarets.[109] Moreover, Indian merchants bypassed both the Portuguese blockade of the Somali coast in the 16th century and Omani traders and used Somali ports of Merca and Barawe. These two ports were out of jurisdiction of Portugal and Omanis and therefore, Indian merchants conducted their trade freely without interference.

In the medieval Islamic period, Somalis developed a new culture of state-building. The first native state they established was Ajuran Imamate, the largest multi-clan and longstanding Somali state that emerged in the fourteenth century and continued until seventeenth century. It was headquartered in Merca and its territory included much of the southern Somalia. Its territory extended from Mareeg in the north (Elder district in Galmudug State of Somalia); to Qalafo in the west; to Kismayo in the south. The sultanate secured trading routes and promoted foreign trade, which flourished in the coastal provinces. Large ships loaded with a variety of commercial goods were coming from Arabia, India, Venetia, Persia, Egypt, and as far away as China.[110]The Ajuran Imamate instituted strong standing army, which had successfully resisted the Oromo invasion/migration from the west, as well as the Portuguese incursion from the Indian Ocean.

Services, 1989.

[109] Joao de Sa Alvaro Velho, *A Journal of the First Voyage of Vasco Da Gama, 1497-1499*. Hakluyt Society, 1898, 88.

[110] Fred M. Shelley, *Nation Shapes: The Story behind the World's Borders*. (ABC-CLIO., 2013), 358.

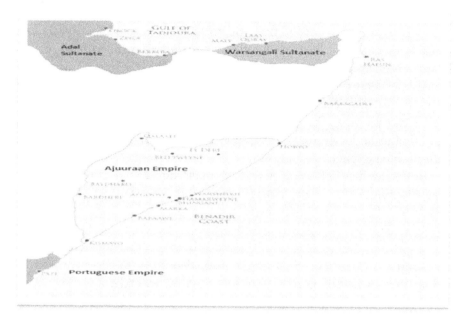

Map 5. The Map of Ajuran Imamate

The Oromo invasion, also known as the Black Infidel War (*Dagaalkii Gaala Madow*) took place in the mid-17th century. This invasion was defeated and some of the invading Oromo were converted to Islam while others shifted their migration away from the Ajuran territory. During the Ajuran rule, many clans of East Africa were converted to Islam. The Ajuran Imamate, also defended its territory from the Portuguese incursion that initially burned and looted Barava under the command of Tristão da Cunha.[111]

The Portuguese plan to attack Mogadishu was averted due to the preparedness of the Ajuran Mogadishu province under the rule of Muzzaffar Dynasty, who mobilized large troops that included many horsemen and battleships in defense of the city. Nonetheless, the Portuguese did not abandon the plan of conquering Mogadishu, and several decades after their earlier attempt, they sent a punitive expedition against Mogadishu under the command of João de Sepulveda, who also failed to conquer Mogadishu.[112] As a reaction to the Portuguese threat,

---

[111]   Duarte Barbarosa, *A Description of the Coasts of East Africa and Malabar in the Beginning of Sixteenth Century* (London: the Hakaluyt Society, 2008)

[112]   Justus Strandes, *The Portuguese period in East Africa* (Kenya Literature Bureau, 1989), 112

the Ajuran Imamate strengthened its relations with the Ottoman Empire in Istanbul. Both parties established military pact to collectively thwart the Portuguese threat in the Indian Ocean. As a result, the marine forces of Ajuran and the Ottoman Navy organized common expeditions to break the Portuguese blockades of the coastal towns of the Indian Ocean. This cooperation reached its peak in the 1580s during Mir Ali Bay's command of the Turkish fleet in the Indian Ocean, when a Somali-Turkish expedition was sent as far as South East Asia.[113] Historical records of the Ajuran Imamate and its encounter with Oromo and the Portuguese is very limited. Certainly, the Ajuran Imamate had played an important role in defending the southern Somali territory and spreading Islam in the whole region of East Africa. Alas, the history of the formation of the Somali state symbolized by the Ajuran Imamate was not given deserved attention. One of the reasons may be that the major Somali nationalist movement, the SYL, were shying away from clan names, and since the Imamate was carrying a clan name, it was simply neglected. Another possibility is the lack of historical awareness and deficiency of the historical records. Another reason that is more plausible may be the dominance of the colonial historiography imaging that the Somalis were fragmented clans with only colonial history in its production and implication. Collectively, these three factors diminished research and recovery of the indigenous history of Somali state formation.

The Adal sultanate was weakened after the death of Amir Nur due to the Oromo raids in 1577 and its headquarter was relocated to the oasis of Aussa in the Danakil desert under the leadership of Mohamed Jasa.[114] The sultanate of Aussa (Afar Sultanate) declined gradually in the next century and was destroyed by the local Afar nomads in 1672. Conversely, Harar flourished and established a new dynasty under Ali Bin Daud in 1647, which was the ruling dynasty until the city was conquered by Egypt in 1875.[115] After the hurried Egyptian evacuation, the city gained short-lived independence, after which Emperor Menelik took over the city and incorporated it into its Empire in 1887. Menelik boastfully declared after conquering Harar "This is not a Muslim country, as everyone

---

[113] Sidney Welsh, *Portuguese rule and Spanish crown in South Africa, 1581-1640*(Juta & Co.; 1st edition,1950)

[114] Lee Cassaneli, *The Shaping of Somali Society*, 120.

[115] Avishai Ben-Dror, The Egyptian Hikimdariya of Harar.

knows."[116]On the other hand, the Ajuran Imamate declined in the seventeenth century after the defeat in its major provinces: the Mareeg province,[117] the Muzzaffar dynasty in Mogadishu in 1624 and the Sil'is Sultanate in Afgoye.[118]

In the pre-colonial history, Banadir coast was under the Omani nominal authority from Zanzibar along with much of the east African coastal cities until the European scramble in 1880s. However, the Hirab Imamate and the Geledi Sultanate who succeeded the Ajuran Imamate in Mogadishu and its surrounding regions were local rulers of the region. Moreover, the Geledi sultanate ruled parts of southern Somalia during the late-seventeenth and nineteenth centuries. It was founded by Ibrahim Adeer who defeated the Sil'is dynasty and made its headquarters in the city of Afgoye (30 km south of Mogadishu). The sultanate was incorporated into the Italian Somali colony in 1908.[119] On the other hand, the Hiraab Imamate that rebelled against the Ajuran Imamate on the watering rights had established an independent rule from 1624 and onwards. The rest of the previous Ajuran territories in southern Somalia were segmented into independent clan sultanates, while the entire region was occupied by Italy at the beginning of the twentieth century. At this time in north-eastern Somalia, the Warsangali Sultanate and the Majerteen Kingdom became highly visible. The Sultanate of Hobbio, the offshoot of the Majeerteen kingdom, under the rule of Sultan Yusuf Ali Kenindid, entered into a treaty with the Italians in 1888, while the Kingdom of Majeerteen, which controlled much of the current Puntland state of Somalia, also entered similar treaty in 1889. Both territories of these mini-states were incorporated into the Italian colony by 1927.

---

[116] David Laitin and Said Samatar, *Somalia: Nation in Search of a State* (Westview Press, 1987),12

[117] According to the hagiography, the last imam of the Ajuran was killed by the confederacy of Dalandoole Mudulood clans at the well called *Ceel Cawl* near Messagaway, one of the towns in the Elder District. This city is located in the old Mareeg province (one of the districts of Galmudug State of Somalia).

[118] The Sil'is controlled a large part of southern Somalia from Afgoye, the headquarters of the dynasty. However, in the late seventeenth century, Ibrahim Adeer took over Afgoye and founded the Geledi Sultanate. For more information, see Luling, *The Somali Sultanate*, 111.

[119] Ibid.

The northern coast of Somalia, in the eighteenth century, similar to the Omanis in the Banadir coast, Shariifs of Mukha (Yemen) exercised nominal rule under Ottoman Empire. However, headquartered in Zayla, local Somali rulers like Haji Sharmarke were exercising actual authority of the trade routes and surrounding areas of Zayla and Berbera. Further East, the Warsangali Sultanate was in operation in the Sanaag region and parts of the north-eastern region, an area historically known as the Maakhir coast. The Sultan of Warsengeli signed the first treaty of the British protectorate in 1884, heralding the new era of British protectorate in the northern Somali Peninsula. The British Government signed protection treaties with the other five clans residing in the British Somaliland: the Gadabursi, Issa, Habar Gerhajis, Habr Toljaala, and Habr-Awal in 1984 and early 1885.[120] In such situation of clan fragmentation, expanding European and Ethiopian powers took the opportunity to seize the strategic Somali Peninsula.

Conclusion

This Chapter undertook a concise overview of ancient history of the Somali Peninsula and exposed that this region was the cradle of the human race and the kernel of ancient civilizations, which traded with other world civilizations of the time including the ancient Egyptians, Phoenicians, Mycenaeans, and Babylonians. Archaeological studies and historic linguistics revealed the original homeland of the Cushitic speaking people, to whom Somalia belongs, have been indigenous people in northeast Africa for the last 7000 years. *The Periplus of the Erythraean Sea* was the first written document in the first century AD, which described the coastal ports in the littorals of the Indian Ocean.

Since the seventh century of the medieval Islamic period and onward, Somalia entered a new phase of its history. The historiography of the Somali peninsula began to receive fresh historical sources from various writers and explorers, such as Chinese, Arab/Islamic, and Portuguese. These travelers left behind some records describing the people, its religion, and commercial connections with world communities. Their descriptions depict that Somali people accepted Islam since seventh century and their total conversion may have occurred

---

[120] D. J. Latham Brown, "The Ethiopia-Somaliland Frontier Dispute." *International and Comparative Law Quarterly*, 5, 2 (1956), 245–264

from the eleventh to the thirteenth centuries. The Somali people were incorporated in the emerging Muslim sultanates of Ifat (1285-1415) and Adal (1415-1577) in the northern part of the Peninsula. Moreover, in the southern part of Somalia, the Somalis established their own state, the Ajuran Imamate, the largest and longest standing state that continued for about 300 years from fourteenth to seventeenth century.

Somali history since medieval period revolved around two poles: Islam and colonialism. Thus, the early history of Somalia is mainly the history of introduction of Islam, spreading Islamic education and conflict with the Christian Abyssinian Empire and other ethnic communities in the region. The Ajuran Imamate was the first Somali state, ruling the largest territory extending from the central regions to the far southern Somali territories. Regrettably, studies on this embryonic formation of Somali state are scant.[121] The little available records depict that the sultanate was headquartered in Merca, applied Islamic Sharia, established strong standing army, and gave priority to building water supplies and building fortifications. The Ajuran Imamate is credited with defending the Somali territory from the Oromo and Portuguese raids and spreading Islam across the whole region. However, the later Ajuran rulers abandoned Sharia law, became oppressive, and introduced heavy taxation, which were the main catalysts for the rebellions against them in the 17th century.[122] All sultanates, in the Islamic medieval period, were invaded by nomadic clans who dismembered them into a patchwork of smaller mini-states in the seventeenth century. It is the nature of the nomads to destroy civilizations according to Ibn-Khaldun's theory of Asabiyah. After two centuries of setbacks in creating different states, the advent of colonialism created the second historical theme, with revolves around colonialism and its impact, the period in which an abundance of literature was produced.

The historiography of ancient and medieval Islamic history exhibits a historical gap which we barely know anything about it and a number of narratives are highly contested. The historical gap is the period between the first century, with its flourishing civilization and commercial cities, as reported in the *Periplus of the Erythraean Sea* and the introduction of Islam in the seventh century. The first contested narrative is the origin of the

---

[121] Mohamed Mukhtar, "Ajuran Sultanate." The Encyclopedia of Empire, http://onlinelibrary.wiley.com, 2016.

[122] Enrico Cerulli, *Somalia: scritti vari editi ed inediti. Vol.2* (Roma: Istituto poligrafico dello Stato,1957-1964), 250-254.

Somali people, who are theorized to be immigrants from the southern Ethiopia since 1000 BC or from the Arabian Peninsula in the eleventh century. The new narrative deriving from archeological evidence puts forth that the people of Somalia are the indigenous dwellers of their current habitat in the last 7000 years. The second contested narrative is the time of the introduction of Islam to Somalia. The narrative of the venture of Islam during the first Muslim migration to Abyssinia was seriously questioned because reliable evidence is missing. However, the puzzle that complicates the case is the presence of a Mosque of two niches in Zayla, which alludes that it was built before 624 (at least two years after the migration to Medina). The third contested narrative was Trimingham's depiction of the Abyssinian Christian Empire as "a beleaguered fortress in the midst of a sea of Islam." The counter-narrative was articulated by Travis J. Owens, who articulated that "the Muslim neighbors of the Ethiopian Empire were besieged by Christian Ethiopia throughout the medieval period." All in all, the ancient and Medieval Islamic history of the Somali peninsula demands more research and attention.

Further Readings

Ahmed, Hussein. "The Historiography of Islam in Ethiopia." Journal of Islamic Studies, 3 (1992).

A.S. Brandt. "The Importance of Somalia for understanding African and World prehistory", Proceedings of the First International Congress of Somali Studies in 1992.

Brereton, George Wynn and Huntingford. The Periplus of the Erythraean Sea. Ashgate Publishing, 1980.

Cassaneli, Lee. The Shaping of Somali Society: Reconstructing the history of the Pastoral People, 1600-1900. Philadelphia: University of Pennsylvania Press, 1982.

Hersi, Ali Abdirahman. The Arab Factor in Somali History: The Origins and Development of Arab Enterprises and Cultural Influence in the Somali Peninsula. Los Angeles: University of California, 1977.

Lewis, Herbert. "The Origins of Galla and Somali." The Journal of African History, vol.7, No.1 (1966), 27-46.

Mire, Sadia. "Mapping the Archaeology of Somaliland: Religion, Art, Script, Time, Urbanism, Trade, and Empire", 2015.

Mukhtar, Mohamed. "Islam in Somali History: Fact and fictions" in The Invention of Somalia, edited by Ali Jumale Ahmed. Lawrenceville: The Red Sea Press, 1995.

N. Chittick H. "An archaeological reconnaissance of the southern Somali coast", Azania, 4.

CHAPTER THREE

RECONFIGURATION OF THE SOMALI SOCIETY: THE IMPACT OF SUFI ORDERS AND COLONIALISM

The Worst thing that colonialism did was to cloud our view of our past
- Barack Hussein Obama, President of the USA

The day will come when history will speak ... Africa will write its own history...
It will be a history of glory and dignity. - Patrice Lumumba

The modern history of Somalia began in the 18th century, about two centuries after the collapse of the Ajuran Imamate and before the European scramble for Africa. This period was characterized by the ascendency of segmented clan-based sultanates, city-states, and the revival of Sufi orders. The geography of Somalia has been strategic since the ancient times and remains so in the contemporary period. The people were mainly pastoral nomads bestowed with rare uniformity of belief in the Islamic religion, language and culture. The region has an abundance of arable land and a long coast along the Indian Ocean, which is rich in natural resources. Alas, Somalis did not develop national state in the pre-colonial period, which could have protected its territories and unified its segmented clans. With such precarious state of affairs, the advent of colonialism in the late nineteenth century created new pervasive conditions for change that reshaped its cosmology and lifestyle.

Since then, Somali history has revolved around two antagonistic domains: Islam and colonialism. Islam, which was introduced to Somalia in the seventh century, has exerted its influence on most Somalis since the eleventh century. Nonetheless, its vibrant revival was noted in the eighteenth century with the rise of the various Sufi orders. The transformative impact of the Sufi orders on the illiterate and pastoral Somali society was enormous because of its innovative mobilization techniques and cultural sensitivity. The early period of modern development of the Islamic call in Somalia is signified as "the Islamic revival." The other three phases include the rise of the Islamic consciousness (1950-1967), the beginning of the Islamic awakening

67

(1967-1978), and the emergence of the Islamic movements (1978-present).[1] On the other hand, colonialism reached Somali Peninsula in the 1880s in the era of European scramble for Africa. Failing to avert colonial dominance, the people of Somalia were gradually integrated into the political and economic systems of the multiple colonial powers.[2] The actual process of integration began with the introduction of colonial education system and the creation of westernized elites. Through education and rudimentary job training, Somali elites were poorly prepared to take over the administrative task of the independent Somali state in 1960.

This chapter looks at the period that begins in the pre-colonial era, which is divided into three major configuration phases that interactively overlap each other. The first phase explores the social impact of the revival of Islam, in particular the role of the Sufi orders. The second phase investigates the incursion of multiple colonialism in the Somali Peninsula which provoked Somali resistance in the form of sporadic militant and peaceful resistances. In the process of interaction with the various colonial administrations, the people of Somalia have learned about modern warfare systems, material production techniques, and modern approaches to politics. The third phase explores the impact of the colonialism on the education sector and production of westernized elites. During this phase, political clannism was developed with the introduction of the political parties. In this phase, the bifurcation of the elites into Islamists, non-Islamists and westernized was witnessed, and their growing tension was apparent. This state of affairs has triggered conflict among the elites imbued with politicized clans and the rising Islamic awakening. At this point, state-society relation drastically deteriorated, succumbing to disastrous implications that finally collapsed the Somali state in 1991.

---

[1]   The author had divided modern development of the Islamic movement in Somalia into four phases. Refer to Abdurahman Abdullahi (Baadiyow), "Somalia: Historical Phases of the Islamic Movements." Somali Studies Journal. Volume 1 (2016), 19-49

[2]   Somali people were subjected to three European colonial powers: Britain, France, Italy, and neighboring Ethiopia, which expanded its frontiers in the Somali territory.

The Islamic Revival and Reconfiguration of Society

Islam laid the foundation for reorientation of the societies regarding its world view, identity, and hierarchy of values by providing a road map and a blue-print of total order. This blue-print derives its basic sources of the Qur'an and prophetic tradition interpreted in a flexible method that accepts multiple opinions within its general framework and objectives. Islam offered orderliness and ethics to barbarous nomads and sedentary dwellers and caused sweeping changes and great transformations in social, political, economic, and moral values. Islam does not aim to wipe out pre-existed cultural norms of communities, rather, it reorients, integrates and perfects. On this point of view, the Prophet Muhammad said: "Indeed, I was only sent to complete/to perfect the noble qualities."[3] Moreover, Allah praised the prophet for his great manners and said: "And, indeed, you are of a great moral character" (The Qur'an, 68:4). Thus, Islam has a long history of transforming nomadic societies into a civilized society and the Qur'an described their character in a number of verses. For instance,

> The Arabs of the desert [nomads] are the worst in unbelief and hypocrisy, and most fitted to be in ignorance of the command which Allah hath sent down to His Messenger: But Allah is All-knowing, All-Wise. (The Qur'an, 9:79).

However, after their belief in Islam, some of the nomads change their characters as the following verse states:

> But among the Bedouins [nomads] are some who believe in Allah and the Last Day and consider what they spend as means of nearness to Allah and of [obtaining] invocations of the Messenger. Unquestionably, it is a means of nearness for them. Allah will admit them to His mercy. Indeed, Allah is Forgiving and Merciful. (The Qur'an, 9:99).

Therefore, Sufi orders played a particular role in the Islamization of the peoples of Africa and Asia through their innovative and sensitive approaches to the different cultural tendencies of the targeted people. Here, we will explore how Sufi orders transformed Somali society from illiterate nomads to settled communities.

---

[3] Al-Adab Al-Mufrad, Book 1, Hadith no. 273

Sufism (*al-Tasawuf*) existed as an individual inner practice of Muslims since early Islamic history. Yet, its organized form emerged as a reaction to the growing worldliness of the expanding Muslim caliphates and the dominance of legalistic school of thought.[4] It is founded on the perfection of the worship of *"Ihsan"*, as described in the prophetic tradition: *"Ihsan* is to worship Allah as if you see Him; if you can't see Him, surely He sees you."[5] In other words, Sufi orders believe that the Qur'an and Hadith have esoteric meaning and symbolist aspect (*Batin*), in addition to their exoteric (*Zahir*) meaning. However, these two dimensions constitute indispensable components of the comprehensive conception of Islam. Further, despite the fact that extreme circles of esoteric and exoteric schools of thought have fanatical voices, notwithstanding, the mainstream Muslim belief combines these two aspects in moderation. In the Somali context, its traditional Islam follows three main genealogies: the Ash'ariyah theology, Shafi'i jurisprudence, and Sufism. The Ash'ariyah theology was founded by Abu al-Hassan Al-Ash'ari (873-935AC) in reaction to the extreme rationalism espoused by the school of Mu'tazilah.[6] The Shafi'yah School of jurisprudence is also one of the major four Sunni schools of jurisprudence and it is rooted in the methodology and teachings of Abu Abdallah al-Shafi'i (767–820).[7] Sufi orders in Somalia belong to the moderate form rooted in al-Ghazali's way, and it had a significant missionary impact throughout Somalia.[8] The rise of Sufi orders as organized movements in the Muslim World dates back to the eleventh, twelfth and thirteenth centuries. For instance, Qadiriyah was founded by Sheikh Abdulqadir al-Jeylani (1077-1166) and Shadaliyah by Abu- Hasan al-Shadali (1196-1258). Other orders, such as Ahmadiyah founded by Ahmad Ibn Idris al-Fasi (1760-1837), were developed later. Islam has been always linked with education, and its tradition is founded to give it utmost priority. In particular,

---

[4]   Abdallah Saeed, *Islamic Thought: An Introduction* (London: Routledge, 2006).

[5]   Muhammad Bin Jamil Zeno, *The Pillars of Islam & Iman* (Darussalam, 1966),19.

[6]   Mu'atazilah is theological school founded by Wasil ibn Ata (d. 748). The main assumption of this school is that reason is more reliable than tradition. See Majid Fakhry, *A History of Islamic Philosophy* (New York: Colombia University Press, 1983), 44-65.

[7]   The four main jurisprudence schools of the Sunni Muslims are Malikiyah, Hanafiyah, Shafi'iyah, and Hanbaliyah.

[8]   Abu Hamed al- Ghazali (1058–1111) is considered the scholar who best succeeded in combining Sufism and Islamic jurisprudence in his works, where he argued that Sufism originated from the Qur'an and was compatible with Islamic thought.

Islamic education which is indispensable to the performing basic rituals has been made priority and obligatory on every Muslim. The first revelation of the Qur'an began with:

> Read! Read in the name of thy Lord who created; [He] created the human being from a blood clot. Read in the name of thy Lord who taught by the pen: [He] taught the human being what he did not know (The Qur'an, 96: 1-5).

In realizing this challenging task, Somali Islamic scholars undertook the project of educating illiterate nomadic/pastoral people in an innovative method. They introduced an inventive and sustainable system of education, using environmentally friendly techniques. The education system was simple in all its elements like the teacher, teaching methods, educational content, learning environment, and funding that was self-centered and community centered. It was based on a curriculum which starts with memorization of the Qur'an and elementary Islamic knowledge in early childhood. To facilitate such memorization in non-Arabic speaking population of Somalia, Islamic scholar Sheikh Yusuf al-Kawnayn invented the notation system for Arabic alphabets in the Somali language around 1150 AD.[9] The Qur'anic school sites are environmentally friendly and constructed from the local materials. Moreover, Qur'anic students use reusable wooden slates and ink made of milk mixed with powdered charcoal as educational materials. These schools provide sustainable educational opportunities that are accessible and affordable for the large populations in the villages, towns, and cities. The second level of Islamic education is situated in the mosques where dedicated graduates from the Qur'anic schools proceed to the higher level of Islamic learning. The curriculum is mainly focussed in the Arabic language, Islamic jurisprudence, interpretation of the Qur'an (exegesis) and Hadith studies. Opportunities for higher education are offered freely by volunteer scholars and mainly confined in the urban centers. Graduates who are more committed to the Islamic knowledge are sent as emissaries of their Sheikhs/Sufi masters to their home territories in order

---

[9]   The tomb of Aw-Barkhadle is located about 20 km north-east of Hargeisa. See Oral traditions on Aw-Barkhadle in the detailed narrations of I.M. Lewis, *Saints and Somalis: Popular Islam in a Clan-based Society* (Red Sea Press, 1998), 89-98. Also, I.M. Lewis, (ed.), *Islam in Tropical Africa* (London: Oxford University Press, 1966), 28.

to propagate Islam. The concept of sending educated emissaries is grounded on the Qur'anic verse:

> And it is not for the believers to go forth [to battle] all at once. For there should separate from every division of them a group [remaining] to obtain understanding in the religion and warn their people when they return to them that they might be cautious (9:112).

They also initiate settlements and urbanization of the pastoral population through establishing permanent Islamic education centers. Some of these scholars focus on the studies of jurisprudence and become judges and teachers, while others may belong to one of the Sufi orders. Others combine their studies with Sufism in the early stage and focus on spreading Sufi doctrines. The third level of Islamic education is purely based on Sufism, dispensed by the masters of the Sufi orders. Sufi orders focus on spiritual purification (Tazkiyahtu al-Nafs) under the guidance of a spiritual master. Followers of Sufism seek a closer relationship with Allah through special disciplines and spiritual exercises. Sufism in Somalia is an extension of the similar phenomenon in the Muslim world with the added Somali specificity and flavour. Following figure demonstrate traditional education system which may vary after the basic education to either early attachment to Sufism or pursuing higher education.

Basic Education	Intermediate/Higher	Sufism
• Memorization of the Qur'an • Elementary Islamic learning	• Arabic Language • Jurisprudence • Exegesis • Prophetic Traditions	• Sufi Studies • Practical application

Fig 2. Traditional System of Islamic Education

The advent of Sufism in the Somali Peninsula was spotted in the early 15th century with the arrival of 44 Islamic scholars from the Arabian Peninsula under the leadership of Sheikh Ibrahim Abu-Zarbai in

1430.[10] However, the revival and reform of Sufi orders was noticeably witnessed from the last quarter of the 19th century to the middle of the 20th century. Professor Said Samatar proclaimed that "these years between 1880 and 1920 can be described as the era of the Sheikhs in Somali history."[11] Sufi reformation entailed shifting from individual piety and warships to institutionalized orders and collective approaches.[12] Sufi masters may belong to all three categories of Islamic scholars in Somalia: Sheikh (Islamic jurist and teacher), Moalim (Qur'anic teacher), and Aw (a person with a rudimentary Islamic education). As described by orientalist historian Spencer Trimigham, the stimulus for the revival of Sufism may have been the emergence of charismatic spiritual preachers with a talent for mass mobilization.[13] However, this raison d'être is not sufficient to explain the phenomenon which seems to have linked with the nature of Islam to revive periodically, as the prophetic Hadith relates that "Allah will raise for this community at the end of every hundred years someone who will restore its religion for it."[14] In addition to that, Sufi orders played the role as civil society organizations after Muslim states declined, and opportunities for passionate missionary activities were availed among peoples of different cultures, particularly in Africa and Asia.

Sufi orders are known mainly for their peaceful approaches to socio-religious reform through Islamic propagation and spiritual revitalization.[15] As such, they dominated religious life, reaching out to populations in the urban and rural areas alike. In that manner, Sufi sheikhs played complementary role in running community affairs hand in hand with the traditional elders and establishing Islamic commonwealth

---

[10] Abdurahman Abdullahi (Baadiyow), *The Islamic Movement*, 38.

[11] Said Samatar, *Oral Poetry and Somali Nationalism: The Case of Sayid Mohamed Abdulle Hassan* (Cambridge: Cambridge University Press, 1982), 97

[12] Scott Steven Rees, *Patricians of the Banadir: Islamic Learning, Commerce and Somali Urban Identity in the Nineteenth Century* (PhD thesis submitted to the University of Pennsylvania, 1996), 306

[13] Trimigham, *Islam in Ethiopia* (Taylor & Francis,1952). Also, Rees, *Patricians of the Banadir*, 302-303.

[14] This Hadith was narrated by Abu Dawood, Hakim and Baihaqi. Another Hadith with a similar meaning, narrated by Hakim, says: *"There will always be in my nation a group who will safeguard the truth until the day of resurrection comes."*

[15] The nature of the peacefulness of Sufi orders may be interrupted because of external provocations, such as colonialism, as in the case of many scholars, exemplified by Sayid Mohamad Abdulle Hasan, and internal doctrinal conflicts, such as the conflict between Bardheere Jama'a and Geledi Sultanates and current fighting between Al-Shabaab and the Sufi order of Ahl al-Sunna wa al-Jama'a.

centers whose dwellers gave their allegiance only to their Sufi masters/sheikhs.[16] Moreover, conventional historiography that considers Sufi orders to be mainly apolitical, which means not interested or involved in politics, is questionable. Firstly, from the Islamic perspective, there is no apolitical conception in Islam since every Muslim must participate in enjoying what is right and forbidding what is evil. Islamic scholars, in general, took the responsibility of what following verse addresses to them:

> And let there be [arising] from you a nation inviting to [all that is] good, enjoining what is right and forbidding what is wrong, and those will be the successful" (The Qur'an 3:104).

Secondly, Sufi orders possess legitimate authority and exercise politics, in the broadest sense, as the activity through which people make, preserve and amend the general rules under which they live. Moreover, in the traditional meaning of politics, many leaders of the Sufi orders and their disciples became the political leaders of their communities. Thus, clan allegiances and loyalties were diluted, and at times transformed into ideological loyalties. Occasionally, both religious and worldly authorities are combined in one leader, thereby creating a strong Sufi master. Professor Said Samatar lucidly wrote that "...The emergence of organized Sufism allowed these religious men to exercise autocratic powers unknown to secular men in the fragmented politics of clan organization."[17] Moreover, most of the Islamic education centers were located in settlements in agricultural areas and around water wells, and many of these were later transformed into villages, towns, and cities. In

---

[16] Certainly, all Jama'a communities in Somalia, estimated by I.M. Lewis in the 1950s to account for more than 80 communities, are under the leadership of a master/sheikh, and the clan factor has not much space. Of these, over half were Ahmadiyah, and the remaining was distributed almost equally between Qadiriyah and Salihiyah (note here Lewis does not include Salihiyah in Ahmadiyah, which is incorrect). See Lewis, *Saints*, 35. Moreover, Professor Mukhtar produces 92 Jama'a in 1920s in the Italian colony, where 50 Jama'a were located in the upper Juba, 30 in Banadir, 4 in Lower Juba, and 8 in Hiran. See Mohamed Mukhtar, *Historical Dictionary of Somalia. African Historical Dictionary Series, 87* (Lanham, MD: Scarecrow Press, 2003), 127.

[17] Samatar, Said. "Poetry in Somali Politics·, PhD Dissertation submitted to the Northwestern University, 1979, 192.

this way, Sufi orders transformed pastoral society into settled communities engaged in agriculture and/or trade.[18]

In the 19th century, Islamic propagation in Somalia was not a monopoly of the Sufi orders alone. There were independent Islamic education centers, such as Galusbo in Hiiraan region, Rooh in Nugaal region, and Hafun in Bari region that did not belong to any Sufi brotherhoods. For example, famous judge Sheikh Abdalla Qoriyow was educated in Galusbo and became a judge for the Darwish Movement led by Sayyid Mohamed Abdulle Hasan (1900-1921). On the other hand, Rooh, located 50 km north of Galkayo town, was the center of Haji Yusuf Mohamed Fiqhi Idris, the teacher of Sheikh Ali Majeerteen and other prominent scholars. Moreover, Hafun education center was well connected to the Arabian Peninsula, and the Salafiyah School was introduced there earlier.[19] In southern Somalia, the seat of Ashraf in Sarman, located near Hudur town and Barave, were center of Islamic learning where many scholars graduated from. For instance, prominent leaders of Bardheere Jama'a, such as Sharif Abdirahman and Sharif Ibrahim, originated from Sarman. This conflict was erroneously called the "Bardheere Jihad" by most historians and, in particular, professor Cassanelli who coined this catchphrase. In fact, internal wars between Muslims should not be called Jihad. This is a misnomer that militant Bardheere Jama'a used to justify their war with the other Muslims in the region. This phrase is a loaded concept that carries Takfir ideology (a Muslim declaring another Muslim as a non-believer) and has to be revised.[20]

There were also early reformist attempts to establish Islamic sultanates in southern part of Somalia in the first half of the nineteenth century. For instance, the Bardheere Jama'a, which was founded in 1819 by Sheikh Ibrahim Yabarow, undertook the ambitious plan of establishing Islamic order. The Jama'a introduced some Islamic reforms such as outlawing tobacco, the ivory trade, and popular dancing, and imposed wearing Islamic dress for women. It had expanded its sphere of influence to parts of the Bakol, Bay and lower Shabelle by 1840. In

---

[18] Laitin, and Samatar, *Somalia: Nation*,45.

[19] Abdurahman Abdullahi (Baadiyow), *The Islamic Movement*. 67-71.

[20] Note that the Sultan of Geledi did not call it Jihad, but was simply defending his area of influence from Wahabiyah intruders. On details of this event, see Lee Cassanelli, *The Shaping of Somali Society: Reconstructing the History of a Pastoral People, 1600-1900* (Philadelphia: University of Philadelphia Press, 1982),136-139.

particular, the Jama'a prohibition of the lucrative ivory trade threatened the interest of traders in the urban cities of Merca, Barawe, and Mogadishu. As Ambassador Salah Mohamed articulates, "The traders considered the prohibition of the ivory trade by the Jameeca [Jama'a] leaders an unjust trade block on Banadir, as well as open act of hostility."[21] This action provoked traders and clans of the inter-river areas to join the Geledi sultanate's raid of Bardheere, the center of the Jama'a. The Geledi sultanate mobilized an expedition force of 40,000 from all clans in the areas, instructing them to storm Bardheere and burn it to the ground in 1843.[22] Another example is the arrival of Sheikh Ali Abdirahman (Majeerteen) (1787-1852) in Merca with hundreds of armed men and substantial quantities of firearms and ammunitions, with the aim of establishing an Islamic emirate in 1846, four years after the defeat of Bardheere Jama'a. The reaction of the Geledi Sultanate was rapid, and Sheikh Ali's followers were defeated in confronting the Geledi Suldaan's forces in 1847.[23] Apparently, Sheikh Ali belonged to the same ideology of Bardheere Jama'a, a new militant tendency that was emerging during this period in many Muslim countries. With the destruction of the Bardheere Jama'a and the foiled attempts of Sheikh Ali Majeerteen at Merca, the objectives of the early reformist movements were aborted until the emergence of a stronger and more organized movement in the dawn of the colonial intrusion, that is, the Darwish movement, under the charismatic leadership of Sayyid Mohamed Abdulle Hassan.

The Sufi orders remained active across Somalia with popular support, despite the fact that modern elites who did not belong to any Sufi order emerged with the development of modern education and modern Islamic movements eschewing Sufism. Briefly, the main characteristics of Sufi orders in Somalia are as follows. They are affiliated with the wider networks of Sufi brotherhoods in the Muslim world. Their leadership is absolute and authoritative, and succession is not necessarily based on heredity; however, the Khalif (Sufi master) designates his successor in his lifetime. Often, most of the Sufi masters nominate their sons, believing that their blessing (Baraka) is dormant in them, and members of the order will pay great respect to the son, deriving from respect for his father. Every Sufi master has an official Sufi genealogy connecting him to

---

[21] Salah Mohamed Ali, *Hudur and the History of Southern Somalia* (Cairo: Nahda Publishing, 2005),33

[22] Abdullahi, *The Islamic Movement, 68.*

[23] Ibid., *70.*

the founder of his order. Membership is acquired by new aspirants through direct formal initiation (allegiance). Every member has to comply with the policies and procedures of the orders that include regular recitation of litanies. Finally, members take the common name of Ikhwaan (brethren) that connote their relation to the pan-Islamic brotherhood.[24]

There are two main Sufi orders in Somalia: Qadiriyah and Ahmadiyah. Each Sufi order has its local offshoots.[25] Qadiriyah has three branches: Zayli'iyah, Rufaiyah and Uweysiyah. Zayli'iyah was founded by Sheikh Abdirahman al-Zayli'i (1815-1882), who was based in Qulunqul near Dhagahbur in western Somalia (Somali State of Ethiopia).[26] Rufaiyah was followed primarily by some Banadiri Sheikhs in Mogadishu, such as Sharif al-Aidarusi, who was one of the founders of the Islamic Leagues, the first Islamic organization after the WW II.[27] Uweysiyah was founded by the spiritual master Sheikh Uweys ibn Ahmad al-Barawe (1846-1907), and its seat was located in Balad al-Amiin near Afgoye, about 40 km south-west of Mogadishu.[28] Ahmadiyah has three offshoots in Somalia: Rahmaniyah, Salihiyah, and Dandarawiyah. Rahmaniyah was founded by Maulana Abdurahman ibn Mohamud (d. 1874). Salihiyah, founded by Sheikh Mahamad Salah around 1890s, has two branches: the southern branch introduced by Sheikh Mohamad Guleed al-Rashidi

---

24 Spencer Trimigham, *Islam in Ethiopia* (Taylor & Francis, 1952), 236-237.

25 Most scholars fail to distinguish between the original Sufi order and their later derivatives. Sometimes these Sufi orders are said to be three, making Salihiyah a separate order from Ahmadiyah and also neglecting the existence of the Rufa'iyah order. See David Laitin and Said Samatar, *Somalia: Nation in Search of State (Boulder: Westview, 1987)*,45.

26 Bradford G. Martin, "Shaykh Zayla'i and the nineteenth-century Somali Qadiriya", in: Said S. Samatar (ed.), *In the Shadows of Conquest. Islam in Colonial Northeast Africa* (Trenton, NJ: The Red Sea Press, 1992), 11-32.

27 Abdurahman Abdullahi, *The Islamic Movement*, 113.

28 A number of valuable papers were written on the Uwayiyah branch of Qadiriyah. These include: Bradford G. Martin, "Shaykh Uways bin Muhammad al-Barawi, a Traditional Somali Sufi", in: G. M. Smith and Carl Ernst (eds.), *Manifestations of Sainthood in Islam* (Istanbul, 1993), 225-37., Said S Samatar, 1992. "Sheikh Uways Muhammad of Baraawe, 1847-1909. Mystic and Reformer in East Africa", in: Said S. Samatar (ed.), *In the Shadows of Conquest. Islam in Colonial Northeast Africa* (Trenton, NJ: The Red Sea Press, 1992), 48-74., and Christine Choi Ahmed, "God, Anti-Colonialism and Drums: Sheikh Uways and the Uwaysiyya." (Ufahamu: A Journal of African Studies, 17(2) 1989), 96-117.

(d.1918) and the northern branch introduced by Sayyid Mohamad Abdulle Hasan (1856-1921). Dandarawiyah was introduced by Sayyid Adan Ahmad and has a limited following in northern Somalia.[29]

In gathering pieces of the early history of the Sufi orders, it is important to note that there were two regional centers of Islamic learning in the pre-colonial Somali territories. These centers were connected with Yemen, Zanzibar, Oman, Saudi Arabia, and Egypt. One of these centers was established in the Banadir region, where the cities of Mogadishu, Barawe, Merca, and Warsheik are located. In these centers, famous Islamic scholars and prominent Sufi sheikhs spread Islam to the clans of the interior. They also established pan-clan networks through common affiliation to one of the Sufi orders. Students traveled to Banadir via trade routes connecting this area with the southern and middle regions of Somali territories.[30] The other Islamic education centers were located in historical cities in western Somali territories (currently the Somali state of Ethiopia), such as Harar, Jigjiga, and the surrounding areas. In particular, Qulunqul is renowned as the Qadiriyah Sufi center and had its special importance as the site of the founder of Zayliyah branch of Qadiriyah, Sheikh Abdirahman al-Zayli'i. Islamic scholars and students of Islamic studies traveled between Harrar, Jigjiga, and the surrounding areas throughout the northern and northeastern Somali regions that include the current Somaliland and Puntland. Other Sufi orders were marginal late-comers. The two main Sufi orders, Qadiriyah and Ahmadiyah, and their offshoots spread their messages along with these Islamic education centers and satellite centers established by their disciples.

---

[29] Cabdirisaq Caqli, *Sheikh Madar: Asaasaha Hargeysa* (biographical work on Sheikh Madar written in Somali Language, no date or publishing house).
[30] See trade routes in early Somalia in Laitin and Samatar, Somalia: Nation, 9-10.

Name of Sufi Order	Founder of the Order	Center of the Order
Qadiriyah: Zaili'iyah Uweysiyah	Sh. Abdirahman Al-Zaili'i (d. 1882) Sh. Uweys al-Barawi (d. 1909)	Qulunqul (Dhagahbur) Balad al-Amin (Afgoye)
Ahmadiyah: Rahmaniyah Salihiyah (North) Salihiyah (south) Dandrawiyah	Sh. Abdirahman Mohamud (d.1875) Sh. Mohamed Abdulle Hassan (d.1921) Sh. Mohamed Guled al-Rashidi (d.1918) Sh. Sayyid Adan Ahmed (second half of 19ᵗʰ century)	Basra (Afgoye) Qoryaweyne (Las-Anod) Mira weyn (Jowhar) Haahi & Sheikh town

Fig 3. The Sufi Brotherhoods in Somalia[31]

Cases Studies: Sufi Orders' Role in Social Change

The following three examples demonstrate the role of Sufi Orders in three different locations of Somalia.[32] In northern Somalia, we pick Sheikh Madar Ahmad Shirwa (1825-1918) as an example. Sheikh Madar Ahmad Shirwa was a Sufi guide, a social reformer, and a jurist. In his early childhood, he memorized the Qur'an and learned Arabic language in a pastoral Qur'anic school, a mobile school moving with pastoral seasonal movements. Berbera was the commercial port connected with the historic Islamic city of Harar, and Islamic scholars, students, and business people frequently traveled between these two cities. While Berbera was the regional trade hub, Harar was the regional seat of Islamic learning. After Britain's takeover of Aden in 1839, Berbera supplied livestock to the British garrison in Aden. Consequently, pastoralists in the area, benefiting from the lucrative business opportunity, became more affluent, and trade between Berbera and Harar was significantly thriving. As a result, many Somalis lived in Harrar for business, work, and as students of Islam. By 1855, as related by Richard Burton, the British intelligence officer, about 2,500 Somalis lived

---

[31] This table is reproduced from the original table prepared by this author in his other book: The Islamic movement in Somalia: A Study of Islah Movement, 66

[32] These three examples could be referred in more detail to Abdullahi, *The Islamic Movement, 44-66.*

in Harar, one third of the total population of the city.[33] Two of the three most prominent Islamic scholars were ethnic Somalis, namely, Haji Jama'a and Kabir Khalil. Kabir Khalil originated from the Berbera area and many students who came from this area were under his custodian. The father of Sheikh Madar was among those affluent pastoralists who benefited from the lucrative business in Berbera and was capable of supporting his son's education in Harar. Sheikh Madar studied in Harar for 20 years, becoming an authoritative Islamic scholar and Qadiriyah Sufi master. He was assigned by his Sufi master Kabir Khalil to return to his home area and spread Islam, Qadiriyah order, and to resolve conflicts between clans disturbing trade routes between Berbera and Harar.[34] Subsequently, fulfilling directives of Kabir Khalil, Sheikh Madar moved to the center of the clan conflict, and founded *Jama'a Weyn* (the big commune) as the seat of the Islamic learning in the 1860s. This commune was later developed to became the city of Hargeisa, the capital city of Somaliland.[35] He also mobilized other Islamic scholars in the area, built homes for his commune, and constructed his Grand Mosque in 1883. From there, Islamic education began to boom, Shari'a was applied in the community, and reconciliations between feuding clans were initiated. Sheikh Madar, benefiting from his experiences gained in Harar, introduced three reforms in the way of life of the pastoral communities. First, he introduced permanent settlements, reforming nomadic life based on following after the rains and pastures. Second, he brought together members from various clans in an affiliation of brotherhood, changing the culture based on single clan loyalties. Third, he promoted and directed his followers toward agriculture, changing the culture of nomadic pastoralism.[36] The impact of Sheikh Madar's introduction of agriculture remains evident in the agricultural firms in the area west of Hargeisa, Gabeley and Borama districts.

Another case study in the central regions of Somalia is Sheikh Dauud Ulusow, who will be our example of the role of Sufi order in establishing urban centers and educating people. Young Dauud left his native area in the district of Eldheer about 300 km north of Mogadishu and traveled to

[33] Richard F. Burton, *First Footsteps in East Africa* (BiblioBazaar, 2009), 139. Also, Caqli, *Sheikh Madar*, 26.
[34] Abdullahi, *The Islamic Movement*, 48-49.
[35] The commune and the mosque established by Sheikh Madar are still active symbolizing the transformational rule of the Islamic scholars in the Somali society.
[36] See Cabdirisaq Caqli, *Sheikh Madar*, 184.

Banadir, seeking Islamic knowledge. He memorized the Qur'an in Barmale, which is about 100 km north of Mogadishu, and then studied for a while in Agaran, a village near Merca. Agaran was the seat of Islamic learning established by the famous Sheikh Ali Majeerteen who migrated from Mudug region. Dauud finally joined the Islamic school of Sheikh Ali Maye in Merca, from where he later successfully graduated. After graduation, Sheikh Ali Maye appointed Sheikh Dauud as his emissary and sent him to his clan, Wa'eysle. He also, appointed with two other disciples from the area, namely, Haji Omar Mudey and Moallim Osman Kulmiye to accompany Sheikh Dauud in his mission. Sheikh Ali Maye, giving them his final directive before their departure, told them: "I made my son Dauud, the neck and you are the two hands," which meant Sheikh Dauud is the leader (*Amir*) and head of the mission and the other two emissaries were his lieutenants. The mission of the Islamic scholars made their headquarter in the town of Mareeg, exactly where Sheikh Ali Maye recommended in the littorals of the Indian Ocean.[37] The mission, initially founded a mosque to comply with Muslim tradition, opened an Islamic court to deal with community disputes, established educational programs and proclaimed for the people a new era of Islamic rule. Sheikh Omar Mudey became the judge of the new court while Moallim Osman initiated the first Qur'anic school. Sheikh Dauud began social mobilization and consultation with the clan elders in his new venture. He organized general congregation of the clan members held at Mareeg, and he directed them to collectively bath in the Ocean in order to make ritual purity, as mentioned in the story known as *Maalinta Bad-galka* (the day of entering the sea). This was an extraordinary event intended to cleanse the bodies and clothes of the people in order to perform ritual purity *(ghusl and wudu)* as required by the Islamic jurisprudence before the prayer is

---

[37] The folklore tale of Mareeg town relates that Sheikh Ali Maye advised the mission at the departure to travel through the littorals of the Ocean and where they find setting gazelles which do not run away from them, they should establish their settlement. The place of sitting gazelles is where Mareeg town was located and still remains intact and could be seen by the visitors of the ruined town. For more details, see Abdullahi, The Islamic Movement, 58. It seems that founding the city which I have related earlier to be founded by the mission under Sheikh Dauud was misleading. The city existed before the arrival of Sheikh Dauud and was the commercial outlet for Ajuran Imamate.

conducted.[38] Sheikh Dauud led congregation prayer, taught his people the importance of the prescribed prayers and trained them how to pray. Since that day, Sheikh Dauud became the *Amir* of his clan and undertook the responsibility of educating them. He declared the supremacy of Islamic Shari'a above the customary traditions (Xeer), resolved clan conflicts though reconciliation or adjudication, restructured clan authorities, and founded strong standing army. He successfully defended his emirates from the encroachment of the Sultanate of Obia ruled by Sultan Ali Yusuf in the north and Darwish forces from the west. The organizational structure created by Sheikh Dauud among his clan still remains functional and his Islamic education center continues producing numerous traditional scholars every year.

In the riverine regions of southern Somalia, our case study will explore Sheikh Bashir's Salihiyah commune in the Region of Middle Shabelle. This Jama'a is one of the 15 Jama'a settlements along the banks of the Shabelle River. It was founded in 1919 by Sheikh Bashir Haji Shu'ayb, who moved from Jama'a Ma'ruf, located near the Bulo-Burte district in the Hiraan Region, after a devastating epidemic in 1917 and 1918.[39] After the death of Sheikh Bashir, Sheikh Hanafi (d. 2002) succeeded as the Sheikh of the Jama'a and continued the tradition. Traditionally, besides the Sheikh of the Jama'a, there are four consultative members, called *Shuruud*, who assist the Sheikh of the Jama'a in the administrative matters. The Jama'a constitutes a small principality in which all members are required to comply with a set of rules and Islamic value system. For instance, all members should regularly frequent congregation prayers and Friday prayer in the Jama'a Mosque, and those who fail to do so should leave the Jama'a.[40] The Jama'a Sheikh undertakes functions such as conflict resolution in the community, provision of legal services, conducting marriage contracts, as well as performing occasional functions such as festivities for the birth of the Prophet Muhammad (*Mawliid*), Eid celebrations, annual commemoration of deceased dignitaries (*Siyaaro*), etc. Members of the local community are known as al-Ansar, while those who arrive from other regions and join

---

[38] Sheikh Osman Hidig, interviewed by the author on December 12, 2014, Mogadishu, Somalia.

[39] Ahmad Rashid Hanafi interviewed through email on November18, 2009.

[40] Conditions for membership are: (1) accepting the Salihiyah order, (2) recommendations from other three members, (3) allegiance to comply with the value system and regulations of the Jama'a.

the community are called migrants (*al-Muhajirun*), emulating the era of the Prophet Muhammad (peace be upon him). In contrast to the Jama'a in northern Somalia which converted nomads into settled communities and pastoralists into agricultural cultivators, the Jama'a in southern Somalia usually is established initially in settled agricultural communities. However, they share with all other Jama'a communities the duty of creating cross-clan community, whose allegiance is primarily to their Islamic leader.[41] Sufi Jama'a communities at the banks of the rivers, Juba and Shabelle, exhibit profound culture of pan-clannism, lack of prejudiced notion of majority versus minority clans, and intermarriages among various clan members.

The above case studies show that Sufi orders laid the civilizational foundation in transforming many people among Somali society from pastoral nomads to settled communities organized mainly in a pan-clan system that supersedes parochial clan affiliations. The major task of Islamic scholars is anchored on teaching Islam, as well as invigorating religiosity, and peace-building and conflict resolution among feuding communities. Sufi orders were also great missionaries who converted many people in various continents to Islam. They have undertaken the extra task of what is generally considered an Islamic scholar's duty. In Somalia, they introduced four major civilizational reforms that sometimes cross-cut non-Sufi Islamic scholars. These reforms had drastically changed the lifestyle of Somali communities. To be accepted to work among various communities, Sufi orders use symbolical activities that are sensitive to the people's culture and innovative mobilization techniques. In the beginning of the social reform, occasional social gathering festivities were established to bring together nomads who could not otherwise assemble.

The first Sufi masters' program was launching annual memorials of deceased common parents (close and distant). This program is called "*Xus*" which aims to assemble sub-clans annually at the graveyards of their ancestral fathers to make prayers to their souls. In gathering clan members, Sufi masters resolved conflicts, promoted Islamic education and undertook leadership in many social affairs. Gradually, other programs were established such as commemoration of the deceased teacher/sheikh/Sufi master of the community, known as "*Siyaro*". This

---

[41]   Jaylani Hanafi interviewed by the author on December 21, 2009, Hargeysa, Somaliland.

program is founded on visiting the tomb of the Sheikh/Islamic scholar annually in his time of death, where all his disciples gather for his memorial, recite Qur'an and make supplication for his soul. Moreover, purely Islamic programs are celebrated and people gather, such as during the memorial of the birth of the Prophet Muhammad (peace be upon him) called (*Mawlid*) and the two Eid festivities (the one after the Ramadan and the Great Eid after annual Pilgrimage to Mecca). In all these occasions, popular and ritualized dhikr ceremonies called "*Dikri*" are performed in which religious poems known as "*Qasaaid*" are chanted in a choral, artistic manner with various rituals. The Qur'an is also recited collectively in the form called "*Subac*", which is very important form of demonstrating Qur'anic students' memorization capability of the Qur'an and performance of the Qur'anic schools.[42] Moreover, the Qur'an is recited on the body of the sick individuals using its proven healing power as recommended by the Prophet Muhammad (peace be upon him).[43] Furthermore, the Qur'an is also recited at the tombs of deceased parents and venerated Sheikhs requesting Allah's blessing, mercy, and forgiveness for them. Other services are also handled, such as conflict resolutions, conducting marriage contracts, and other religious services. These occasions create collectiveness, a sense of belonging, and mutual support for the adherents of the Sufi orders. They also create a web of trans-clan networks, which enable their members to undertake business contracts and bolster their family relations through inter-marriages of their progenies.

The second reform program was the establishment of Islamic education centers with all its components, such as Qur'anic schools, high

---

[42] "Subac" derives from the Arabic Sab'a, meaning seven, designating the seven chapters of the Qur'an recited in the seven days of the week. It is one of the many ways of reciting the Qur'an in Somalia. Memorizers of the Qur'an sit in a circle and everybody recites.

[43] There are numerous verses and prophetic traditions which provide selected prayers for healing. Following Qur'anic verse and Hadith are just examples. "And We send down of the Quran that which is a healing and a mercy to those who believe..." (The Quran,17:82). One of the prophetic supplication for healing is "O Allah, Lord of mankind! remove our suffering, heal us you are the Healer, and none can heal but you. I beg to bring about healing that leaves behind no ailment" (Bukhari, no. 5675, Muslim, no. 2191).

learning centers, and circles of Sufism. The system of education usually follows a tradition of self-supporting model with the community support including scholarships for students from poor families, or those from distant locations. This scholarship package encompasses free education offered by the learned scholars and free accommodation provided by the community members. This system is called "*Jilidda Xer-cilmiga*" (feeding seekers of knowledge) and members and followers of Jama'a provide food for the students. The third reform program of the Sufi orders was the introduction of permanent settlement and urbanization in reforming the lifestyle of the nomadic pastoralism based on tracking after the rain falls and pastures. As result, they established villages, towns, and cities. Moreover, the culture of agricultural development, held as the work for the low cast by the "noble" nomads, was introduced and trade networks with other urban centers were promoted. Indeed, the beginning of human civilization began with settlements and dependence on agriculture. In particular, grain farms which produce surplus food that can be stored and traded. As H.G. Wells puts it, "civilization was the agricultural surplus."[44] The fourth reform program was to bring together members from various clans in the affiliation of brotherhood, changing the culture based on simple clan loyalties. They established supra-clan affiliation without discrimination of the minority clans, which resembled the concept of one community *(Umma)* based on brotherhood and cooperation, with pious individuals are placed as the leaders of the community. In this context, it was observed that most of the early Sufi Sheikhs belonged to the minority clans in Somalia. Sufi communes had changed the cosmology of clannishness to strong believers of universal Islamic principles, such as peace, benevolence, and brotherhood. In doing so, they did not abolish clan affiliations but mitigated its strong primordial loyalties and its divisive impact.

Colonialism and its Impact in Social Reconfiguration

The second phase of the reconfiguration of Somali society begins with the colonial incursion of the Somali Peninsula and integration of its society in the multiple colonial administrations. The Berlin Conference of 1884–885, which legitimized, mapped and divided the continent of

---

[44] H.G. Wells, *The World Set Free: A Story of Mankind.* (Macmillan and Co. Ltd, 1914), 194.

Africa among various European powers, was horrendous tribulation for the Somali people. As a result, the Somali Peninsula was seized and partitioned by four powers, namely, Italy, Great Britain, France, and Ethiopia. In order to legitimize their occupation, the three European powers signed various agreements with the Somali Sultanates, while the eastward expanding Ethiopian Empire captured Somali-inhabited territory by force. Britain and Italy approached administrations of their Somali colonies differently through indirect and direct rule respectively. For instance, Italy built its Somali colony through agreements with local powers through commercial companies.[45] The Italian objective of colonialism consisted of, according to Luigi Giglia, "three main elements: direct rule, racism, and demographic colonialism".[46] Its motivation was also three-fold: to relieve population pressure at home, to offer the "civilizing Roman mission" to the Somalis, and to increase Italian prestige through overseas colonization. The first such agreements were conducted in Banadir in 1986 under the nominal sovereignty of Oman Sultan of Zanzibar and followed by the Sultanate of Obbia under the leadership of Yusuf Kenadid in 1888. A similar agreement was also concluded with Boqor Osman over the Majeerteen Sultanate in 1889. The protectorate agreements between these two sultanates and Italy were later abolished unilaterally by Italy in 1925.[47] The Banadir region that was nominally under Sayyid Bargash of Zanzibar jurisdiction was purchased by Italy in 1905.[48] On April 5, 1908, the Italian Parliament enacted a basic law to unite all of the parts of southern Somalia into an area called "*Somalia Italiana*". Italy gradually expanded territorial possessions during the fascist rule, in particular under the Governor Maria De Vecchi who took over the rule of the colony on December 15, 1923, and completed the creation of a fully-fledged Italian colony by 1927.[49] The final part of

---

[45] For example, the Italian company that administered Banadir was the Filonardi company (1889-1893).

[46] Poalo Tripodi, *The Colonial Legacy in Somalia: Rome and Mogadishu: from Colonial Administration to Operation Restore Hope* (Macmillan Press Limited, 1999), 5.

[47] The annual emolument for the sultan was 120,00 Dollars according to Salah Mohamed, *Hudur*, 3. Also, Mohamed Osman Omar, *Somalia: Past and Present* (Somali Publications Pvt. Ltd.),53.

[48] Italy agreed to pay 144,000 pounds to the Sultan of Zanzibar. See Mohamed Osman Omar, Ibid., 63.

[49] The creation of a fully fledged Italian colony occurred during fascist rule after capturing the last independent Somali sultanate, and the submission of Boqor

the Italian colonial territory in Somalia, Jubaland, was acquired from Britain in 1925 as a reward for Italy's joining the Allies in WW I, according to the Versailles Peace Treaty. This treaty had officially ended the state of war between Germany and the allied powers and was signed on 28 June 1919.[50]

On the other hand, Britain signed various treaties with various clans throughout northern Somalia. The first treaty was signed with Warsangaly Sultanate Mohamud Ali Shire in 1888 who ruled what are nowadays known as the Sool, Sanaag, and Ayn provinces.[51] Other clans residing in the Somaliland protectorate also signed similar agreements. Thus, Somaliland Protectorate was officially proclaimed in 1887 and its border with French Somaliland (Djibouti), Ethiopia, and the Italian Somali colony was successively delineated until 1889. The protectorate was initially ruled from the British India until 1898 after which foreign office took over (1887-1905), and colonial office in 1905. Since 1990, the Somaliland protectorate was engaged in war with the Darwish Movement led by charismatic leader Sayyid Mohamed Abdulle Hassan until February 1920.[52] France also signed various treaties with the ethnic-Somali Issa and Afar Sultans between 1883 and 1987 and proclaimed its colony under the governorship of Léonce Lagarde, who played a prominent role in extending French influence into the Horn of Africa.

Osman Mohamud, the ruler of Majeerteen in November, 6, 1927. See Robert Hess, *Italian colonialism* (University of Chicago Press, 1966),156.

[50] Roland Anthony Oliver, *History of East Africa, Volume 2*. Clarendon Press, 1976, 7.

[51] World Heritage Encyclopedia, *Mohamoud Ali Shire* (World Heritage Encyclopedia, no publishing date). Available from http://www.ebooklibrary.org/articles/eng/Sultanate_of_Mohamoud_Ali_Shire(accessed on March 19, 2017).

[52] After failing to defeat Darwish state with ground forces, Britain sent 12 aircraft of Royal Airforce to Somaliland in the beginning of the Fifth Expedition. The campaign began in the first January, 1920 and was concluded on 9 Feberuary,1920 when Taleh, the capital city of the Darwish state, was bombed by the Royal Air force and was occupied. Dawrish forces had never seen an aircraft before and were terrified and scattered. Sayyid Mohamed evacuated to Ogaden where he died on 21 December 1920 at the age of 64. This was the first-time air force was used in Africa and strategic lessons learned were used in other countries afterwards. See, Douglas Jardine, *The Mad Mullah of Somaliland* (London: 8vo., 1923).

Colonial historiography belittles the importance of the Somali Peninsula, which connects Asia, Africa, and Europe through the Indian Ocean, the Red Sea, and the Suez Canal waterways. It depicts as if Somalia had no attractive interest to the colonizers. The colonial powers had claimed that their interest in Somalia was merely to use it as a stepping stone and a communication nexus to maintaining or capturing other vital geographic locations. For example, Britain claimed that its primary purpose of establishing Somaliland protectorate was to secure supplies of meat for their British Indian outpost in Aden, which they occupied in 1839. As such, Somaliland was nicknamed "Aden's butcher's shop".[53] Moreover, other British objectives included, as articulated by Professor Abdi Samatar, to "check the traffic of slaves, and to exclude the interference of foreign powers."[54] Nonetheless, historical records show earlier British strategic interest in the northern Somali territory when concluded commercial treaties with the clans of the coastal cities as early as 1927.[55] France claimed that their interest of the Somali coast, known today as the Republic of Djibouti, was to set up coaling facilities for its ships on their way to the French colonies in Indo-China and Madagascar. Thus, Britain and France took over part of the Somali territories, giving them the names of British Somaliland (1885) and French Somaliland (1887). The two countries recognized each other's sphere of influence and demarcated their colonial borders in 1888. Furthermore, Britain got hold of another Somali-populated tract of land, later called the Northern Frontier District (N.F.D), located in the far south of Somali territory adjacent to its colony in Kenya. The Italian interest in the Somali territory was unambiguous in aiming to boost its image as one of the great European powers in the scramble for Africa. It also aspired to extend its sphere of influence in Eritrea and Somalia to the Ethiopian highlands as part of image building and prestige seeking among other rival European powers. However, after a surprise Italian

---

[53] Ahmed Samatar, *Socialist Somalia: Rhetoric and Reality* (London: Zed Books, 1988),16.

[54] Abdi Ismail Samatar, *The state and rural transformation in Northern Somalia, 1884–1986* (Madison: University of Wisconsin Press, 1989), 31.

[55] In April 1825, the Ship Mary Anne under the command of Captain Linguard anchored in Berbera Port for trading purpose. He was attacked by the Somalis and in 1827 an expedition consisting of two Ships Tamar and Pandora arrived Berbera and forced the inhabitants to agree on a treaty on 6 February, 1827. See Mohamed Osman, *Somalia: Past and Present* (Publications Pvt. Ltd, 2006), 2. Also, Mark Bradbury, *Becoming Somaliland* (Progresso, 2008), 23.

defeat at Adwa in 1896 by Ethiopian forces, Italy claimed that the occupation of Somalia was in support of their strategic plan to avenge and recapture Ethiopia.[56] Interestingly, Italy's colonial venture was supported by Britain so as to thwart the French colonial plans. Initially, Italy set off its Somali incursion with a commercial treaty in 1885 and taking over the total administration of Banadir region, which they leased from the Zanzibar Sultanate in 1892. The Italian dream was briefly realized in the period (1936-1941) after it conquered Ethiopia and integrated it with Eritrea and Italian Somaliland creating a unitary colonial state called Italian East Africa (*Africa Orientale Italiana*).[57] Mogadishu was the capital city of the Italian East Africa and over 50,000 Italian settlers were living in the Italian Somaliland by 1935, 40% of whom were residents of Mogadishu which had estimated residents of 50,000.[58] Finally, Ethiopia was an emerging African empire in the 19th century and, being recognized as an independent African state on good terms with the major Western powers, it pushed its claim for its part of the pie of Somali territory. The Ethiopian Emperor Menelik II, competing with Europeans and expanding frontiers of the Ethiopian Empire to the eastwards, conquered and annexed parts of the Somali territories by 1897. The Ethiopian Empire impressed the European powers, in that it was a local African power to reckon with in grappling and sharing the Somali territorial booty. Consequently, the Somali people, who are culturally quite homogeneous but politically fragmented, entered the 20th century divided into five parts among four countries. This multiple colonial domination has inflicted enormous psychological distress and touched their mind and heart, provoking uncoordinated spontaneous resistances. The new era of reconfiguration of Somali society and state formation commenced that had a great impact on the whole history of Somalia in 20th century and beyond.

---

56 Robert Hees, *Italian Colonialism*, 172.
57 Francesco Marion, *Military Operations in the Italian East Africa, 1935-1941: Conquest and Defeat* (MA thesis submitted to Marine Corps University Quantico VA school of Advanced War-fighting, 2009).
58 W. Mitchell, Journal of the Royal United Service Institution. Whitehall Yard, Volume 57, Issue 2, 997.

Somali Reaction to Colonialism

The Somali encounter to colonialism can be generally divided into two phases. The first phase (1889-1927) was the era of traditional leaders' encounters with colonialism. This phase was concluded with the defeat of the Majeerteen king, Boqor Osman who dramatically consigned his sword to the Italian Fascist Governor De Vecchi in November, 1927.[59] The early Somali reaction against colonialism was sporadic and spontaneous, being segmented clans and small sultanates. In the meantime, colonial powers approached their colonial plans with steak and carrot, and used modern arsenal of weapons.[60] The sporadic resistance is evident from the first reaction that occurred in the town of Warsheik (40 km north of Mogadishu), where two Italian navy officers, Zavaglio and Bertorello, were killed in 1890.[61] This event was followed by other resistance that took place in the town of Adale in May 1891 where forty-five Somalis and six colonial solders were massacred.[62] Adale was the first headquarter of "*Somalia Italiana*" under Vincenzo Filonardi, the first Italian governor in 1889. These two incidents led to a drastic change in the colonial policies in dealing with the local population. Sheikh Ahmed Abiikar Gabyow (1844-1933) composed a patriotic poem instigating to resist Italian colonialism translated into English as follows:

> Fight against the enemy of Somalia! Reject the infidel colonial settlements!Do something before you die; Soon you will turn into ash and warms will eat your flesh; Set a model for later generations.[63]

---

[59] Boqor Osman consigned his sword at Hurdia coastal town (in the current Puntland State of Somalia). For more details consult, Abdisalam M. Isse-Salwe, *The Collapse of the Somali State: The Impact of Colonial legacy* (Haan Publishing; 2nd edition (1996), 45.

[60] For example, Britain used military aircraft to bomb the Headquarter of the Darwish Movement in Taleh in 1920. See, Laitin and Samatar, *Somalia*, 58.

[61] Mukhtar, Historical Dictionary, 204.

[62] When the people of Adale rose up against colonial occupation, three persons were arrested. This action provoked more anger and incited more resistance which cause so many deaths for Abdalla Arone lineage of Harti Abgal. See Salah Mohamed Ali, *Hudur and the History of Southern Somalia*. (Cairo: Nahda Publishing, 2005), 5-6.

[63] The original Somali version of the poem is as follows:
Somalian u dagaalamayna; Kuwa dulmaaya la dood gelayna; Kufriga soo degay diida leenahay; Dabeysha mawdka intey I daadeyn; Hilibka duud cunin ooan deeb noqon; Dadka tusaan danahiisa leeyahay; Kuwa dambaan udariiq falaaya! Mukhtar, Historical Dictionary, 204.

This poem may have inspired the people of Warsheikh in their uprising against Italians. Moreover, Italy sent a punitive expedition, which destroyed both Warsheikh and Adale, and killed more than 80 people in 1891. Sheikh Ahmed Gabyow composed another poem describing suffering the people after Italian massacre translated into English as follows:

> Manhood is wounded by these aliens; they are not prophets sent by God; we rejected then, but they did not heed us; Woe to those who come late; when we were fighting against such powerful force; our manhood is wounded by these alien.[64]

Moreover, in October 1893, Italian officer Maurizio Talmone was stabbed to death in Merca "on the day the Italian flag was hoisted in the town."[65] Furthermore, another Italian officer, Giacomo Trevis was killed in Merca in 1897.[66] These sporadic resistances have matured and became more organized later. In the first phase, the leadership of defending Muslim land from invading Christians was primarily on the shoulders of the Islamic scholars.

In the second phase (1943-1960), the Somali encounter to colonialism was led by new nationalist elites. The difference between the two periods is that the first encounter was a complete rejection of the Christian invaders of Muslim land, and people were mobilized under the banner of Islam. The second phase was founded on gaining the status of independent state, in line with the established world order of nation-states. This phase was a new direction for Somalia, shifting the paradigm from early anti-colonial resistance led by the Islamic scholars to a modern elite struggle, with the objective of establishing a modern state of Somalia. The 15-year gap between 1927 and 1943 is regarded as the years of "Somali disorientation", a transitional time from the dominance of the traditional elites to the emergence of nationalist elites. During these years, the Somali people went through harsh experiences, such as

---

[64] The original Somali version of the poem is as follows:
Ragow hadoo qalbi waa rafaadaa! Rujulka kaafira oo rugtaan yimid; Sidii Rasuul Rabi nooma soo dirin; mana rabne naga reed bax waa niri; Hadaase ruux la dagaasho kaa roon; reekaad u kasha laheedna raagaan;
Ragow hadda qalbi waa rafaada!). Mukhtar, Historical Dictionary, 205

[65] Salah, Hudur,7.

[66] Ibid.,8. It is reported that a young Somali, Omar Hassan Yusuf, assassinated the Italian resident, Giacomo Trevis.

participating in the Italian-Ethiopian war (1935-1941) and the WW II (1941-1945) as colonial soldiers of the warring sides. For instance, historical records show that "Somali colonial troops eagerly fought against Ethiopians, their traditional enemy" and more than 6,000 regular Somali soldiers and 40,000 irregulars participated in the Italy-Ethiopian war.[67]Also, a large number of Somalis, including 22 notables, had fought on the Ethiopian side against Italian occupation.[68] Likewise, in the WW II in the Horn of the African theater, Somali colonial soldiers fought for both Britain and Italy in the war of 1940-41. Also, Somali soldiers participated in the Burma war theatre as part of African brigades of the British forces in the WWII.[69] Moreover, Somali soldiers from Djibouti as part of African soldiers in the French army were used as cannon fodder in the WW I and also participated in the liberation of France in 1944.[70] It is worthy to note here that Somali military history is a black hole in the history of Somalia and "in search for historians."

The Somali resistance to colonialism became better organized under the leadership of the Islamic scholars of the Sufi orders. For example, the Darwish Movement led by Sayyid Mohamed Abdulle Hasan (1856-1921) was well organized militant that waged relentless wars against the British, Italians and Ethiopians for more than 20 years. Hence, Sayyid Mohamed became a symbol of Somali nationalism for his unchallenged poetical polemic and pioneering anti-colonial movement. Sufism is known to have formed an obstacle against colonial administration and westernized system of education.[71] Various approaches of resisting colonialism were

---

[67] Robert Hees, *Italian Colonialism*, 174.

[68] The names of the 22 notables are listed in Pankhurst, *Ex-Italian Somaliland*, 17. It seems that the stated 2000 notables, as given by Samatar, is highly exaggerated. See Samatar, *Socialist Somalia*, 52. See also Abdurahman Abdullahi, "Tribalism, Nationalism and Islam: The crisis of the political Loyalties in Somalia" (MA thesis, Islamic Institute, McGill University, 1992), 66.

[69] Ashley Jackson, *The British Empire and the Second World War* (London: Habledon Continuum, 2006), 213.

[70] Jonathan Sutherland and Diane Canwell, *Vichy Air Force at War: The French Air Force that Fought the Allies in World* (Pen and Sword Aviation, 2011), 32.

[71] Qadiriyah in the north strongly opposed attempts by the British administration to open secular schools. I.M. Lewis, *A Modern History of the Somali: Nation and State in the Horn of Africa* (Ohio University Press, 2003), 37. Also, I.M. Lewis, *Saints and Somalis: Popular Islam in a Clan-Based Society* (Sea Press,1998), 9.

used by different Sufi orders in different circumstances. The widespread assumption that depicts Salihiyah order as the champion of anti-colonial struggle, while Qadiriyah order is considered acquiescent, and even the collaborators with the colonizers have no historical basis. The well-known historical fact is that "Sheikh Aweys promoted resistance to the European colonizers in German-occupied Tanganyika, and even Uganda and eastern Congo."[72] Historical evidence shows that Qadiriyah encounter with colonialism was circumstantial, and any singular approach or prioritization of militancy over peaceful resistance is simply not borne out. These approaches should be seen to complement each other, depending on the situations and assessment of the available options. For instance, a colonial encounter that emerged from the pastoral areas was mainly armed resistance, while anti-colonial movements in the urban and agro-pastoral regions were mainly peaceful. This viewpoint could be used as theoretical backdrop in explaining the approaches of the Darwish Movement, led by Sayyid Mohamed Abdulle Hasan and that of Sheikh Aweys al-Barawi in Somalia.

On the other hand, the approaches mainly used by Qadiriyah order in the Southern Somalia, even though the concept of Jihad was present, were simply due to their environment of agro-pastoral and urban settlements. At times, followers of Qadiriyah opted for armed resistance as exemplified by the Lafole encounter of 1896. Warriors belonging to Wa'adan and Geledi clans who were disciples of Qadiriyah Sheikh Ahmad Haji Mahadi (d. 1900) were accused for the incident. On 20 April 1897, the Italians bombarded Nimow, the seat of Sheikh Ahmed in retaliation for the Lafole incident massacring the civilian population.[73] Another southern resistance movement is exemplified by the Biyamal resistance (1896-1908) led by Mo'alin Mursal Yusuf and Sheikh Abikar Gafle, which had continued resisting colonialization for 12 years.[74]

---

[72] Ibid., 36.

[73] Sheikh Ahmed Haji migrated from Mogadishu in deviance to the Italians and considered it as the abode of non-believers (*Dar al-Kufr*) and established *'Dar al-Islam'* in Nimow. The Lafole incident was also implicated two Arab individuals who lived in Mogadishu, Filonardi's interpreter Abu Bakr Bin Awod and Islam bin Muhammed. *See Exploration of History and Society.*
Available from https://operationoverload.wordpress.com/category/anti-colonization-wars/(accessed on 14 February, 2017).

[74] Isse-Salwe, The Collapse of Somali State, 22.

Ambassador Salah Mohamed lucidly writes "The resistance of the Bimal [Biyamal] in Somali history could only be compared with that of Darwish of Sayyid Mohamad in its bitterness, duration, and determination."[75]

The southern resistance movement networked with the northern Darwish Movement, demonstrating unity of purpose and Islamic consciousness. Moreover, resistance against Italian expansion in Banadir region led by Sheikh Hasan Barsane (1853-1927) of Ahmadiya/ Rahmaniya order. Furthermore, Sheikh Bashir Yusuf (1905-1945), a Salihiyah Sufi master continued the path of Jihad of Sayyid Mohamed Abdulle and the nationalistic teachings of Farah Omaar against British colonialism in the Burao area, Togdheer Region. Alas, most of these movements had been suppressed by 1924 and their leaders were either eliminated or contained. Finally, the independent Majeerteen Sultanate was brutally suppressed after two years of resistance in 1927, finalizing the Italian occupation of Somalia. Since then, the era of independent leadership in the Somali society was over. It took 100 years to conquer the Somali territories completely, since the first British agreement with the Somali clans in Berbera in 1827 to the Italian victory over the Majeerteen Sultanate in 1927.[76] The early colonial policy of containing traditional elders through persuasion and intimidation were accomplished. On the other hand, Islamic scholars were oppressed, marginalized, and excluded because of their resistance to the colonial project using both armed and non-violent means. Those who opted for violent means have been recorded and commemorated in the Somali historiography, while peaceful activists were neglected and marginalized. Colonial scholars studied armed resistance and wrote about them as a threat to their rule. It seems that Somali nationalists, who appropriated all forms of armed encounters as part of the history of Somali nationalism, were tilted toward militarism in the struggle against hegemonic Ethiopia. Perhaps, for that reason, Islamic scholars who engaged in the cultural activities and reform programs, and those who were invigorating internal resilience to the colonial cultural hegemony as a whole, have not been given enough attention in the Somali historiography.[77]

---

[75] Salah Mohamed, *Hudur*, 17.

[76] Ahmed Samatar, *Socialist Somalia: Rhetoric and Reality* (Zed Books Ltd, 1988), 19.

[77] Exceptions are the interest of Professor Mukhtar in this issue in the *Historical Dictionary of Somalia* and the work edited by Said Samatar, who questions conventional historiography in re-examining the Qadiriyah and Salihiyah and

Colonial states developed policies to deal with the traditional leaders after their total occupation of all Somali territories. Traditional leaders, comprising of clan elders and Islamic scholars, were the supreme leaders of their communities before the colonial states reconfigured the societal equation and changed the praxis of power. The colonial regimes dealt with these leaders through "bureaucratic integration" of the clan elders. At the onset, clan elders signed agreements with the colonial powers and were recognized as local partners. What facilitated their commonality was that the secular laws of the colonial states were, by their nature, closer to the Somali customary law known as Xeer, administered by the clan elders. As such, since there are some convergences between the two laws, Somali elders were easily convinced to collaborate with the colonial powers. Putting into practice policy guidelines, colonial states employed clan elders, provided salaries, and used them as official representatives of their communities. In this way, colonialism established hierarchical system of governance in the equalitarian society where the culture of leadership was the first among equals. Historical records show that in the late 1950s, there were 950 salaried clan elders in Italian Somaliland and 361 in British Somaliland.[78] On the other hand, Islamic scholars, through the policy of containment, were oppressed and marginalized, although some of them were later incorporated to the colonial administration. For instance, Sorrentino, who was the Italian commissioner in Mogadishu in 1896, distributed 296 Thalers to the notables and Islamic scholars "to gather friends for Italy."[79] Islam was perceived by the colonial power as a menace to the colonizers' so-called "civilizing mission" and cultural hegemony, and therefore, had to be sidelined. Most of these Islamic scholars were either actively resisting colonial incursion through violent means, or sought to persuade the masses against collaborating with the infidels.

---

emphasizes the need for more research.

[78] For example, those offered fixed salaries during this period included 8 chiefs from Shangani, including the Imam [of Abgal], Sharif Haddad Mawlana and Sharif Habiib bin Hamet, and other 10 from Hamarweyne including Hassan Geedi Abtow (Reer Matan) and Hassan Sokorow (Murusade). See the footnote of Salah Mohamed Ali, *Hudur and the History of Southern Somalia.* (Cairo: Nahda Publishing, 2005), 10. Also, Abdurahman Abdullahi, "Tribalism and Islam: The Basics of Somaliness." In *Variations on the Theme of Somaliness,* edited by Muddle Suzanne Lilius (Turku, Finland: Centre of Continuing Education, Abo University, 2001): 227-240, 229.

[79] Robert Hess, *Italian Colonialism* in Somalia (University of Chicago Press, 1966),33.

However, after the failure of the armed resistance and the triumph of colonialism, peaceful resistance continued and new approaches were gradually adopted. On the other hand, colonial powers also adopted more sensitive methods to satisfy the religious sentiments of the population and initiated a policy of winning people's hearts and minds. The strategy of Italy during fascist rule in Somalia was to gain the support of the Muslims against the Orthodox Christians of Ethiopia. Mussolini proclaimed himself as the protector of Islam in 1937 during his visit in Libya.[80] This approach led colonial governments; in particular, the Italian fascists, to construct mosques, respect Islamic scholars, accept Islamic laws in their most sensitive aspects such as the family affairs, and to establish Islamic courts employing Islamic scholars as magistrates and judges.[81] Moreover, Britain adopted indirect rule, empowered clan elders and also supported Qur'anic schools to gain the support of the population. In addition, Christian missionary activities were prohibited in the Somaliland protectorate in 1910, and that strict rule was enforced afterwards.[82] The activities of the Catholic missions in the southern Somalia was also restricted to avoid provocative actions.

The second phase of resisting colonialism began with the long process of creating new elites with new vision for the society and the state. The colonial powers endeavoured to employ more Somalis in the lower echelons of the colonial civil and military labour force and initially opened selective schools, where children of the traditional elite were given priority and privilege.[83] In line with this strategy, the Somali territories were gradually incorporated and absorbed into the colonial economic and political system. However, the anti-colonial sentiment of the early years did not dry out entirely but was transformed into a modern and peaceful political struggle for independence.[84] In practice,

---

[80] Jakob Krais, "Shakib Arslan's Libyan Dilemma: Pro-Fascism through Anti-Colonialism in La Nation Arabe"? (Orient-Institut Studies 1, 2012). Available from file:///C:/Users/Abdurahman/Downloads/krais_dilemma.doc.pdf (accessed on 19 April, 2017).

[81] Italian built mosques remain functioning in Baidoa, Beledweyne, and Dhagahbur.

[82] Lewis, A History, 103. The Swedish Church wanted to return to Somalia after the Second World War but was refused entry by British Military Administration.

[83] Sylvia Pankhurst, *Ex-Italian Somaliland* (London: Watts, 1951), 212- 214.

[84] On the development of Somali nationalism, see Saadia Touval. *Somali Nationalism: International Politics and the Drive for Unity in the Horn of Africa* (Cambridge: Cambridge University Press, 1963).

the modern state formation in Somalia had begun with the establishment of civil society organizations that were different in form and function from the traditional institutions such as religious establishments of predominantly Sufi orders and clan leadership. These organizations initially began in the British Somaliland and later in southern Somalia, under the rule of British Military Administration (BMA) in 1941. In the southern Somalia, during the Italian fascist rule, all forms of organizations were prohibited.[85] The early social organizations began with the formation of the Somali Islamic Association in 1925 in Aden by the exiled Haji Farah Omaar to support his political activism and to advocate for the improved conditions of the Somali employees of British administration.[86] Gradually, other organizations appeared, such as Khayriyah in 1930, which promoted welfare and education, the Officials' Union, founded in 1935 to lobby for equal rights with expatriates for Somali employees, and the offshoot of the latter, the Somali Old Boys Association (SOBA). The earlier social organizations in southern Somalia were Jamiyat al-Kheyriyah al-Wadaniyah (Patriotic Beneficiary Union), founded in 1942;[87] Native Betterment Committee (NBC), founded in 1942;[88] and the Somali Youth Club (SYC), founded in 1943. The modern political development of Somalia began in the early years of the WW II, after the 1941 defeat of Italian Fascism in the Horn of Africa and the establishment of the BMA in most parts of the Somali territories. The BMA, although had completely destroyed existing small economic projects and infrastructures established by Fascist administration, brought improved political environment by abolishing "restrictions of the Italian regime on local political associations and clubs."[89] The destroyed or removed industry and infrastructures by the BMA include the railway line connecting Mogadishu, Afgoye, and Villagio Della Abruzi (Jowhar); Afgoye Bridge; salt production machinery in Hafun; and the

---

[85] M. Lewis, *A Modern History of the Somali: Nation and State in the Horn of Africa* (Ohio University Press, 2003), 121.

[86] Touval, *Somali Nationalism*, 65.

[87] Mohamed Mukhtar, *Historical Dictionary of Somalia: African Historical Dictionary Series, 87* (Lanham, MD: Scarecrow Press, 2003), 106. Also, Salah Mohamed Ali, *Hudur and the History of Southern Somalia* (Cairo: Mahda Bookshop Publisher, 2005), 340.

[88] Abdurahman Abdullahi, "Non-state Actors in the Failed State of Somalia: Survey of the Civil Society Organizations during the Civil War (1990-2002)." *Darasat Ifriqiyah,* 31 (2004): 57-87. See Salah Mohamed, *Hudur,* 361.

[89] I. M. Lewis, *A Modern History,* 121.

Majayaan and Qandala mines.[90] The BMA's new policy encouraged advances in the political consciousness of the Somalis after many of them have participated in five wars: the Somali resistance wars (Darwish movement, Biyamal resistance and others, the Italian–Turkish War (1911-12), the WW I (1914-18), the Italian-Ethiopian War (1935-36) and the WW II (1941-45). As a result, the Somali Youth Club (SYC), a pan-Somali youth organization, was formed on 15 May 1943 in Mogadishu with the encouragement of the BMA.[91] From its founding membership of 13 men, this club developed into a political party in 1946 and was renamed the Somali Youth League (SYL).[92]

A comparable rise in political consciousness began to appear in the British Somali Protectorate, and this led to the establishment of the party known as the Somali National League (SNL) by 1950s. These two parties, the SYL, SNL adopted corresponding nationalist platforms by the 1950s. At the same time, other smaller and particularistic parties were shifting toward a similar nationalist agenda. The fate of Somalia was decided after five-year debate on the future of the Italian colonies which was defeated in the WW II. Finally, the United Nations opted to grant Italy administrative power over Somalia under the UN Trusteeship on November 21, 1949. Paradoxically, this decision was taken after the UN mission to Somalia witnessed Somali nationalist's violent rebellion against Italians in January 11, 1948, where 24 Somalis and 51 Italians were killed.[93] In the first April, 1950, the former Italian colony was officially returned to Italy. Returning Somalia to Italy was a disastrous defeat of the Great Somali project advocated by Ernest Bevin, the foreign Minister of Great Britain.[94] The diplomatic defeat of the Great

---

[90] See Poalo Tripodi, *The Colonial Legacy in Somalia: Rome and Mogadishu: from Colonial Administration to Operation Restore Hope* (London: Macmillan Press, 1999), 45.

[91] On the relations between SYC and BMA, refer to Cederic Barnes, "The Somali Youth League, Ethiopian Somalis and the Greater Somali Idea c1946-1948". Journal of East African Studies, v.1, no.2, 2007, 277-291.

[92] The founding fathers of modern Somali Nationalism are: Haji Mohamed Hussein, Mohamed Hirsi Nur (Sayidi), Abdulqadir Sakhaa-Uddin, Ali Hasan Mohamed (verduro), Dheere Haji Dheere, Mohamed Ali Nur, Dahir Haji Osman, Mohamed Abdullahi Farah (Hayesi), Khalif Hudow Mohamed, Mohamed Farah Hilowle (Farnajo), Yasin Haji Osman, Mohamed Osman Barbe, and Osman Gedi Rage. See, Abdulaziz Ali Ibrahim "Xildhiban", *Taxanaha Taariikhda Somaaliya* (London: Xildhiban Publications, 2006), 13.

[93] Poalo Tripodi, The Colonial Legacy, 46-47.

[94] Salah Mohamed, *Hudur,* 229-324.

Somali project was rationalized, in that the four powers (USA, Soviet Union, France, and Britain) disregarded the aspirations of the Somali people for unity and were sympathetic to the Ethiopian claim to keep the Somali territories it had previously seized. Moreover, another factor was that Italy was nostalgic about retaining its former colony, while Somali political elites, in particular, SYL were suspicious of the British rule.[95] Therefore, disregarding Somali wishes to be placed under a large four-power trusteeship, the former Somali Italian colony was returned to the Italian administration under UN trusteeship in 1950. According to the UN mandate, Italy had to manage the colony and bring it to full independence in 1960. This episode concludes one chapter of southern Somalia's experience in changing administrations.

Southern Somalia had experienced 62 years of colonialism which include 24 years of formative years of Italian colonialism (1989-1923), followed by 18 years of Fascist rule (1923-41), 10 years of BMA (1941-1950), and 10 years of UN trusteeship under Italian Administration (1950-1960). During these years, in two instances, majority of the Somalis were placed under one administration. The first instance was the five years' rule of the "Italian East Africa" when two Somali territories, the Ogaden and Italian Somalia was placed under Italian Fascist rule besides Ethiopia and Eritrea. Somaliland was included in the Fascist administration for a period of 8 months (August 1940- March 1941).[96] Mogadishu became the capital city of the Italian East Africa. The second instance was after the defeat of Fascist rule in the Horn of African theatre of operations and BMA conquered southern Somalia. During this period, all Somali territories except French Somaliland, were placed under BMA. Italy took the responsibility to prepare southern Somalia for independence in a very short time, with a significant shortage of financial resources.[97] During this formative period, some prominent Islamic

---

[95] The Somali political elite were very angry with the British Military Administrations' policies, and were therefore against both returning Somalia to Italy and the continuation of the British administration. Ibid., 313-320.

[96] Sally Healy argues that perhaps because of "frequently shifting colonial administrations", Somali nationalists envisioned the possibility of new territorial arrangement. See Sally Healy, "Reflections on the Somali state: What Went Wrong and why it Might not Matter." In *Milk and Peace, Drought and War: Somali Culture, Society and Politics* edited by Markus Hoehne and Virginia Luling (London: Hurst&Company, 2010), 271.

[97] In 1951, the budget of the Italian administration was cut by a quarter. See Tripodi,

figures were incorporated into the process for the trusteeship to gain popular support and legitimacy. However, most Islamic scholars were focusing on socio-cultural activities, watching suspiciously for the rise of the new elites and colonial domination. Northern Somalia remained in the British protectorate since 1888 until the Somali independence in 1960, aside from 8 months under Italian occupation (August 1940-March 1941). It was spared from changing colonial hands and its implications. Britain also used indirect rule where traditional institutions were given power to administer their people under the supervision of the colonial authority. Thus, traditional authorities were not destroyed comparing to the direct Italian rule in the southern Somalia which had marginalized traditional institutions.

The Impact of Colonialism on Education and Politics

Colonialism primarily used two instruments to transform Somali society. The first instrument was westernized education system, which enabled the creation of the second instrument, the westernized political elites. This section will examine the process used to achieve these goals. The timeframe available for introducing required reform was very limited and resources were minimal. Therefore, the process produced low capacity political elites and a poorly trained bureaucratic apparatus. Moreover, this process alienated traditional leaders, particularly Islamic scholars, and created a bifurcation of the elites and state-society conflict.

The Establishing of Modern Education

The impact of colonialism in reconfiguring Somali society begins with the introduction of modern education in Somalia, which was the most important factor in the rise and spread of Somali nationalism and the emergence of modern elites. In the pre-colonial era, political and religious power was in the hands of the traditional elites that included clan elders and Islamic scholars. The traditional elites were systematically marginalized with the rise of modern education and its production of modern elites. However, modern education was comparatively recent in the Somali territories, because the Christian missions that pioneered education in colonial Africa were challenged, and their educational

---

The Colonial Legacy, 60-61.

activities were blocked by the Somali Islamic scholars.[98] Also, because of political unrest, volatile security, and the lack of vested interests, colonial governments did not allocate enough resources to develop modern education. With such slow process, the formation of the Somali elite was sluggish, deficient, and divergent mired within the Cold War atmosphere and Muslim-Christian tensions.

Indeed, educational systems in the Somali territories could be classified into traditional and modern, non-state and state education. The traditional education remained essentially Islamic, with Qur'anic memorization and the studies of the Arabic language and jurisprudence being its core subjects. Most of the modern elites passed through Qur'an memorization in their early childhood. Modern education was introduced during the colonial era and was taught in the colonial languages, adopting colonial curricula that promoted Western world outlook. Thus, Italian and English became the official languages of education, while the Arabic language was kept as insignificant part of the curricula. Moreover, modern non-state education embodied a hodgepodge of different schools and curricula, such as Christian Mission schools, Egyptian Arabic schools, Italian schools, and others.[99] Some graduates from these schools were granted scholarships to study overseas.[100] In examining elite formation in Somalia and its impact in creating ideologically conflicting society, our focus will turn to the state education system.

Modern elites are the product of modern education that began with the arrival of colonialism, which was essentially secular. It introduced and nurtured Western values and governance system based on the Western notion of the separation of religion and politics. The early involvement of Christian missionaries in education created the idea in the minds of the Somali population that modern education is correlated with

---

[98] As late as 1942, they controlled 99 percent of the schools, and more than 97 percent of the students in [Africa] were enrolled in mission schools. By 1945, there were comparatively few literate [Africans] who had not received all or part of their education in mission schools. Magnus O. Bassey, *Western Education and Political Domination in Africa: A Study in Critical and Dialogical Pedagogy* (Bergin & Garvey, 1999), 27. In Somalia, Christian missionaries were either expelled or were very conservative, fearing the resentment of the Muslim population.

[99] Some of these schools are: Russian Banaadir High School, Italian schools, and Saudi Islamic Solidarity School.

[100] After 1960, many Somali students were sent to Russia, Eastern Europe, China, Italy, Egypt, USA, Syria, Iraq, and many other countries.

Christianity and that it has to ensure permanent colonial domination through Christian conversion and cultural assimilation. As Abdirahman Ahmed Noor noted, "The amount of education offered by colonial government depended on (a) the African people's level of religious conversion and cultural assimilation; (b) the nature of trained labour required by colonial administration, and (c) the degree of people's acceptance of, or resistance to, that education."[101] Therefore, before the WW II, minor education programs in the former Italian colony were bequeathed to the Roman Catholic Church (RCC). The objective of the education was limited to provide qualified workers for jobs unsuitable for the "superior race" of Italians.[102] Moreover, the Italian Fascist regime that effectively took power in 1923 prohibited education in all Italian colonies.[103] A document discovered in 1939 after the defeat of Italy in the East African war states that "the goal of education was to train the pupil in the cultivation of soil or to become qualified workers in the jobs not admissible for the Italian race."[104] Moreover, this goal was discriminatory in that "cultural" schools were reserved only for the sons of "obedient" notables, and these children were expected to succeed their fathers in serving colonial masters as interpreters, clerks, and office "boys".[105]

In British Somaliland, the expulsion of the Christian Mission in 1910 and the subsequent atmosphere of suspiciousness, as well as the impact of the Jihad of Sayyid Mohamed Abdulle Hasan, delayed all attempts of introducing modern education until after the WW II.[106] Indeed, a combination of the Somali resistance to taxation, suspicions of mixing Christianity with modern education, and the insufficiency of the colonial financial allocations contributed to postponing the introduction of modern education in British Somaliland. However, a new trend transpired with the concerted efforts of small Somali elites educated in Sudan and the substantial Somali participation in the WW II. As a result,

---

[101] Abdirahman Ahmed Noor, "Arabic Language and Script in Somalia: History, attitudes and prospects" (PhD diss., Georgetown University, 1999), 48.

[102] Italy was ruled by a fascist regime from 1922 to 1943, with a far-right ideology based on racism and authoritarianism.

[103] Mohamed Sharif Mohamud, "*Abdirizaq Haji Hussein, Rais Wasara al-Somali (1964-1967)*, 2009", availablefromhttp://arabic.alshahid.net/columnists/6110 (accessed on April 21, 2010).

[104] Pankhurst, *Ex-Italian Somaliland*, 212.

[105] Abdullahi, *Tribalism*, 63.

[106] Touval, *Somali Nationalism*, 64.

in 1945, 400 students attended seven elementary schools, besides numerous Qur'anic schools supported by the British authority. The growth of modern education was very slow because of the resource deficiency, and only in 1950, the first two intermediate schools were opened. Questions asked UK Secretary of State for the Colonies Mr. Lyttelton on the education of the Somaliland protectorate in 1952 in the UK parliament, he replied as follows: The estimated population of 640,000, "there are 1,130 pupils at Government primary and intermediate schools and 50 at secondary schools, of whom 25 are maintained by Government at schools abroad".[107] The secretary stated that the education budget was £48,511 from Protectorate funds and £17,000 from the Colonial Development and Welfare. The number of schools were 13 elementary schools with 815 pupils, three intermediate schools, including one trade training school with 315 pupils, and one junior secondary school.[108] However, modern education expanded gradually afterward and, according to the records of the public office reproduced by Ahmed Samatar, the total number of students in Somaliland had increased from 623 in 1948 to 6,209 in 1959.[109]

In the former Italian Somali colony under the BMA, modern education began "without ceiling."[110] For a variety of reasons after the WW II, the Somalis took great interest in modern education through local initiatives of social activists and political parties. Emerging political parties were competing with each other in attracting public support by investing in the field of education. A pioneering role in this race was taken by the SYL, which made the advancement of modern education one of its major objectives.[111] The party had opened many adult night classes with the generous contributions of its members, and by 1948,

---

[107] See questions and answers of the UK Secretary of State for the Colonies Mr. Lyttelton. Available from http://hansard.millbanksystems.com/written_answers/1952/nov/12/education-british-somaliland (accessed on April 12, 2017)

[108] Ibid.

[109] Samatar, *Socialist Somalia*, 47.

[110] This terminology used by Salah Mohamed means that freedom of establishing schools and even local organizations was granted. During the fascist rule, these activities were prohibited. See, Salah Mohamed, *Hudur*, 358.

[111] The Somali Youth League (SYL) was the first political party in Somalia. It was founded as youth organization in 1943 and transformed into a political party in 1947. Being the major nationalist party, it became the ruling party (1956 -1969).

65% of its classes were taught in English compared with 35% in Arabic.[112] These schools proliferated in the major cities such as Mogadishu, Merca, Kismayo, Baidoa, Bosasso, and Hargeisa.[113] Other political parties were also following suit and conducting similar education programs, albeit smaller in scope and magnitude. In 1947, in the former Somali Italian colony under the BMA, besides various non-state schools, there were only 19 state-funded elementary schools that taught predominantly in Arabic with English as the second language. Their budget was £16,198 out of a total BMA expenditure of £1,376,752, or 1%.[114] During this period, Moallin Jama'a Bilal became famous as director of one of the early schools in Mogadishu.[115] The trend spread horizontally, and within three years, by 1950, there were 29 schools with an enrolment of 1,600 students and employing 45 teachers.[116] It is noteworthy that the first secondary school in the history of Somalia was founded by Sharif Bana Abba in the Hamar-Jajab district of Mogadishu in 1949 with the support of the Native Betterment Committee (NBC), a local charitable organization.[117] Sharif Bana was a benevolent Somali merchant and the chairman of NBC. The organization was selling sugar with the aim of using its profits to finance social developmental projects in education, orphanage development, and humanitarian assistance.

When the Italian UN Trust Administration for Somalia, AFIS (Administrazione Fiduciaria Italiana in Somalia) was mandated in 1950 to prepare Somalia for independence within 10 years, the objective of education changed radically. As related by Tripodi, these objectives were: "To provide the majority of the Somalis with at least primary education,

---

[112] Noor, *Arabic Language*, 63.

[113] Hassan Makki, *Al-Siyasat al-Thaqafiya fi al-Somali al-Kabir (18871986)* (Al-Markaz al-Islami li al-Buhuth wa al-Nashri, 1990), 141.

[114] The policy of teaching the Arabic language in elementary schools had been in line with prevalent practice in British Somaliland. See, Salah Mohamed, *Hudur*, 358-359. The first intermediate school was opened by the SYL in Mogadishu in 1949, and Mr. Ismael Ali Hussein was appointed the principal of this school. See Makki, *Al-Siyasat*, 141.

[115] Noor, *Arabic Language*, 52.

[116] Lee Cassanelli and Farah Sheikh Abdulkadir, *"Somali Education in Transition"* (*Bildhan*, vol. 7, 2007), 91-125. There is a discrepancy with the statistical data of the numbers of student enrolment. Bildhan journal gives 1,600 while Tripodi gives 2,850. See Tripodi, *The Colonial Legacy*, 59.

[117] In 1948-49, the charity constructed a school with the capacity of 500 students and building for orphanages. See Salah Mohamed, *Hudur*, 361-62.

to offer the small intelligentsia already existing in the country higher education, and to promote the formation of a new, well-educated elite."[118] Accordingly, a five-year development program was launched in 1952 in collaboration with UNESCO. Within this plan, modern schools, technical institutes, and teacher training programs were established. As a result, according to Professor Lewis, "by 1957, some 31,000 children and adults of both sexes were enrolled in primary schools, 246 in junior secondary schools, 336 in technical institutes, and a few hundred more in higher educational institutions."[119] Indeed, this was a notable advance in the modern education compared with the conditions before the 1950s, when fewer than 2,000 students were receiving education. However, there were only eight intermediate public schools and seven of them used Italian language as the language of instruction.[120] Besides the general trend of expanding public education, specialized schools such as School of Politics and Administration were established in Mogadishu in the 1950s. The main objective of this institute was to train Somali officials and political leaders and integrate them into the Italian system of governance. Many of the students admitted to the institute were either members of the SYL or members of other political parties. Some of the graduates of this institute were offered scholarships for further studies at Perugia University in Italy. Others were employed during the speedy Somalization program in the government administration after 1956. During this period, 4,380 Somalis were absorbed in the government employees, which constituted (88%) of the labour force. Indeed, this was a large number compared with the British Administration in Somaliland during the same years, where only 300 persons were employed in the state administration with only 30 (10%) of them being Somalis.[121] Other institutes were also opened in 1954, the most important of which was the Higher Institute of Law and Economics, later converted to Somalia's University College. It subsequently developed into the Somali National

---

[118]   Tripodi, *The Colonial Legacy*, 59.

[119]   Lewis, *A History*, 140

[120]   Noor, *Arabic Language*, 59

[121]   Somalization of administration was a program giving Somalis responsibility of administering the country through training and coaching by Italian administrators. The great difference in administrative style and nurturing of the new elites is evident in the two colonies of the British and Italians under the UN trusteeship. See Tripodi, *The Colonial Legacy*, 75.

University in the 1969.[122] Moreover, scholarships, seminars, and official visits to Italy were provided to the Somali elites to familiarize them with the Italian language and culture. Gradually, through better modern education and improved employment privileges, new Somali elites with the Italian culture emerged. These elites became leaders of the political parties, senior administrators, district councillors, and provincial governors. They were also employed in the security apparatus of the state.[123] The role of the new elites grew even more rapidly as they emerged as the ruling elite by 1956, when they replaced Italians in all senior administrative positions to prepare Somalia for the independence in 1960. Nonetheless, in the higher echelons of education, there was not much development to boast. "According to UN report on Somalia, three years prior to independence, there was not a single Somali medical doctor, professional pharmacist, engineer, or high school teacher in Somalia."[124] However, there were 37 Somali students in the Italian universities in 1957-58, among whom 27 were expected to graduate in 1960.[125]

With the Somali independence in 1960 and the unification of the British protectorate and the Italian Somalia, the modern elites became the national leaders of the Somali state. This time, the issue of competing Arabic and Italian languages was expanded to include the English language, the official language of elites from British Somaliland.

---

[122] Lewis, *A History*, 141. Also, see the Somali National University website, http://snu.edu.so/overview/ (accessed on 19 April, 2017).

[123] The first eight police officers were sent to Italy for training in 25 August, 1952. They were Mohamed siyad Barre, Hussen Kulmiye Afrah, Mohamed Ibrahin (Liiq-liiqato), Mohamed Abshir Muse, Abdalla Ali Mohamed, Daud Abdulle Hirsi, Mohamed Aynanshe Guleed and Mohamed bin Khamis. Also, first 13 civilian officers were sent in 1953. They were Haji Omar Shegow, Haji Bashir Ismael, Abdirashid Ali Sharmarke, Dahir Haji Osman, Ali Shido Abdi, Ali Omar Shegow, Nur Ahmad Abdulle (Castelli), Ahmed Adde Munye, Osman Omar Sheegow, Hasan Mohamed Hassan (Waqooyi), Abdi Sheikh Adan, Mohamed Sheikh Gabyow and Aweys Sheikh Mohamed. See Maxamad Ibrahin Maxamad "Liiq-liiqato", *Taariikhda Somaaliya: Dalkii Filka Weynaa ee Punt* (Mogadishu: 2000), 127.

[124] Noor, *Arabic Language*, 52.

[125] "In 1960, the year of independence, only 27 Somalis would receive university degrees in Italy; one in medicine, six in political science, one in social science, nine in economics and business administration, one in journalism, three in veterinary medicine, two in agronomy, one in natural science, one in pharmacy, and one in linguistics." See Mohamed Osman Omar, *The Road to Zero: Somalia's self destruction* (HAAN associates, 1992), 45.

Therefore, the language problem became even more complicated and the adopted education policy was based on a mixed system of three languages: English, Arabic, and Italian. Arabic became the language of elementary education, and English took precedence in the intermediate and secondary education. However, Italian language was still the language of administration and maintained its role through specialized Italian schools and scholarships to Italy. Moreover, the Italian language took over the university level in the 1970s. Furthermore, after independence, Somalia's future political orientation began to take shape, and stiff competition between the Eastern bloc and the Western bloc was tearing Somalia apart. This competition focused on three major intervention areas: education, military, and economic development.

In the education sector, the external actor's competition mainly focused on providing scholarships to the graduates from the secondary schools to shape the future elites' socio-political orientations. For instance, the incomplete statistical data shows the following trends: in the 1960s, about 500 civilian students were studying in the Soviet Union, 272 in Italy, 152 in Saudi Arabia, 86 in the USA, 40 in Sudan, 34 in the UK, 32 in France, and 29 in India.[126] This indicates that the total number of scholarships from the Western countries was less than that from the Soviet Union alone. However, these data are incomplete as Arab nationalist countries that provided generous scholarships, such as Egypt, Syria, and Iraq are missing in these statistics. Moreover, scholarships from China and other Eastern bloc countries such as Czechoslovakia, Poland, Romania, and East Germany are also unaccounted for. Obviously, Somalia was turning its face to the East and the new elites trained in the socialist countries and their allies in the Arab world would play a major role in the future Somali politics. Looking into the military sector, this trend is even more evident. After the Somali dissatisfaction with the small size of the Western assistance in military purposes, the Soviets agreed in 1962 to help the Somalis build a strong army as part of its Cold War strategy to balance the U.S. presence in Ethiopia. According to Laitin and Samatar, a joint western countries' proposal for the military assistance to Somalia was $10 million for an army of 5,000 persons. However, the Soviet offer was a loan of $52 million and an army of

---

[126] Luigi Pastaloza, *The Somali Revolution* (Bari:Edition Afrique Asie Amerique Latine, 1973), 350.

14,000 persons. Thus, the Soviets succeeded in taking over the training of the Somali army.[127]

As a result, Somali military officers trained in the Soviet Union alone were estimated more than 500 by 1969. Thus, the majority of modern elites, though initially educated in the Western education system, were in one way or another indoctrinated with the socialist ideology.[128] Elites trained in the socialist countries were adding a far-left drift to the growing westernization; the ramifications of this phenomenon was experienced during the military regime in 1969.

The Emergence of Political Clannism

The colonial policy of selecting sons of clan elders to be educated in cultural schools was aimed at establishing a line of genealogical continuity of the ruling elites. The traditional elites now had the opportunity of dwelling in the cities, towns, and the villages, because most of them were salaried and were connected with the colonial administrations. Moreover, many traditional Islamic scholars were also settled in the urban areas or even founded their own settlements and villages.[129] Dwelling in the cities and towns offered children of these traditional elites the opportunity to be educated in modern schools and to gain early employment in state institutions. Of course, another competitive line of urbanized Somalis was those who had early contact with the Italians and the British, or were former irregular warriors who participated in the various wars, and afterward settled in the cities. Moreover, there were small merchant elites that, in combination with the original urbanized people of the Banadir coast, constituted majority in urban areas. Educated children of the traditional elites provided continuity through blood relations between the traditional and modern elites. It seems that the marginalization of the traditional elites had been compensated by empowering their progenies within the modern state institutions. In this way, blood-related elites with clearly demarcated roles

---

[127] See David D. Laitin and Said Samatar, *Somalia: Nation in Search of a State* (Boulder: Westview Press, 1987), 78.

[128] Ahmed Samatar, *Socialist Somalia*, 78.

[129] Towns in Somalia were established near water sources. These sources can be rivers, sea, and wells. Early traders were those literate people who received the traditional Islamic education. Moreover, in every settlement, a mosque, a Qur'anic school, and Islamic education circles were established.

were created where fathers and cousins managed social affairs and their children dominated the modern political landscape.[130] It is also worth mentioning that traditional elites had a long history of intermarriages for a variety of reasons, including bringing about harmonious society and, therefore, many clan elders and Islamic scholars had next of kin relations with one another. Moreover, the early Somali elites were mainly new immigrants to the urban cities or soldiers recruited during the colonial era. Thus, the gap between traditional and modern elites was very narrow, and some of them even represented traditional elites that were transformed into modern ones. This process took place after 1950 with the establishment of the Territorial Council, where among its 35 members, traditional elites were dominant. In British Somaliland, this phenomenon was even stronger and the Advisory Council consisted of only clan elders.[131]

The gap between traditional and modern elites was expanding along with the expansion of modern education and urbanization. When educated children of the traditional elites became urbanized, they acquired urban culture and norms. This is an area where change occurred gradually or sometimes even through cultural breach. Modern education provided universal education for the entire population and the earlier privileges of the notables' sons were expanded to other social segments as well. In the urban setting, children tended to interact with their neighbourhoods and not with the members of their clans. They played differently, watched films, and frequented cinemas. Some of them even went to nightclubs, smoked, drank alcohol, and had extramarital sexual relationships. They dressed in European dress, read European books and journals, and ate European food. This process of acculturation began to transform the urbanite Somali generation by inducing them to mimic the dominant white European cultural norms. With the influx of pastoral migrants to the cities after the independence in 1960, rapid social mobility and a hybrid urban culture were developing, combining conservative pastoral Somali culture and the urbanized European culture. During those years, the nationalist elites were seemingly at crossroads between their inherited outlook and the emerging elite values; between conservative religious education and liberal modern education, and between inter-clan dependency and self-reliance of urban life. This

---

[130] On the formation of modern elites, see Abdullahi, *Tribalism*, 62-75.
[131] Lewis, *A History*, 144.

growing westernized culture that was affecting social life provoked resentment among conservative Islamic scholars.

In the political activities, modern elites failed to overcome traditional cleavages and allegiances. Most of the political parties in the 1950s were based on clan divides, except the SYL, which were articulating nationalist ideals and sentiments.[132] The main parties in Italian Somaliland in the 1950s were the SYL, Hizbia Digil and Mirifle (HDM), the Somali National Union (SNU), the Great Somali League (GSL), and the Liberal Somali Youth Party (PLGS).[133] On the other hand, in the same period, the main political parties in British Somaliland were the Somali National League (SNL), the United Somali Party (USP), and the National United Front (NUF).[134] All these political parties advocated against clannism and were campaigning to discredit it at every occasion. They were attempting to speak in the language of modernity, promoting national ideology that disdained clannism and called for its elimination. Nevertheless, during political elections, political clannism usually brought out its ferocious clout without ignominy, since there was no way to hold political office in the parliament or in the government, other than through first passing the knotty test of political clannism. Political clannism was the only place where everybody mobilized his/her clan to get elected by their home constituency. During early years of the political experiences in the 1950s, the foundations of the Somali political culture were developed.[135]This

---

[132] The SYL was a nationalist party; however, most of its members were drawn from Darood (50%) and Hawiye (30%), failing to recruit other major clans, such as Digil and Mirifle, that had formed their own party, HDMS. See Lewis, *A History*, 146. However, these statistics seem highly speculative and only indicate that early years of SYL was dominated by these two clan families.

[133] These five parties participated in the municipal and general elections of 1954, 1958, and 1959. In these elections, the SYL received an overwhelming majority, while HDMS was registered as the second opposition party. For details on the performance of these parties in these elections, see Touval, *Somali Nationalism*, 88.

[134] The SNL was formed in 1951 with the same nationalist program as the SYL, and with the development of the Haud question, where Somali territory was given to Ethiopia. The NUF emerged as a convention and common platform for all parties and organizations; however, it developed later into a political party with a strong nationalist agenda. The USP appeared in 1960, attracting former members of the SYL in British Somaliland. See Touval, *Somali Nationalism*, 104-108.

[135] Details on political clannism refer to Aweys Osman Haji and Abdiwahid Osman Haji, *Clan, sub-clan and regional representation 1960-1990: Statistical Data and findings* (Washington D.C., 1998). Also, Maryan Arif Qasim, *Clan versus Nation* (Sharjah: UAE, 2002).

culture was partially implanted within the political system and partially emanated from the traditional Somali culture. It could be mainly summarized in the following points: the imperativeness of clan affiliation and subsequent nepotistic behaviour; the commoditization of politics for economic gain; falsification, fraud and violence as political means; ambivalence; and dependence on foreign patronage. This ambivalent political culture that depends on clan attachment and personal interest breeds endless proclivity and personal voracity; it can be extinguished only through raiding the national coffers and seeking external patronage.

As a result, the new urban phenomena of political clannism developed within the modern Somali elites during their early political participation in the 1950s. This phenomenon is distinct from the traditional clan system dictated by the ecological setting and mode of life based on subsistence and collectivism. Developed in the urban milieu as a continuation of extended family networks, political clannism was a form of cooperation and socialization among clan members dwelling in the cities. These clan members cooperated and socialized in assisting new rural immigrants and vulnerable members of the community, and organizing marriage events and burial services. Clan members created informal organizational networks with recognized representatives in the urban setting. In this way, in the urban setting, clans sustained their clan networks by reorganizing them and collaborating with the clans based in their original home territory. However, this network gradually developed particularistic political consciousness, which resulted in comparing the political role of its clan members with that of other clan members. The leaders of the clan take stock of the employment, economic well-being, and political role of the clan members. This "book-keeping" is very important in collecting social contributions called *Qaaraan*. Therefore, this web of networks functions effectively, each seeking privileges and developments of his particular community networks. These networked clan organizations were used by the political elites vying for elections in their home districts, and thus, clans were extremely politicized. The electoral system introduced by the Italians also promoted the emergence of political clannism and weakened nationalistic agenda. Mario d'Antonio, criticizing the electoral system in Somalia, as quoted by Tripodi, writes:

Even in this circumstance, it was necessary to proceed carefully in introducing radical innovative measures. Two tendencies with different social structures, life styles, and mentality in Somalia, had to be reconciled. On the one side, the old Somalia, tribal, traditionalist, pastoral, strongly tied to the past and to its ethnicity and religion; and on the other, modern developing Somalia, with its working people of cities and small villages, which created elective municipalities organized in several political parties that quickly adopted a modern style of life and introduced some of the productive techniques of the West.[136]

Such reconciliation did not occur institutionally though the traditional clan system, and political parties were accommodating each other, and beyond the nationalistic rhetoric, political clannism was sprouting its roots deep into the new elites. Moreover, instead of exploring some form of reconciliation and accommodation, modern elites were pushing to confront what they considered the greatest threat to nationhood: the virulent effect of political clannism or "the cancer of the Somali state."[137] They attempted in vain to apply three methods. The first was the proportional representation of the clans in the government, and the rank and file of the public service to create a balanced society where all citizens would have a share based on clan differentiation. However, maintaining this balance was not easy in practice. Some clans that received better economic and educational opportunities and benefited from these privileges occupied important government positions. This situation created resentment of the other marginalized clans. The second method was the glorification of the Somali nation and denying and shaming clans and clannism. In doing so, nationalist elites entertained the notion that the less is said about clannism the easier it would be to eradicate it. Therefore, nationalism was praised and glorified in the public mass media and through songs and poetry, while clannism was depicted as the greatest national challenge and malady. The third method suggested that clannism should be dealt with through legislative powers and laws intended to curb the influence of clannism. These laws were intended to reduce the authority of the clan elders and to lessen clan solitary. In applying this legislation, the use of clan names was

---

[136] Tripodi, *The Colonial Legacy*, 77-78.

[137] Abdalla Omar Mansur, "Contrary to a Nation: The Cancer of the Somali State," in Jumale (ed.), *The Invention of Somalia* (Lawrenceville: The Red Sea Press, 1995), 107-116.

banned. The military regime of 1969 employed even more radical approach by abolishing the Diya system (blood compensation paid collectively by clan members), renaming clan elders, and introducing a compulsory insurance system for vehicles to eliminate the collective Diya system in urban settings. This means that in the case an accident occurs, the insurance pays damages instead of the clan. Finally, during the military regime, modern elites buried the effigy of clannism publicly within socialist propaganda, and the elimination of insidious clannism became priority program called *Dabar-goynta qabyaaladda* meaning "eliminating clannism." However, none of these approaches produced tangible results. According to another perspective advocated by the Islamic scholars, clan cleavage could be diluted, but not eliminated, and the Somali people could be united by reviving Islamic values of brotherhood and solidarity, an argument which found its historical practices in the Jama'a of the Sufi orders. From that point of view, Islamist elites put forth a different agenda for Somalia. However, in addition to promoting Islamic and nationalistic values, structural change should be introduced in the electoral laws and political party system that weakens political clannism and dried it toxic environment.

The Resurgence of the Islamist Elites

Modern Islamist elites were developed through two processes. The first was formal education in Arabic/Islamic schools, where some graduates of these schools had an opportunity to further their studies at Arab higher education institutions such as Egypt, Sudan, Syria, Iraq, and Saudi Arabia. This does not mean, however, that these students were automatically subjected to the Islamic agenda, since most Arab institutions of higher learning had been secularized during the colonial period and in the subsequent Arab nationalist movements. Nevertheless, students of Arabic schools were imbued with Islamic/Arabic culture, and some of them, either through direct contact or by reading published literature, became aware of the new Islamist trends in the Muslim world. The second process was through those who, after becoming traditional Islamic scholars in Somalia, traveled abroad and joined Islamic higher learning institutions. These scholars contacted Islamic scholars and students from many Muslim countries where modern Islamic revivalist movements were active. They could be called "transitional Islamic scholars" since they bridged the divide between the traditional and modern Islamic educations. Indeed, these scholars were the pioneers of the modern Islamic movements in Somalia. The most notable among them were: Sheikh Ali Sufi, Sayyid Ahmad Sheikh Muse, Sheikh Abdulqani Sheikh Ahmad, Sheikh Nur Cali Olow, Sheikh Mohamad Ahmed Nur (Garyare), Sheikh Mohamed Moallim Hasan, Sheikh Abdullahi Moallim and Sheikh Abdirahman Huseen Samatar, Sheikh Ali Ismael, Sheikh Ibrahim Hashi, Sharif Mohamud, and others.

The marginalization of the Islamist elites began from the unequal job opportunities. For instance, graduates from the Arabic high schools and universities could not compete for local jobs with graduates from the government schools or other non-state schools because of the language barriers. The language of the administration in Somalia remained either Italian or English until the Somali language was committed to writing in 1972. Moreover, Arabic high schools were limited in scope and offered general high school diploma in arts and science, while the al-Azhar schools focused on Islamic jurisprudence and Arabic language. In comparison, the two Italian high schools in Mogadishu offered both general high school scientific diploma and specialized technical education.[138] This technical education aimed at providing trained workforce for the government civil service and private companies. Such schools offered specialization in the fields of accounting, administration, and technical training in civil engineering. Consequently, Arabic education could not compete in the local market linguistically and qualitatively. Therefore, the only jobs available for the graduates of Arabic schools and universities were low-paying jobs as either judge, teacher of Arabic and Islamic subjects in the schools, or as conscripts in the national army.

This structural inequality, through diversified curricula and languages, created bifurcation of the elites. Discrimination against elites educated in the Arabic language in otherwise equal-opportunity jobs for all citizens forced many of them to explore alternative ways and contemplated changing the system. The Islamic students saw their colleagues who graduated from the Italian and English schools were given more opportunities, sent to the USA and Europe, or given high-salaried jobs in the government institutions. Those students educated in the Arabic

---

[138] These two schools were "liceo scientifico" and "Scuola Regineria and Geometero". Graduates had a high potential for finding local jobs. Axmad Cali Culusow interviewed by the Author on June 120, 2009, Nairobi, Kenya.

language realized that the only equal opportunity for them was to join the national army or explore scholarships in the socialist countries such as the Soviet Union, East Germany, and China. In these countries, all Somalis were equal, since new languages had to be learned. Exceptions were a small number of civilian scholarships and cadet officers sent to Italy who had to be graduates from Italian schools, while civilian scholarships and cadet officers sent to Egypt, Syria, and Iraq had to be conversant in the Arabic language too.

The trend of sending young Somalis to Eastern and Western countries with either Socialist or capitalist ideologies eventually brought cultural and ideological schism orchestrated through the Cold War fever. A significant number of professional Somalis who had graduated from many universities in the world could not get jobs in the government institutions upon their return. They were unemployed because of the corruption and nepotism in the government. In this situation, only those who had strong clan backing or recommended by influential political leader were able to get a good job and received easy promotion. Therefore, there were two main forms of marginalization: linguistic and clan. This condition ultimately created numerous strains that necessitated a change in the system. With respect to the Islamic scholars with their meagre resources and capacity, they were simply advocating the revival of the Islamic culture and respect for the Arabic language.

The bifurcation of the elites and their development demonstrates the four types of elites in Somalia. These are traditional elites consisting of clan elders and traditional Islamic scholars, and modern elites consisting of westernized non-Islamist and Islamist elites. The modern elites were super-structural, which was created mainly through modern education. The dynamics of Islam (traditional and modern), clan (represented by elders), and the state (represented by westernized non-Islamist elites) is the most challenging issue in Somalia.

The relations between the traditional elites were cordial and collaborative in order to maintain community cohesion; however, westernized non-Islamist and the Islamist elites were antagonistic because of their different position on the nature of the state. Westernized non-Islamist elites, the inheritors of the post-colonial state, resolutely covet retaining secularity of the state, whereas Islamists advocate zealously for its Islamization.[139] The free choice of the citizens through

---

[139] The diagram of the Somali elite formation and their relations was developed by the

democratic process, as a peaceful resolution of the conflict, was blocked by the westernized non-Islamist elites with the support of the western powers, the consequence of which was the breeding of extremism and curtailing moderate Islamism in general.

Conclusion

This chapter explores historical overview of the reconfiguration of the Somali society from the pre-colonial period. Two factors were the main agents of change: Sufi orders with their Islamic manifestations and multiple colonialism with their modernization venture. Sufi orders laid the civilizational foundation in Somalia by transforming the lifestyle of pastoral nomads to settled communities, founding urban centers, and introducing cooperative farming. Moreover, they established orderly communities of pan-clan believers adhering to the Islamic principles and following a Sufi master of their own choice. Furthermore, the Sufi communities established Islamic propagation centers where students of the Islamic knowledge arrived and are provided with free community scholarships. While doing all above stated programs, Sufi scholars do not challenge authorities of the clan elders, but cooperate with them in order to create harmonious society. In their Islamic propagation approach, they are very sensitive to the culture of the communities and approached their reform mission in evolutionary manner.

The second factor of reconfiguration was colonialism, which was perceived by the colonizers as a symbol of prestige, greatness, and economic opportunities. The colonizers exported their political, social, and economic values to the colonized people through acculturation and education. In particular, Somalia was a victim of its strategic location, which attracted multiple colonialism, thus, dividing Somali people among four colonial powers. This form of colonialism had aggravated existing social divisiveness (segmented clans) in adding extra segmentation (the colonial divide of the Somalis into five parts). In that obnoxious double segmentation, Somalia entered 20th century as divided nation and was subjected to different cultural and administrative systems. The Somali

---

author. See Abdurahman Abdullahi, "Tribalism, Nationalism and Islam: The crisis of the political Loyalties in Somalia (MA thesis, Islamic Institute, McGill University, 1992), 92-101.

people's early reaction was sporadic resistance, though this undertaking was improved later under the leadership of the Sufi orders.

The colonial powers finally dominated Somalia by 1927 after quashing the last pockets of resistance. The new form of struggle began in 1943 with the formation of the Somali Youth Club (SYC). This trend was further bolstered in establishing political parties by 1947. Political development and education, though denied during the fascist rule, were encouraged under the BMA. This trend has continued after the return of Italy to Somalia as UN trusteeship administrator in 1950. With constrained time and budget of Italian administration, education was improved, and Somali elites were hurriedly prepared to administer modern state institutions. Similar and parallel processes were happening in the Somaliland British protectorate, albeit with lesser magnitude. During this period, political clannism was promoted through the system of governance, electoral laws, and the political party system, while lip-services were given to fight political clannism.

After gaining independence in 1960, political elites began to mimic colonial cultural values, leaving aside the culture of good governance. Moreover, two elite groups who were marginalized in the early years of the independence emerged: socialist elites and modern Islamists. Furthermore, the Somali Republic founded on nationalism in quest for idealized unity marginalized both Islam and clans. As a result, harmonious Somali society, where clan elders and Islamic scholars worked hand in hand, was weakened. The modern development of Islam that focused on fighting innovations in Islam had focused its fight on the Sufi orders and frustrated historic cooperation between Islamic scholars and traditional elders. Finally, westernized Somali elites while promoting nationalism and modernity, and demeaning clans and Islam, marginalized traditional leaders. Apparently, imported ideologies regarding state building, extreme interpretation of Islam, and colonially promoted politicization of clans, tore apart harmonious Somali society. In sum, unless these ideologies are domesticated, the crisis and agony will continue.

Further Reading

Abdullahi, Abdurahman (Baadiyow). The Islamic Movement in Somalia: A Study of Islah Movement (1950-2000). London: Adonis & Abbey Publishers, 2015.

Hess, Robert. Italian colonialism. University of Chicago Press, 1966.

Lewis, I.M. A Modern History of the Somali: Nation and State in the Horn of Africa. Ohio University Press, 2003.

Martin, Bradford G. "Shaykh Zayla'i and the nineteenth-century Somali Qadiriya", in: Said S. Samatar (ed.), In the Shadows of Conquest. Islam in Colonial Northeast Africa. Trenton, NJ: The Red Sea Press, 1992.

Martin, Bradford G. Martin, "Shaykh Uways bin Muhammad al-Barawi, a Traditional Somali Sufi", in: G. M. Smith and Carl Ernst (eds.), Manifestations of Sainthood in Islam. Istanbul, 1993.

Rees, Scott Steven. Patricians of the Banadir: Islamic Learning, Commerce and Somali Urban Identity in the Nineteenth Century. A PhD thesis submitted to the University of Pennsylvania, 1996.

Samatar, Said. 1992. "Sheikh Uways Muhammad of Baraawe, 1847-1909. Mystic and Reformer in East Africa", in: Said S. Samatar (ed.), In the Shadows of Conquest. Islam in Colonial Northeast Africa (Trenton, NJ: The Red Sea Press, 1992).

Tripodi, Poalo. The Colonial Legacy in Somalia: Rome and Mogadishu: from Colonial Administration to Operation Restore Hope. Macmillan Press Limited, 1999.

CHAPTER FOUR

THE RISE AND FALL OF SOMALI NATIONALISM: MODERATION AND RADICALIZATION IN PURSUIT OF UNITY

The Somali Peninsula is a kernel of ancient civilizations that developed sultanates in the medieval Islamic period. Nevertheless, its pre-colonial history was characterized as being divided into separate nomadic sultanates and city-states. The historical theme of this period is marked by the role of the spiritual authority of Sufi orders, followed by the political hegemony of multi-colonial powers that began in the late nineteenth century. These two factors have reconfigured and reshaped Somali society, with particular regard to colonialism, which introduced a new system of governance. Moreover, southern Somalia experienced changing hands of colonialism from early formative period of Italian rule, the Italian Fascist rule (1923-41) with its harsh policies and ambitious projects, British Military Administration (1941-50), and Italian administration AFIS under UN trusteeship (1950-1960). The frequency of change was so great and disturbing to the level that within 27 years, Somalia had changed hands with the colonial rulers of three regimes, thereby changing not only its administrative apparatus but also its style of governance, administrative language and legal system. In addition, within 45 years, the Somali people had participated in five major wars from the Jihad of Darwish Movement (1900-20),[1] Italian-Turkish War (1911-12),[2] WW I (1914-18),[3] the Italo-Ethiopian War (1934-35),[4] and WW II (1939-

---

[1] The Darwish resistance resulted in the death of an estimated one-third of northern Somalia's population.There are a number of academic works on Siyyid Mohamed Abdulle Hassan and the Darwish Movement. See Said Samatar, *Oral Poetry and Somali Nationalism: The Case of Mohamed Abdulle Hassan* (Cambridge University Press, 1982); Abdi Sheikh Abdi, Divine Madness: Mohamed Abdulle Hassan (1856-1920) (Zed Book, 1993); Aw Jama'a Omar Isse, Taariikhdii Daraawiishta iyo Sayid Moxamed Cabdulle Xassan (1895-1921) (Wasaaradda Hiddaha iyo Tacliinta Sare, Edited by Akademiyadda Dhaqanka, 1976).

[2] Over 1,000 Somalis from Mogadishu fought along with the Eritrean and Italian soldiers. Most of the Somali troops returned home in 1935, how many of them were killed or died during the war is not known. See W. Mitchell, Journal of the Royal, 1997.

[3] Antoby Beevor, *The Second World War* (Little, Brown and Company, 2014).

45).[5] All the above occurrences have spurred political awareness and paved the way for the emergence of Somali nationalism, the third factor on reconfiguring the Somali society.

Nationalism is an ideology that moulds public and private life on the idea that every nation has the right to self-determination and to create its own nation-state.[6] This idea is historically associated with the triumph of the French and American Revolutions in the 18th century that spread in Europe in the 19th century and to the rest of the world in the 20th century. Becoming the dominant political ideology, the idea was instigated by different factors in the various nations. Regarding Somali nationalism, this was part of similar phenomenon that was taking place in the colonized nations in Africa and Asia, which was energized after the initiation of the decolonization program worldwide.[7] The idea of decolonization was officially adopted as a policy statement in the meeting between the President Franklin Roosevelt of the United States and British Prime Minister Winston Churchill in the Atlantic Charter on 14 August 1941.[8] The Atlantic Charter consists of 8 principles, including the right of the colonized people to self-determination, and was incorporated later in the United Nations' Charter in 1945. Article 1(2) of the UN Charter states that one of the purposes of the UN is to "develop friendly relations among nations based on respect for the principle of equal rights

[4] David Nicole, *The Italian Invasion of Abyssinia 1935–1936* (Westminster, Maryland: Osprey, 1997).

[5] Anthony Adamthwaite, *The Making of the Second World War* (New York: Routledge, 1992), and Angelo Del Boca, *Italiani in Africa Orientale: La caduta dell'Impero* (Roma-Bari: Laterza, 1986). Also, F. Marino, "Military Operations in the Italian East Africa, 1935–1941: Conquest and Defeat." A thesis submitted to the United States Marine Corps, Command and Staff College, 2009.

[6] This author examined the following three books on the study of nationalism. Hans Kohn, *The Idea of Nationalism: A Study in its Origins and Background* (New York: the Macmillan Company, 1956). Also, Benedict Anderson, *Imagined Communities: Reflections on the Origins and Spread of Nationalism* (London: Veso, 1983), and Eric Hobesbawn, *Nations and Nationalism since 1780: Programme, Myth, Reality second Edition* (Cambridge: Cambridge University Press, 1992).

[7] Assa Okoth, *A History of Africa: African Nationalism and the De-Colonialism Process* (East African Publisher, 2006).

[8] See The text of the Atlantic Charter. Available from file:///C:/Users/Abdurahman/Downloads/Atlantic%20Charter.pdf (Accessed on January 23, 2017).

and self-determination of peoples, and to take other appropriate measures to strengthen universal peace." This policy was a paradigm shift in the new world order laying the basis for the liberation of the colonized people. Thanks to President Roosevelt, who was the promoter of the self-determination principle, even though this principle was not popular in Europe, which held sway of the most colonized nations.[9]

In the Somali context, political consciousness and the institutional expression of nationalism were delayed in the Somali Italian colony during the Fascist era (1923-41), in which all socio-political activism was banned. However, this situation changed after the defeat of Italy in WWII in the Horn of Africa theater of operations in 1941. The British Military Administration (BMA), who took over the administration of Somali territories, tolerated freedom of speech and association.[10] Thus, the process of Somali liberation from colonialism began with the emergence of the first nationalist movement, the Somali Youth Club on 15 May 1943. The rise of Somali nationalism and the process of state-building and nation-building was a long process and its fall did not occur suddenly. It is rather passed through different stages of ups and downs. Both processes were intermittent and cross-cutting until the final fall, the breakdown of order and the collapse of the state was completed. This paper explores the history of the rise and the fall of Somali nationalism and its iconic nation-state by traveling through the historical stations of the emergence and formation of the nationalist elites. Moreover, it examines the performance of the nationalist elite in the process of the state-building and dealing with the political clannism and the Greater Somalia project. The final section of the paper will be the conclusion section.

The Rise and Fall of Somali Nationalism (1943-1991)

The idea of the early Somali nationalism began to express itself with the formation of civil society organizations (CSO), some of whom were later developed into full-fledged political parties. These new forms of

---

[9]   Elizabeth Borgwardt, *A New Deal for the World* (Harvard University Press, 2007)

[10] Robert Patman, *The Soviet Union in the Horn of Africa: The Diplomacy of Intervention and Disengagement* (Cambridge: Cambridge University Press, 1990),34. Also, Cedric Barnes, "The Somali Youth League, Ethiopian Somalis and the Greater Somalia Idea, 1946-48." Journal of Eastern African Studies Vol. 1, No. 2, 277-291, 2007, 80.

organizations were totally different in the form and functions of the traditional institutions, such as religious system of Sufi orders and clan system, the only two organizational systems known to the Somalis before the colonial incursions. This process started after the total defeat of the struggle of the traditional leaders epitomized in the subduing Darwish movement (1921) and the last independent Majeerteen sultanates (1927).[11] Establishing CSO was the product of the early emergence of new elites through modern education and interaction with other colonized people similarly striving for freedom and independence. The early CSOs began in the British protectorate, whereby its proximity to Aden, its trade connections, and shared British rule had enabled Somali expatriates to initiate the first CSO, the Islamic Association in 1925. As the name of the organization shows, its founder Haji Farah Omar was influenced by the rising Islamic awareness of that time and his belonging to the religious family affiliated to the Qadiriyah order in Berbera.[12] The Islamic Association was founded to express the people's resentment of the "neglect and abuse" of British administration.[13] Haji Farah was educated in Aden and India, where he had been influenced by the early awakening of the Muslim World and the anti-colonial struggle of Mahatma Gandhi and Mohamed Ali Jinah in India, becoming the pioneer for the early nationalist leaders.[14] In the following years, other CSOs gradually appeared in the protectorate. These organizations included Khayriyah (1930), Atiyatu al-Rahman (1935), Officials Union (1935), and the Somali National Society (SNS) (1936).[15] Similar CSOs,

---

[11] Abdurahman Abdullahi, *The Islamic Movement in Somalia: A case Study of Islah Movement, 1950-2000* (London: Adonis & Abby, 2015), 79.

[12] Muse Eid, "What do you know about Haji Farah Oomaar" (Somaliland young politicians, 2008). Available from http://somalilandyoungpolitician.blogspot.ca/2008/11/what-do-you-know-about-haji-farah.html (accessed on April 13, 2017).

[13] Abdi Samatar, *The State and Rural Transformation in Northern Somalia (1884-1986)* (University of Wisconsin, 1989), 49

[14] Mohamed Ali Jinnah (1876- 1948) was the leader of the All-India Muslim League from 1913 until Pakistan's independence on 14 August 1947. Mahatma Gandhi (1869-1948), the preeminent leader of the Indian Nationalist Movement renown for his use of nonviolent civic disobedience.

[15] Abdurahman Abdullahi, "Non-State Actors in the Failed State of Somalia: Survey of the Civil Society Organizations in Somalia during the Civil War." Darasaat Ifriqiyayyah 31 (2004): 57-87, 65.

prohibited during the Fascist rule of southern Somalia, appeared after the defeat of Italy in 1941. These CSOs included *Jamiyat al-Kheyriyah al-Wadaniyah* (Patriotic Beneficiary Union) (1942), the Native Betterment Committee (1942), and the Somali Youth Club (SYC) (1943).[16] Some of these organizations developed later into full-fledged political parties by 1947. For instance, SYC was renamed the Somali Youth League (SYL) while the Patriotic Beneficiary Union was transformed to Hisbia Digil and Mirfle (HDM). The difference between these two parties was that SYL was a nationalist party while SDM was a regional particularistic party confined mainly to the speakers of the "Maay" dialect of the Somali language. They also differed in their vision for the structure of the Somali state in a way that SDM advocated for a federal system, while SYL pushed for a centralized system of governance. In the British Somali protectorate, the Somali National Society (SNS) was transformed to the Somali National League (SNL) in 1948 and became a de facto party. The trend of party politics became a new model, and many other small political parties were formed for different reasons and mostly expressed clan slogans and claimed interests.

After the end of WWII, when the question of what to do with the former Italian colonies came to the fore, Britain proposed to the four-power conference (USA, Britain, USSR, and France) held in 1946, to put all Somali territories under BMA.[17] Whatever was the real objective of the British plan for the Somali unity; it was very much hailed by the people of Somalia and the British foreign minister Ernest Bevin's proposal ignited nationalistic aspirations for Greater Somali unity. Alas, this proposal was utterly repudiated by the United States, France, and the Soviet Union for a variety of reasons. For instance, the USA yielded to the strong Ethiopian lobby and voted in favor of Ethiopian wishes in return for the military base in Eritrea (former Ethiopia).[18] Ethiopia,

---

[16] Abdullahi, "Non-State Actors," 82

[17] On the whole issue of how deal with the Italian colonies, refer to S. Kelly, *Cold War in The Desert: Britain, the United States and Italian Colonies* (Macmillan Press Ltd, 2000).

[18] The Radio Marina, the communication center of Italy in Eritrea was seized by Britain during the WWII. The United States received access to the base from the British in 1942. Moreover, President Franklin Roosevelt announced the Ethiopian eligibility for the Lend-Lease Military Aid program. The USA began to operate this communication site in 1943, which was later renamed Kagnew station. See Getachew Metaferia, *Ethiopia and United States, History, Diplomacy and Analysis* (Algora Publishing, 2009), 49. Also, Jeffery Lafebvre, *Arms for the Horn: US Security Policy in Ethiopia and Somalia 1953-1991* (Pittsburgh: University of Pittsburgh Press, 1991), 55-

according to Bevin's plan, would have lost the Somali territory it had captured during the eastward expansion in the 19th century. On the other hand, the Soviet Union was supportive for the Italian return to Somalia to influence the leftist parties' win in the forthcoming Italian elections. Soviets were expecting that, in the situation where the Popular Democratic Front, the leftist alliance parties, win the election in 1948, Italy would have eventually become allied with the Soviets. Moreover, France was interested in its French Somaliland (Djibouti) colony and believed the creation of united Somalia territories under British influence would lead to total Somali unity, which jeopardizes its influence in Djibouti.[19]

Therefore, after more than four years of intense deliberations and disagreements between the four powers influenced by the Cold War realignments, the issue was referred to the UN general assembly. Subsequently, on 21 November, 1949, the UN voted in favor of returning the former Somali colony to Italy under a new mandate of UN trusteeship.[20] Hence, Somalia became a "victim of UN decision" as Ambassador Mohamed Osman described.[21] Deplorably, Somalia was the only former Italian colony returned to Italy, while the other two former Italian colonies, Libya and Eritrea, were dealt with differently. Libya was granted independence on 24 December, 1951 due to strong Arab League advocacy, while Eritrea was loosely federated with Ethiopia against the will of its people.[22] According to the UN mandate, Italy had to develop and manage Somali territory and bring it into full independence in 1960.[23] However, in the fragile democracy and the broken economy after WWII, Italy took the responsibility to prepare Somalia for independence in a

---

58.

[19] Detailed narration on Bevin plan for Greater Somalia and various meetings held to agree on the future of Somalia refer to Mohamed Osman Omar, *The Scramble in the Horn of Africa: History of Somalia (1927-1977)*, 500-526. Also, Tripodi, 92.

[20] S. Kelly, *Cold War in The Desert*, 110-131.

[21] Mohamed Osman Omar, *Somalia Past and Present* (Somali Publications Pvt. Ltd.),138.

[22] Ibid. Also, refer to Ronald Bruce St John, *Libya and the United States, Two Centuries of Strife* (University of Pennsylvania Press,2002).

[23] Lawrence S. Finkelstein, "Somaliland Under Italian Administration: A case Study of in United Nation's Trusteeship" (Carnegie Endowment for International Peace, 1955). Available from https://archive.org/stream/somalilandunderi00fink/somalilandunderi00fink_djvu.t xt (accessed on January 23, 2017).

very short time of 10 years. Retrospectively, the implication of the UN decision to place Somalia as a trust territory under AFIS could be considered as the first seed in creating a deficient, economically dependent state comprising a divided Somalia in conflict with its own people and its neighbors. It was also a lost opportunity for the Greater Somalia project aspired by the people of Somalia.

The nationalist movement was expressed in the form of institution on May 15 1943, when 13 young Somalis from different clans assembled in Mogadishu to promulgate the Somali Youth Club (SYC). The BMA nurtured this movement and encouraged Somalis in the service of the administration to become members of the SYC, including civil and military servicemen such as police, judges, and clerks, contrary to their assumed neutrality as public servants. Explaining the timing of the emergence of the Somali nationalist movement, professor Said Samatar and professor David Laitin wrote as follows: "A complex number of factors helped to foster this new attitude: the memory of Darwish nationalist resistance; the recent unification of the country and specter of another dismemberment, the public humiliation of the colonial masters (first the British, then the Italians) hitherto presumed invincible; the progress in education and in economic complexity; the growth of an articulate elite; and the lifting of the ban of an open political debate by the new administration."[24] Moreover, Professor Saadia Touval, who studied Somali nationalism profoundly, provided the common factors shared with other colonized people and the other factors specific for the Somalis. The common factors underlying the rise of nationalism in the colonized people included social and economic change, the appearance of determination, equality, and the liberty of nations.[25] The specific factors that contributed to the development of Somali nationalism included three additional factors, according to Saadia Touval. The first factor is resentment against colonial governments that had ruled but never subjugated the Somalis. As a result, Somalis who had never been

---

[24] David Laitin and Said Samatar, *Somalia: Nation in Search of a State* (Boulder: Westview, 1987), 63.

[25] Saadia Touval, *Somali Nationalism* (Harvard: Harvard University Press, 1963), 76-78. See also James Colman, "Nationalism in Tropical Africa", In *African Politics and Society*, (ed.) Irving Markovitz, (New York: The Free Press, 1970),153-178. Also, Abdi Sheikh-Abdi, Somali Nationalism: Its origin and Future. *The Journal of Modern African Studies, Vol. 15, 7 (1977), 657-665.*

subject to an institutionalized government had to bear the burden of heavy taxation, forced labor, and racial policy imposed by the Italian colonialism during the Fascist rule, in particular.[26] In addition, colonial authority applied the policy of appropriation of agricultural land, thereby interfering with that of traditional authority.[27] Moreover, "the confrontation of the nomadic, individualistic, and independent Somalis with an organized government inevitably led to the resentments and conflicts."[28] The second factor relates to religious antagonism towards both the European powers and Ethiopia. The colonial powers represented Christian faith, whereas the Somalis were staunch Muslims. Since there is no separation of religion and state in the conception of Islam, it was "exceedingly difficult and humiliating for the Muslim society to accept non-Muslim rule."[29] The third factor is that of "the deliberate encouragement by various governments" to achieve their strategic objectives. For example, the policy of the Italian Fascists in creating a strong East African Italian Empire (*Africa Orientale Italiana*) and their invasion of Ethiopia in 1935 had rewarded Somalia. Italy included Somali territories formerly occupied by Ethiopia to the administration of Somalia as part of its design of "*La Grande Somalia.*" In addition, British Foreign Minister Ernest Bevin's proposal in 1946 that the British House of Commons consider "a Greater Somaliland more objectively" also inspired Somali nationalists.[30] Moreover, in the 1950s, revolutionary Egypt played an important role in spreading nationalist sentiments by introducing modern education in the Arabic language and the idea of Arab nationalism.[31] It is also important to note that Somali nationalism emerged as an antithesis to political clannism in the quest for national unity. Somali nationalism is geared towards weakening and suppressing clan consciousness and replacing it with the national consciousness. Thus, the Somali people were taught by their nationalists to identify with

---

[26] Touval, Somali Nationalism, 61.

[27] The number of concessions of arable land given to Italian nationals grew considerably, from 4 in 1920 to over 115 in 1933. By the end of 1933, a total of 87,487 hectares of choice land had been granted; of the 1192 owners, none was a Somali native. See Abdullahi, *Tribalism, Nationalism and Islam*, 65.

[28] Touval, *Somali Nationalism*, 62.

[29] Ibid.

[30] Bevin was Foreign Secretary of Britain in 1946 and, in a "speech delivered in the house of Commons on June 4, 1946, he proposed the unification of the Somalis under the British Administration. See Saadia Touval, *Somali Nationalism*, 79.

[31] Abdullahi, *The Islamic Movement*, 105-113.

the nation and to pledge their allegiance exclusively to the nation-state. With respect to Islam, the Somali nationalists did not deny Islam as a religion, but rather chose to look it as being apolitical, in line with the secular view, and according to the early conception of modernity and nation-states.

Even though Somalian's feelings of solidarity and awareness of their own identity had been present all the time, Somali nationalism emerged after their contact with European colonialism. As such, the emergence of nationalism depended on the advancement of modern education, socio-economic advancement, and political development. Therefore, understanding educational, economic, and political development of the 10 years of AFIS is very important to trace the development of Somali nationalism. Also, comparative analysis of the socio-economic and political development in the British Somaliland and southern Somalia under AFIS sheds some light on the crisis that emerged between the two entities after the independence and unification. During this period, political elite culture was developed, and the educational deficiency and economic dependence of the Somali Republic were laid down. To explore these factors briefly, we will look into the statistical data of the colonial education, trade index, military service, political parties and elections.

In the southern Somalia, education was deliberately limited during the Fascist era because the main objective of colonial education was to provide selective training intended only to serve colonial masters.[32] That policy was intact until the trusteeship period (1950-60) when the doors for free education were opened for every child and enrolment rates increased sharply. For example, only 6 elementary schools managed by the Catholic Mission had been operating in the Somali territory prior to 1939, who were mostly orphans and bastards.[33] Enrolment in these schools rose from 1390 in 1930 to 1776 in 1939. A comparative study of the expenditure of the colony in 1931-36 and 1936-40 shows that the military expenditure rose from 39% to 55% and economic development

---

[32] Abdullahi, *Tribalism, Nationalism and Islam*, 62.

[33] Catholicism came to Somalia in the late-19th century and believers were Italian immigrants and some former slaves who were converted from the Bantu ethnic group. The Catholic cathedral in Mogadishu built in 1928 was the largest on the African continent. It is ruined during the civil war. Back in 1950, there were 8,500 Catholics living in Somalia.

fell from 3% to 2%. Education quota was only 1% of the total budgetary allocations.[34] Moreover, public education declined even further in the early years of BMA, which took over after the Italians were defeated in 1941. However, the Catholic Church had maintained its activities and its orphanages received British support of 0.65 shilling per day per orphan.[35] The number of pupils attending schools fell to 399, and quota for education accounted for 0.5% of the total expenditure.[36] From 1950 to 1958, during AFIS, enrolment in elementary schools jumped from 6,459 to 31,524 pupils, while in secondary schools, the number increased from 193 to 1,029 and in post-secondary schools from 14 to 58.[37] Moreover, "in 1957 there were 2,000 students receiving secondary, technical, and university education in Italian Somaliland and through scholarship programs in China, Egypt, and Italy."[38] In British Somaliland, the emergence of modern educated elites was relatively slow due to the low development of modern education in the protectorate, for which there were three reasons: the unavailability of government funds for education, the unwillingness of the population to accept imposed taxation to finance education, and the opposition of religious leaders to modern education because of their fear of using it as an instrument for Christian missionary propaganda.[39] Therefore, in 1934, only one government elementary school with 120 pupils was operating in the protectorate, and the allocated budget for education was only $500.[40] In 1952, there were 13 elementary and intermediate government schools with the total student population of 1,130 pupils including 50 in the secondary school. However, according to the records of the public office reproduced by Professor Ahmed Samatar, the total number of students had increased

---

[34] See Pankhurst, *Ex-Italian Somaliland* (Publisher, Watts, 1951), 96; and Ahmed I. *Samatar, Socialist Somalia:* Rhetoric and Reality (Zed. Books, London, 1988), 51.

[35] Salah Mohamed Ali, *Hudur and the History of Southern Somalia* (Cairo: Nahda Publishing, 2005), 360.

[36] Pankhurst, *Ex-Italian Somaliland*, 192.

[37] Muhammad Ahdul-Mun'im Yunus, *Al-Somal: Wadanan wa Sha'ban* (Al-Qahira: Dar al-Nahda al-'Arahiyyah, 1962),112-24.

[38] Helen Chapin Metz (ed.), *Somalia: A Country Study* (Washington: GPO for the Library of Congress, 1992), 21

[39] Tauval, *Somali Nationalism*, 64, 65.

[40] Ibid., 64.

from 623 in 1948 to 6,209 in 1959 in the estimated population of 650,000, while the percentage of enrolment was 4.9%.[41]

In the colonial economic development, adopted policy played a role in the emergence of the modern elite. For instance, agricultural development was directed toward attracting more European settlers and the proletarianization of Somali farmers. In the Italian colony, during the Fascist era (1923-41), the number of concessions of arable land given to Italian nationals grew considerably, from 4 in 1920 to over 115 in 1933. By the end of 1933, a total of 87,847 hectares of choice land had been granted; of the 1192 owners, none were Somali natives.[42] During 1919-39, the value of exports represented only 20% of the value of imports and Somalis were forbidden by decree from participating in the import\export business.[43] As a result of the application of deliberate underdevelopment policies and the efforts to create an attitude of dependence among Somalis, 60% of the colony's revenue in 1931-36 consisted of grants.[44] When AFIS took over Somalia under the UN trusteeship in 1950, the Italian economy was in a shambles, with an individual average income of about $300, the lowest in Europe.[45] Therefore, an economically-constrained Italy shrunk the budget of the AFIS by a quarter, reducing it from 8,000 million Lire to 6,000 million in 1951.[46] Moreover, out of the total expenditure of $18.3 million US dollars in 1951, $13.5 million comprised Italian government subsidies.[47] Although that amount decreased sharply in the subsequent years, still, in 1957, out of the expenditure of $14.1 million, 6.9 million and 7.2 million comprising local revenues and Italian grants, respectively.[48] This means that more than 50% of the salaries of Somali employees were paid through Italian grants. The following table (1) shows the budgetary index of AFIS from 1951-57. It was constructed from the table provided by

---

[41] Ahmed Samatar, *Socialist Somalia: Rhetoric and Reality* (London: Zed Books, 1988), 47.

[42] Ibid, 50.

[43] Pankhurst, *Ex-Italian Somaliland*, 197

[44] Ibid.

[45] Poalo Tripodi, *The Colonial Legacy in Somalia: Rome and Mogadishu: from Colonial Administration to Operation Restore Hope* (Macmillan Press Limited, 1999), 60

[46] Tripodi, *The Colonial Legacy*, 61. The exchange rate of Lira to Dollar was US$1 = 625 lire on 21 September 1949.

[47] Ahmed Samatar, *Socialist Somalia*, 55.

[48] Ibid.

Professor Ahmed Samatar, quoted from Mark Karp's studies of the economy of AFIS in 1960.[49]

Item/Million	1951	1952	1953	1954	1955	1956	1957
Expenditure	18.3	14.2	12.8	12.3	14	14.9	14.1
Revenue	4.8	4.8	4.3	5.2	5.8	6.2	6.9
Italian subsides	13.5	9.4	8.5	7.1	8.2	8.7	7.1
Total	18.3	14.2	12.8	12.3	14	14.9	14.1

Fig.4. Expenditure/Revenue index and Italian subsidies

Examining the trade index as an indicator of economic development, it is noticeable that the trade deficit continued from -5.2 in 1951 to -5.7 in 1957 with the export/import ratio of 13.2/8 and 16.4/10.7, respectively. The following table (2) shows comparative data of the export/import index from 1951 to 1957. It was also constructed from Professor Ahmed Samatar's reproduced index of import/export of AFIS from 1951 to 1957 from the Mar Karp statistical data.[50]

Item/Mill	1951	1952	1953	1954	1955	1956	1957
Import	13.2	14.7	10.9	11.5	14.1	16.1	16.4
Export	8	10.4	8.6	9.2	11.4	10.9	10.7
Trade/deficit	- 5.2	- 4.3	- 2.3	- 2.3	- 2.7	- 5.2	- 5.7

Fig.5. Import/Export Index of Somalia and trade deficit

With respect to the British economic policy in the protectorate, sorghum was introduced and cultivated in the western part of the territory in areas such as Borama and west of Hargeisa. In 1949, the estimated area under cultivation was 50,850 acres which almost tripled in the following years of 1954-55 and reached 140,000 acres.[51] Moreover, at

---

[49] Mark Karp, *Economics of Trusteeship in Somalia* (New York University Press, 1960), 147.
[50] Mark Karp, *Economic of Trusteeship*, 153 and Ahmed Samatar, *Socialist Somalia*, 55.
[51] Abdi Samatar, The State and Rural Transformation in the Northern Somalia, 1884-86 (The University of Wisconsin Press, 1989), 60.

the independence in 1960, there were only 1,400 small farms with about 130,000-140,000 acres producing mainly sorghum and maize. Somaliland exported only livestock with the total export of 1,020, 088 pounds ($2,866,447) in 1959.[52] Comparatively, this constitute about 26% of the southern Somalia export of 1957 ($10.7 Million). The Somaliland budget of 1958-59 was $ 4,584 million of which $3,263 was generated from local revenues with the deficient of $1,321 Million.[53] Moreover, comparing the two budgets, northern/southern budgets in the 1959/1957 (4,584/14.1) constitute 33%. No considerable urban growth occurred in British Somaliland and no other economic development projects were carried out by the administration before 1951. Regarding the protectorate policy, Brock Millman states that "it was understood that little development was possible, permissible or even desired."[54] The British showed less inclination to even try to undertake any considerable development program, and "thus, the north experienced little in the way of social or economic development."[55] Douglas Jardine attributes Britain's lack of economic development of Somaliland on three causes: The war with the Darwish Movement which devastated peace; the unproductive nature of great part of the country; and conservative and independent character of the people.[56] The only opportunity and flourishing business in the north was shipping, which is why large numbers of Somalis were employed as seamen. Furthermore, northern Somalia was lagging behind its southern counterpart in the AFIS development program, the disparity which was to later period have a negative impact on the integrated Somalia.

The military service was another factor that contributed to the emergence of modern elites. Somalis were recruited into colonial military

---

[52] Ibid., 64. The exchange rate of Pounds to US dollar in 1959 was 2.81. Therefore, the total Somaliland export in 1959 was $2,866,447. The exchange rate is available from Lawrence H. Officer, "Dollar-Pound Exchange Rate From 1791," Measuring Worth, 2017URL: http://www.measuringworth.com/exchangepound/

[53] S. Steinberg, The Stateman's Year-Book: Statistical and Historical Annual of the states: The statistical and Historical Annual of the states of the World for the Year 1961 (London: McMillan &Co. LTD, 1961), 1376. The pound was converted to US dollars, the rate of 2.8.

[54] Brock Millman, *British Somali land: An Administrative History, 1920-1960* (Routledge, 2014), 4-5.

[55] Peter Woodward, *The Horn of Africa: Politics and International Relations* (London: I.B. Tauris &co., 2003), 26.

[56] Mohamed Osman Omar, *The Scramble in the Horn of Africa: History of Somalia (1827-1977)* (Mogadishu: Somali Publications,2001), xxviii

service in both the British protectorate and Italian Somalia. In particular, during the Italo-Ethiopian War in 1934-35, the number of Somali recruits to armed forces increased drastically. It is estimated that 6,000 regular soldiers and more than 40,000 Somali irregulars participated in the war from the Italian front.[57] It is interesting to note that Somalis were rewarded for participating in the war to remove the title "native" from them, and were instead honorably called "the Somalis."[58] Somalis also participated from the Ethiopian front fighting against the Italians led by 22 notables, and their names were recorded by Pankhurst.[59] As a result of social mobilization and adaptation to the new way of life during the war, many veterans of the war dwelled in the urban centers and became part of the emerging Somali nationalists. Rapid urbanization occurred, particularly in the city of Mogadishu, where the Somali population doubled within the decade 1933 to 1940, raising the population to more than 60,000 people.[60] Despite the lack of statistical data on the number of Somalis who participated in WWII, it is believed that many Somalis joined the armed forces of Italy, Britain, France, and Ethiopia. Moreover, there were more than 2,400 Somalis in the security service in 1952.[61] Unfortunately, after 1948, in incidents known in the Somali history as *"Dhagax-tuur"*, Somali Gendarmerie, most of whom were members of SYL (60%), drastically suffered due to accusations of participating in the 1948 uprising. As a result, 13 infantry companies were entirely dispended and only 600 servicemen were retained.[62] Lastly, the legacy of the Darwish Movement and contact with the nearby Muslim countries like Yemen and Sudan had also contributed to the emergence of nationalism in the British Somaliland. Unsurprisingly, however, modern educated elites expressed their political ideas differently from the traditional elites. They opted for accommodation and imitation, and hence formed political parties.

The political party formation and elections were something new to the Somalis and clan factor played a crucial role. It should be noted that

---

[57] I.M. Lewis, *A Modern History of Somalia: Nation and State in the Horn of Africa* (London: Longmans, 1980),113.

[58] Lewis, A Modern History, 111.

[59] Pankhurst, *Ex-Italian Somaliland*, 17. It seems that 2000 notables given by Ahmed Samatar is highly exaggerated. See A. Samatar, *Socialist Somalia*, 52.

[60] Lewis, *A Modern History*, 113.

[61] Tripodi, *The Colonial Legacy*, 53.

[62] Ibid., 48.

most important problem in Somali politics concerns having multiple loyalties to the kinship groups and political parties. Professor Saadia Touval ardently suggested that "the most significant fact about Somali politics is its essentially tribal basis."[63] However, the essentialization of the clan factor belongs to the anthropological school of thought and in reality, is not the only factor. Of course, the presence of a strong clan factor in the Somali politics is undeniable, but other factors and trends must also be accounted for. Modern elites who espoused the ideology of nationalism were in a real dilemma within the multiple loyalties. It can be noted that within multiple polities, "modern elites are not, and they cannot be of their tribal connections."[64] Thus, clan divisions had an important influence on the formation of political parties. Political parties and non-clan organizations were not entrenched in the Somali political culture, and the only socially acceptable trans-clan organizations were Sufi orders. It would be expected, therefore, that forming of such an organization in the urban centers would consequently suffer from organizational weakness, fluidity of ideology, and traditional alignments. For example, in southern Somalia, 20 political parties which participated in the municipal election of 1954 represented national, regional, socio-economic, and clan interests.[65] SYL was the only pan-Somali party in terms of its vision and agenda. It enjoyed wide support across Somali territories, even though it was dominated by the Darood and Hawiye clan-families.[66] The other major clan in the south, the Digil and Mirifle clan-families, were mainly members of Hisbia Digil & Mirifle (HDM). It is also worthy to note that all of the Darood or Hawiye clan-families were not supporters of SYL. For instance, the Hawiye Youth League formed before 1956 detached a part of the Hawiye support from the SYL. In addition, the Majeerteen in Banadir and Juba regions supported the Great Somali League (GSL), which splintered from SYL.[67] Moreover, the Liberal Somali Youth Party (PLGS) also acquired most of its support from the Abgal branch of the Hawiye and the Biyamal of the southern

---

[63] Touval, *Somali Nationalism*, 85.

[64] Ibid.

[65] Mohamed Abdullahi, *State Collapse and Post-Conflict Development in Africa: The Case of Somalia (1960-2001)* (Indiana: Perdue University Press,2006), 74.

[66] A 1956 estimate of distribution of SYL members among the main clan groups was as follows: Darood, 50%; Hawiye, 30%; Digil and Rahanwayn 10%. See Lewis, A Modern History, 146. It seems that these data are highly speculative.

[67] Abdullahi, Tribalism, Nationalism and Islam, 69.

Dir.[68] Other parties included the Somali National Union (SNU), the main supporters of which were Banadiri people, and the Marehan Union, the only sub-clan party frankly bearing tribal name.[69] In the north, tribal divisions among political parties were even more evident. The Somali National League (SNL), the major northern party, was based on the Isaq clan-family, while SYL branch in the north drew its support from the Darood clans of north (Dhulbahante and Warsangeli). The third party, the Somali United Front (NUF), was even narrower in its base of support and confined to Habar Toljala branch of the Isaq.[70] The fourth party, the United Somali party (USP), which was formed in the early 1960s, represented the alliance of non-Isaq clans in the north such as Dhulbahante, Warsengeli, Issa, and Gadabursi. It was created primarily to counter-balance SNL party dominated by Isaq. It is interesting to note that political parties were illegal in the British protectorate until 1959 and civil servants were not allowed to join these political parties.[71] Conversely, since 1943 in southern Somalia, BMA encouraged political parties and allowed civil and military servicepersons to join the SYL. Therefore, party politics in Somaliland appeared much later than the Italian Trust Territory of Somalia.

The first election in the history of Somalia occurred in May 1954 when AFIS initiated the first ever municipal election. In this election, only 50,740 males, registered voters in the municipal districts, were allowed to vote, with very high participation ranging up to 75% of the registered voters (38,119).[72] The electoral law was promulgated on 31 March 1955 in a degree by Ambassador Anzilotti, the administrator of AFIS. The basis of the law was as follows:

> The territorial council is elected with male universal suffrage: from people living outside municipal districts with second-degree elections, through the shir [assembly of the clan] and electoral representatives, and the people living inside the municipal districts with direct elections. The preference of the electoral representatives and of voter resident in the municipal districts is direct, free and

---

[68] Ibid.

[69] Ibid.

[70] The prominent leader of the party was Michel Mariano, a Christian political figure in Somalia.

[71] Maria Brons, *Society, Security Sovereignty and the state of Somalia: From Statelessness to statelessness* (International books, 2001), 153.

[72] Tripodi, *The Colonial Legacy*, 66.

secret, and it goes according to the list of the candidates in competition. The representation is proportional.[73]

In this election, SYL received a decisive victory of 47% of the total votes cast, which means 141 out of 281 councilors. The second party, HDM, received 57 councilors and the remaining seats were distributed to many other small parties.[74] The result of this election had changed the relations between SYL and AFIS, which were hostile, and hence the period of rapprochement had begun.

The SYL gradually improved relations with AFIS and was contained through a variety of means of persuasion. The enthusiastic nationalist orientation of SYL began to moderate; indicating the effect of what Johannes dubbed as "Political domestication" and Mohamed Sharif Mohamud called the "wisdom and insightfulness of some leaders of SYL."[75] This shift of policy was natural development since the SYL was recognized by AFIS as the majority party and was preparing to become the ruling party of the country. However, this new party policy did not please some prominent personalities in the party, such as Haji Mohamed Hussein who was elected as the party chairman in 1957. Haji Mohamed represented the Nasserite model of a non-aligned movement of positive neutrality and, as such, was considered by Italy and the USA to be anti-Western and pro-Communist. The categorization of party leaders into moderates as pro-Western and radicals as anti-Western had begun within the Cold War atmosphere and political vocabulary of the time. Haji Mohamed's strong articulation of the "Greater Somalia" issue, using his exceptional communication skills and mastery of the Arabic language spiced with Somali poetry and Qur'anic verses had captured the

---

[73] Ibid., 78.

[74] Ibid., 66.

[75] The USA and Italy orchestrated a policy of keeping Somalia aligned with the West. Their approach was to cultivate pro-Western orientation in the dominant SYL party. Reciprocally, this had warranted the SYL the support of the West to overshadow other parties in 1956. See, Okbazghi Yohannes, *The United States and the Horn of Africa: An Analytical Study of Pattern and Process* (Westview Press, 1997), 204-212. Moreover, the moderate SYL leadership, in particular Adan Abdulle Osman, convinced the majority of the party central committee to follow a peaceful path and to cooperate with Italy to smoothly gain the independence within the mandated date. On this matter, see Mohamed Sharif Mohamud, "al-Ra'is Ādan Abdulle Osman Awal Raīs li al Ja mhūriyah alSomāliyah," 2009, available from See http://arabic.alshahid.net/ columnists/ 1 458 (accessed on June 6, 2010).

imagination of the masses and religious circles. In particular, Haji Mohamed received the support of many Islamic scholars for his strong Islamic tendency and support for the Arabic language and culture. However, in an orchestrated conspiracy with the participation of the USA and Italy, he was expelled from the SYL party in May 1958.[76] Haji Mohamed and other prominent politicians represented unwarranted competing ideologies in Somalia and established the Great Somali Party (GSP). He was characterized by the Western media as "extremist and with an anti-Italian position of the SYL," "an old-time nationalist rabble-rouser," and the advocate of the "pro-Egyptian policy."[77] Indeed, as later events revealed, and contrary to conventional rhetoric, Western powers prevented the emergence of democratic political culture in Somalia under the pretext of confronting communism.[78]

The election law was a mixed system which was necessitated because of the difficulty of organizing a census for the nomadic population and registering them as voters due to the time pressure and paucity of resources. The people living in the municipal districts numbered 230,000, and only 50,000 were eligible to vote who were residing and registered in the specific districts. Those living outside of the districts were estimated to be about 1.5 million.[79] In the first general elections of 1956, 10 political parties participated to elect 60 seats of the constituent assembly allocated for the Somalis. The outcome of the election was 43 seats for SYL and 13 seats for HDM. The remaining 10 seats were reserved for Italians, Indians, Pakistanis and Arabs. The election system has reinforced political clannism and "the clan's male population was forced to find a representative party of the clan, and the coincidence between the clan and party became intense."[80] Speculatively, adopting mixed electoral law was intended to fragment SYL supporters and give more opportunities to the pro-Italian parties.[81] Thus, political clannism was not only essential to the segmented clan system in Somalia, as

---

[76] Tripodi, *The Colonial Legacy*, 87.

[77] Tripodi characterizes Haji Mohamed Hussein's policies as "extremist," while Touval considers him as merely pro-Egyptian. See Touval, *Somali Nationalism*, 91; and Tripodi, *The Colonial Legacy*, 87. Also, the Time Magazine, branded Haji Mohamed as "an old-time nationalist rabble-rouser," quoted from Elby Omar, *Fifty Years, and Fifty Stories: the Mennonite Mission in Somalia, 1953-2003* (Herald Press, 2003), 31.

[78] See Yohannes, *The United States and the Horn of Africa*, 211.

[79] Tripodi, *The Colonial Legacy*, 78-79.

[80] Tripodi, *The Colonial Legacy*, 67.

[81] Ibid.

anthropologists portrayed, but was deliberately promoted by the colonial powers who sought that it facilitates their control over the population.

The idea of promoting clannism started with the policy of indirect rule and creating salaried clan elders, which corrupted the egalitarian system, and instituted instead a hierarchical system and colonial collaborators. Moreover, the lack of reliable census to base distribution of the electoral seats aggravated fair representation of the various clans in the assembly. The planned census, to be completed in 1957, failed miserably in three of the total six administrative regions: Majeerteen, Mudug, and Lower Juba, while it was successful in Banadir, Upper Juba, and Hiran.[82] As a result of the shortcoming of AFIS to accomplish reliable census, early unfair representation of the seats in parliament began, which also led to the early culture of rigging elections. The new electoral system was adopted precipitately by 1959 as the easiest system for the illiterate people. It was based on a district constituency and a single-wining voting method, also known as "winner-takes-all." This system of voting allows each voter to vote for one candidate choice, and the individual that receive the most votes wins the seat, even if he receives less than a majority of votes. Thus, in accordance with the new electoral law, the first parliamentary election on the basis of universal suffrage was conducted on March 1 1960. Nonetheless, most of the parties boycotted this election and SYL received, for fait accompli, 83 seats out of 90 seats.[83] The adopted electoral system promoted clan divide, conflict, and ensured that only majority clans in each constituent district won parliamentary seats. Also, this election system led later to the proliferation of the districts and Gerrymandering electoral constituencies. The following table (3) indicates the political parties of 1960 and their clan affiliation. As noted, only SYL had the widest clan representation, and all other parties were either regional or sub-can parties.

---

[82] Tripodi, *The Colonial Legacy*, 86.
[83] Nohlen, D, Krennerich, M & Thibaut, B, *Elections in Africa: A data handbook* (Oxford University Press, 1999), 812.

Parties 1960	SYL	SNL	HDMS	GSL	NUF	PLGS	SNU	USP
Clans	Darood & Hawiye	Isaq	Digil & Mirifle	Majeerteen	Toljala (Isaq)	Abgal/ Biyamal	Banadiri	Non-Isaqs in the north

Fig.6. Political Parties and their clan affiliations before the independence 1960

At the time of the independence, programs of all political parties were unanimous regarding fundamental nationalist goals, such as the establishment of the Somali state and the struggle for pan-Somalism. The process of indoctrination of these ideas took about a decade between the 1940s and 1950s; SYL being the only party with pan-Somali ideology in 1940s, whereas all political parties started to advocate for pan-Somalism in 1950s. The only issue that was controversial was the structure of the Somali state. Federalism remained the point of view of the HDMS party, as the party leader Jaylani Shaykh bin Skaykh articulated its goals in 1958.[84] However, other major nationalist parties in the north and south, the SNL and SYL, "favored a unitary centralized state."[85]

Somali Nationalism: Moderation and Radicalization in the Pursuit of Unity

As we have seen in the above section, political clannism had been growing since Somalia's engagement with the state-building project in 1954. Divisive clan alignments and unified nationalistic agenda were intertwined influencing the whole nation-building process. The initial objectives of SYC were to unite all Somalis through eradicating harmful social prejudices and clannism, to educate the youth in modern ideas and civilization, to eliminate any condition antithetical to Somali interest, and to create an indigenous script for the Somali language. As its constitution indicates, the SYC initially focused on dealing with the prevailing social malady such as pervasive and divisive clan culture while promoting education and other social programs. Thus, the most important objective of SYC was to fight against clannism that was the root cause of the

---

[84] "The party leader stated that the party had become convinced that the only system of unifying the Somalis is through a federal constitution that accords full regional autonomy". Touval, *Somali Nationalism*, 96.

[85] Ibid., 105.

friction among the Somalis. Evidently, their program was initially confined to the realization of the internal Somali unity. However, after the Bevin declaration of Britain's wishes to establish Greater Somalia under its tutelage, the SYC, which was transformed into a de facto political party in 1946, took up the cause of Greater Somalia with momentous vigor. Therefore, the internal Somali unity, which should be realized through weakening clannism, and the external Somali unity of all five Somali territories seized by the four colonial powers, became the major nationalist agenda. Both agendas were approached with high emotions and perfectionist approaches. Let us now turn to how the nationalist movements approached their quest for unity and what they have achieved.

The Moderate Nationalist Approaches

Two factors have been the major concerns of the Somali nationalists: weakening clannism and strengthening nationalism. These two factors were depicted by the nationalists as completely antithetical, which means that the weakening one of them necessarily strengthens the other; in other words, a zero-sum-game approach. Nonetheless, clannism was a factual and societal culture, diminishing of which requires more than nationalistic slogans of shaming and begrudging. On the other hand, nationalism is a new intruder and a prerequisite ideology for national mobilization, modernization, and state-building. As a matter of fact, Somali nationalists went through two stages in dealing with clannism and the Greater Somalia projects: the moderate approach on the one hand, and the radical approach on the other, characterized by its militarized and conflictual approach.

The major problem of Somali state-building as identified by Somali nationalists was clannism, upon which they focused all their efforts to mitigate its negative impact. Scholars of state-building in the tribal/clannish societies recommended the application of the following three approaches: (1) proportional representation (PR); (2) maximum devolution into regional governments; and (3) the use of broad political coalition.[86] The devolution to regional governments in the form of regional autonomy or federalism was totally refuted by the Somali nationalists prior to the independence. Moreover, building broad-based

---

[86] S. Sharma, *Politics of Tribalism in Africa* (Delhi: Kay Printers, 1973), 145-55.

political coalition never became the nationalist agenda, since the SYL party's policy was to weaken other competing parties and to incorporate their prominent members. What Somali nationalists attempted to implement was PR of the clans in the government and the rank and file of the public services. In addition, weakening political clannism was approached through propagandizing and glorifying nationalism and through some legislative actions. However, it was not easy to maintain proportional representation, and in the course of time, specific clans received more government jobs. The reason was that some clans received earlier opportunities for colonial education and were employed in the colonial administrations thereafter. Moreover, specific clan culture and ecological factors may have contributed to the collapse of the proportional system.[87] For instance, when the first Abdullahi Isse government in 1956 was formed, from which 6 ministers were chosen from certain clans of Hawiye and Darood, the Digil & Mirifle clan was outraged even though their HDM did not receive enough seats. In addition, some resentment felt by the Darood sub-clans because of Hawiye majority in the government.[88] Therefore, to address this resentment and give consideration to the national unity, the 15 ministers and under-secretaries of the government of 1959 were evenly distributed among the Darood, Hawiye, and Digil & Mirifle clan-families.[89] Moreover, the proportional approach was also applied after the independence, and the first unity government consisting of 14 ministries was proportionally distributed to the northern and southern proportions of the seats in the parliament. For example, for the 33 northern seats, 4 ministries were allocated (2 Isaq and 2 Darood), while out of 90 southern seats, 10 ministries were distributed [4 Hawiye, 4 Darood, and 2 Digil & Mirifle].[90] Although this balance was based on the proportionality of south versus north, it has ruined clan balance. This form of balance did not satisfy the Isaq and Digil & Mirifle clan families. Even though the concept of clan balancing became a standard procedure in the Somali Republic, it did not offer the legitimacy that governments required due to

---

[87] It is my view that clans whose members were raised as nomads despised menial jobs and preferred to join government employment, while others clans from the agricultural areas had expertise working in the private sector.

[88] Of six portfolios, including the premiership, three were allocated for Hawiye, two for Darood and one for Dir. See Lewis, *A Modern History*, 140.

[89] Lewis, *A Modern History*, 160.

[90] Ibid., 168.

the lack of criteria to base proportionality. In the absence of reliable census of the country and clans, criteria of proportional representation were based simply on the whimsical assumptions of the dominant clan families of Hawiye and Darood. Second, there was excessive glorification of the Somali nation, just as there were extraordinary mockery and denial of the prevailing clannism. Glorification of nationalism was expressed in the mass media, especially in the form of poems and songs, and Somali "nationalist heroes" such as Imam Ahmad Gurey and Sayyid Mohamed Abdulle Hassan were well commemorated as the national heroes. Some nationalists, applying radical approaches, even denied that clannism was a force in Somali politics. They thought that the less they said about clannism the easier it would be to eradicate it. Third, clannism was dealt with by legislation mitigating its impact on the public spheres. For instance, three important laws were passed prior to 1969 to curb the influence of clannism. The first law was intended to reduce the authority of clan elders, the second one to lessen clan solidarity, and the third resulted in the banning of political parties that utilized tribal names.

Despite the fact that political clannism was on the rise and politics of factionalism was evident among Somali nationalists, the unification of the British Somaliland protectorate and *Somalia Italiana* under UN trusteeship in 1960 was a great leap and triumph for Somali nationalism. In 1960, for the first time in the history of Somalia, an independent state was born, encompassing two territories with a long history of separation from the medieval Islamic period up to the colonial era: the Somaliland Protectorate and Italian Somalia. The Somali Republic became an independent state among 17 independent nations in Africa in the year of 1960, which was dubbed as the Year of Africa when the wind of change blew in the continent. However, Somali nationalists, despite their success in realizing the first phase of Greater Somali project, remained discontented as long as their brothers still yearned under the yoke of brutal colonialism. Somali nationalists considered the unification of the two parts of Somalia as both the stepping stone and the ladder for the complete unification of all five Somali territories represented in the five-pointed white star emblazoned on Somalia's national flag. The hope of the Somali people for complete unity was memorialized in Halima Khalif's famous song *Somalidayne hadii ii midowday, saddexdii maqnaana wey soo socdaane* (when our two parts have united, the three missing lands will soon are joining us).

In the first civilian administrations (1960-1969), Somali nationalists were very moderate in adhering to the constitution of the land, which stipulates, "The Republic repudiates war as a means of settling international disputes (Article (6:2). Moreover, the constitution highlights the means to peruse Somali unity in the Article (6:4), which states, "The Somali Republic shall promote, by legal and peaceful means, the union of Somali territories and encourage solidarity among the peoples of the world, and in particular among the African and Islamic peoples."[91] As part of promoting pan-Somalism, citizenship of the Somali Republic was granted to the ethnic Somalis in all "missing" territories.

Immediately following independence, the new Republic faced great challenges such as; poorly trained human resources, a politicized clan system, huge rural migrations to the cities, low economic performance, pressure from the hostile neighboring countries, and problems with the administrative integration of British and Italian systems. The first sign of dissatisfaction in the power-sharing relationship between the southern and northern elites was expressed when the presidency and premiership were given to the southern politicians. This way of power sharing was seen in the north as humiliating and unfair. The northern Somalis expressed their early grudges and dissention toward Mogadishu politics in rejecting the constitution by a 54% majority in the referendum held on 20 June 1961. Their grievance had reached to the boiling point, and a failed coup d'état of the northern officers was organized with the aim of seceding Somaliland from Somalia on 9 December 1961.[92] Nevertheless, it seemed that Somalia had been rapidly learning democratic system of governance, whereby freedom of association and political participation was granted. In practical terms, two parliamentary and presidential elections were held and embryonic social organizations emerged, strikes and demonstrations were tolerated, and political prisoners were not known. However, the hasty application of the alien model of democracy in a tradition-bound society had brought about clan conflict, political anarchy, and immeasurable political turmoil. The democratic experience of this period could be characterized, to quote Abdulla Mansur, as "democracy gone mad."[93] It had caused the emergence of clan-based

---

[91] Somali Constitution of 1960. Available from
   http://somalitalk.com/dastuur/1960.html (accessed on January 18, 2017).
[92] The officers included Abdullah Saeed Abbi, Mohammed Ahmed, Hassan Kayd, and many other officers.
[93] Mansur Abdulla, "Contrary to a Nation: The Cancer of Somali State'" in Ahmed,

politics, which did not satisfy the real aspirations of the general population, the educated elites and officers of the Somali Army. The Somali masses, dismayed with the prevalent corruption and economic stagnation, looked to the army as the only possible instrument of change to the political impasse. During this period, in pursuit of pan-nationalist ideals, Somalia established closer relations with the USSR in 1963 and received substantial military and economic aid.[94] It is noteworthy that the rivalry of USSR and USA in the Horn of Africa was taking great strides allaying Somalia and Ethiopia respectively.

Pursing the Greater Somalia project, after achieving Somali independence in 1960, the civilian government undertook moderate policies in two phases. The first phase was characterized as more aggressive pursuit of the pan-Somali project in the international forums, supporting local insurgences in "the colonized territories", and strong advocacy of the self-determination for the people of Somalia. This phase continued in the period (1960-1967) under the Premiership of Abdirashid A. Sharmarke (1960-1964) and Abdirizak Haji Hussein (1964-1967). The second phase took place during the premiership of Mohamed Ibrahim Egal who introduced a major policy shift pursuing regional détente. The new policy was based on mitigating conflicts and improving relations with the Somali neighbours. For example, in 1963, the people of the Somali territory held by Ethiopia formed the Western Liberation Front (WSLF) and demanded self-determination; and after refusing their demand, the WSLF started guerrilla operations. The Somali government was supportive to the insurgency, and as a result, in January 1964, border skirmishes broke out between the two countries. The conflict was contained within few months and Somalia and Ethiopia agreed to a cease-fire and signed an accord in Khartoum under the auspices of the OAU on 6 March 1964.[95] Both countries pledged to withdraw their troops from the border, cease hostile propaganda, and to start peace negotiations. As a result of this agreement, Somalia had to terminate its

---

Ali Jimale (ed), *The Invention of Somalia* (Lawrenceville, NJ, Red Sea Press, 1995),114.

[94] Abdullahi, The Islamic Movement in Somalia, 146. Also, Laitin and Samatar, *Somalia: Nation*, 78

[95] Keesing's Record of World Events (formerly Keesing's Contemporary Archives), Volume 10, July, 1964 Ethiopia, Somalia, Page 20176. Available from https://www.google.ca/webhp?sourceid=chrome-instant&ion=1&espv=2&ie=UTF-8#q=somalia+ethiopian+agreement+in+Khartoum+1964 (Accessed on January 25, 2017).

support of the Somali guerrillas. Subsequently, the border war of 1964 cooled down tensions to a certain level. However, as part of the Egal government's new policy, the two countries released a communiqué on September 22 1967 in which they had agreed to "eliminate all forms of tension" between themselves, establish a joint military commission to examine complaints by either side, and to "perfect co-operation" by means of quarterly meetings between their administrative authorities.[96] This new political direction in dealing with Greater Somali project faced stiff oppositions in the domestic front, but was hailed by the African and other states interested in peace and security in the Horn of Africa.[97] However, Premier Egal turned to the parliament, his power base, who ratified the agreement on November 23, 1967. Having received the endorsement of the parliament, Prime Minister continued his endeavours to settle outstanding differences between Somalia and her neighbours.

Moreover, Somalia severed diplomatic relations with Britain (1963-68) after its disregard, the outcome of the plebiscite in the Northern Frontier District (NFD) which demonstrated the overwhelming desire of the region's population to join the Somali Republic.[98] On this occasion, the Somali government issued the following statement: "It was evident that the British Government has not only deliberately misled the Somali Government during the course of the last eighteen months, but has also deceitfully encouraged the people of the NFD to believe that their right to self-determination could be granted by the British Government through peaceful and legal means."[99] As a reaction, Somalia supported the armed insurgence of the Northern Frontier District Liberation

---

[96] Keesing's Record of World Events (formerly Keesing's Contemporary Archives), Volume 13, November, 1967 Kenya, Somalia, Ethiopia, Kenyan, Somali, Ethiopian, Page 22386. Available from http://web.stanford.edu/group/tomzgroup/pmwiki/uploads/1378-1967-11-KS-a-RRW.pdf (accessed on January 22, 2017)

[97] Upon the return of Prime minister Egal from Arusha, he was received by hostile demonstrations, and Abdirizak Haji Hussein (the former Prime Minister), the secretary-general of SYL, criticized the Arusha agreement. Ibid.

[98] David D. Laitin, *Politics, Language, and Thought: The Somali Experience*, (University of Chicago Press: 1977), 75

[99] Tom Wanambisi, "The Somali Dispute: Kenya Beware". Marine Corps Command and Staff College,1984. Available from http://www.globalsecurity.org/military/library/report/1984/WTL.htm (accessed on January 23, 2017).

Movement (NFDLM) in their fight for the unification with Somalia.[100] This situation provoked a Mutual Defense Treaty between Kenya and Ethiopia in 1964.[101] Kenya and Ethiopia, the two countries allied with the Western block, were in fear of Somalia's military buildup with the assistance of the Soviet Union. To ease this tension, according to the constitutional principle of the peaceful means of settling international disputes, premier Egal began to solve the conflict with Kenya. The mediation of the conflict was initiated under the auspices of the Organization of the African Unity (OAU) and agreement was signed in Kinshasa in September 1967. The major article regarding Somali unity was the clause stating that: "Both Governments have expressed their desire to respect each other's sovereignty and territorial integrity in the spirit of paragraph 3 of Article III of the OAU Charter".[102] A memorandum of Agreement was signed at a follow-up meeting held in Arusha (Tanzania) on October 28 1967, by President Kenyatta of Kenya and the Prime Minister of Somalia, Mohammed Ibrahim Egal. The accord was interpreted differently by the two governments. In a public speech on October 20, President Kenyatta described the dispute as "a little quarrel" which had been reconciled. In contrast with this, Prime Minister Egal, addressing political parties, said that his Government's policy was to "stand with one leg ready for war and the other ready for peace."[103]

Furthermore, with respect to the French Somaliland (formerly Djibouti), the first referendum was held in 1958 to decide whether or not to join the expected independent Somali Republic by 1960 or to remain with France.[104] The result of the referendum was in favour of a continued

---

[100]   Moshe Terdman, Somalia at War – Between Radical Islam and Tribal Politics, The S. Daniel Abraham Centerfor International and Regional Studies,Tel Aviv University, Research Paper No. 2, 2008, 27.

[101]   Vincent Bakpetu Thompson, *Conflict in the Horn of Africa: The Kenya-Somalia Border Problem 1941-2014* (UPA, 2015), 247.

[102]   Declaration on Kenya -Somalia Relations: The Assembly of Heads of State and Government of the Organization of African Unity meeting in its Fourth Ordinary Session in Kinshasa, Congo, from 11 to 14 September 1967. Available from http://www.peaceau.org/uploads/ahg-st-1-en.pdf (accessed on January 23, 2017).

[103]   Ogenga Otunnu, "Factors Affecting the Treatment of Kenyan-Somalis and Somali Refugees in Kenya: A Historical Overview. Available from file:///C:/Users/Abdurahman/Downloads/21678-22090-1-PB.pdf (accessed on January 24, 2017).

[104]   David Laitin, *Politics, Language,*75.

association with France. Evidently, this referendum was a triumph for pro-French political forces while Somali nationalists under the leadership of Mohamud Harbi were defeated. The reason given was that the referendum reflected the wishes of non-Somali inhabitants, such as the Afar, Arab and French population.[105] There were also allegations of widespread vote-rigging and the expulsion of thousands of Somalis supportive of the union with Somalia before the referendum.[106] The second plebiscite was held on 19 March 1967 and the result was the continued association with France. Vote-rigging was reported too, plus the expulsion of more than 10,000 Somalis under the pretext of not having a valid identity card.[107] The declaration of the plebiscite results ignited civil unrest. In addition, in reaction to the Somali agitation for unity, the name of the former *Côte française des Somalis* (French Somaliland) was replaced to become the *Territoire français des Afars et des Issas* after the plebiscite of 1967 to reward pro-French Afar and to discourage Somali nationalists' longing for unity with Somalia.[108] Pursuing his détente policy, Premier Egal had met the French President De Gaulle on September 21 1967, to improve strained relations. The issued communique after the meeting emphasized the commitment of both parties to the right of all peoples to self-determination, and to the principle of non-interference by states in the internal affairs of others.[109] Somalia had changed its policy regarding Djibouti, and instead of previous advocacy for unification with Somalia, it had shifted to advocating for the independence of Djibouti. The Somali delegate at the UN stated on November 10, 1976 that Somalia would be "the first to recognize the new state's sovereignty and territorial integrity."[110] Since then, both Ethiopia and Somalia solemnly declared

---

[105] Berouk Mesfin, Situation Report, Institute for Security Studies, 2011. Available from
http://dspace.africaportal.org/jspui/bitstream/123456789/32288/1/15Apr11Djib outi.pdf?1(Accessed on January 25, 2017).

[106] Kevin Shillington, *Encyclopedia of African history*, (CRC Press: 2005), p. 360.

[107] Jean Strouse, *Newsweek*, Volume 69, Issues 10-17, (Newsweek: 1967), p.48.

[108] Abdallah Abdo Adou, "The Ethnic Factor in the National Politics of Djibouti." The Oromo Commentary, VOL. II, no.1, 1992, 23.

[109] Djiboutian Independence 1967-77. Available from
http://www.usc.edu/dept/ancntr/Paris-in-LA/Database/Case-DB/Erit-In-50-93/DIS67A07.TXT (accessed on January 25, 2017).

[110] Ibid.

that they would "recognize, respect, and honour the independence and sovereignty of Djibouti and its territorial integrity after its accession to independence".[111] Finally, the territory gained independence on 27 June 1977 as an independent state of Djibouti. The independent Djibouti state that did not join Somali Republic was the first crack in the Greater Somalia project.

The Radical Nationalist Approaches

During civilian governments, the pursuit of national unity through moderate approaches was founded in weakening political clannism, raising awareness for national issues and peaceful advocacy for the self-determination of the "Missing Three."[112] However, this approach was radicalized after the coup d'état of 1969 and the militarization of the whole public life of the Somalis. The year 1969 could be considered as the first milestone towards the failure of the Somali nationalists in their pursuit of democratic Somalia and curbing political clannism. The rigging of the election, followed by the assassination of the president Abdirashid A. Sharmarke on October 15 1969, marked the first step towards state failure. The earlier years of the multiparty system and democratic culture were faltering and elections were overtly rigged by all means possible. In the elections of 1969, more than 60 sub-clan based parties participated, fielding 1002 parliamentary candidates for 123 seats. This means 8 candidates were vying for each parliamentary seat. However, the ruling party of SYL abusively rigged the election and received the majority of the seats.[113] Moreover, the SYL absorbed almost all members of the parliament from the opposition parties and created a one-party rule.[114] Therefore, the nationalist SYL party of the earlier years of struggle for independence (1943-1954), domesticated by colonial powers (1954-1960), had been gradually drifting towards one-party rule in 1969. Consequently, the grievances of the overt rigging of the election, rampant bureaucratic corruption, and widespread unemployment,

---

[111] Ibid.

[112] The famous nationalistic song of Halima Khalif Magol memorialized Somali unity and gave hope that the other Somali territories would soon be on the way to join the unity.

[113] Lewis, *A Modern History*, 204.

[114] Mr. Abdirizak Hagi Hussien, former Prime Minister alone stayed in the opposition; quipping; Allah is one and I am one".

especially among small educated elites delegitimized the government. Moreover, the public discontentment with the moderate Egal government policy towards pan-Somalism had culminated in the political turmoil and the assassination of president Sharmarke on October 15 1969. During this period, the prestigious national army mainly trained and equipped by the Soviet Union and Egypt was the only qualified organization to take the lead in saving the collapsing Somali state.

As the dreams of the Somali people shattered in the postcolonial state in the first nine years of independence, the Somali National Army launched a bloodless coup d'etat on 21 October 1969 and received overwhelming support from the majority of disgruntled Somali people.[115] After a short period, however, the new regime, contrary to the expectations of the people, curtailed freedom of speech and banned all social and political organizations, exercised heavy-handedness against oppositions, and practiced extra-judicial detentions and persecutions. Moreover, the regime, proclaiming rigorous socialist and nationalist programs, developed closer relations with the Soviets and initiated application of clan-loaded socialist programs, such as recruiting members of specific clans for the sensitive departments such as security, the presidential guard, and foreign services. Initially, the regime gained considerable support and respect from the people due to the improved economic performance, expanding social services, generating employment opportunities and introducing better culture of governance. Nevertheless, after the first few years of socialist rhetoric campaigns, the real nature of the dictatorial regime was unveiled, and oppositions expressing itself in a variety of ways began to mount. The first political challenge to the military regime stemmed from within the Revolutionary Council when some prominent leaders of the regime organized a failed coup d'etat as early as 1971 and their leaders were publicly executed.[116] The second challenge came from the Islamic scholars who voiced their opposition with respect to the regime's interference with the Islamic family law by introducing secular law overtly contradicting the Qur'anic verses.[117] The reaction of the regime to the peacefully protesting scholars

---

[115] Samatar, *Socialist Somalia*, 87.

[116] Mohamed Osman, *The Road to Zero: Somalia's Self destruction* (HAAN Associates, 1992), 125.

[117] Abdurahman Abdullahi, "Women, Islamists and the Military Regime in Somalia: The new family Law and its Implications." in Markus Hoehne and Virginia Luling (ed.), *Milk and Peace, Drought and War: Somali Culture, Society and Politics* (London:

was imprudent and barbarous. On 23 January 1975, 10 leading Islamic scholars were executed and hundreds more indiscriminately prosecuted.[118]

The execution of the leaders of the coup plotters and religious scholars mark the initial operational cause that hastened the weakening of Somali nationalism, growing clannism, and collapse of the Somali state. The consequences of the execution of the attempted coup leaders in the course of Somali history have been disastrous since the executed officers belonged to three major clans. As a result, clannish sentiments took a new dimension and grew drastically from within the regime, bureaucracy, and the population at large. To counter the worsening situation, the regime adopted a new covert policy of targeting specific clans and offering particular privileges to others in the pretext of promoting revolutionaries and eliminating anti-revolutionary elements. On the other hand, with the execution of the Islamic scholars, hitherto underground Islamic movements took new momentum and underground organizations proliferated in every region in defense of the faith against the *"Godless socialists"*. From this historical moment, contemporary Islamic movements formulated their ideological foundation and launched socio-political programs. Gradually, these two forces, stemming from the indigenous ideologies of clannism and Islam, united in their ardent desire for the regime change but disagreed on the means, were each in his own way had engaged in the active subversion of the regime. Apparently, the military regime clashed with these two indigenous Somali ideologies, clannism, and Islamism, thereby creating a crack in the fabric, cohesion, and solidarity of Somali society.[119]

Hurst&Company, 2010), 137-160.

[118] Ali Sheikh Ahmed Abukar, *Judur Al-Ma'sat Al-Rahina* (Bairut: Dar Ibn Hazm. 1992), 181-185; also, see the complete text of the agreement of cooperation and friendship between Somalia and Soviet Union in the attachment. P.247. Executed officers belonged to the Isaq, Majertain, and Abgal clans. From then, their close relatives and sub-lineages were targeted and dealt with as ant-revolutionaries. See complete and firsthand account of the campaign of the military regime against Islam in Ali Sheikh, *Judur Al-Ma'sat*, 109-137.

[119] There is Somali proverb that posits: "two are inviolable in Somalia: the clan and Islam". The regime had toyed with these two strong bases of "Somaliness". See Abdurahman Abdullahi, "Recovering Somalia: the Islamic Factor." African Renaissance, 3, 5, 2006, 34-58. Also, see Abdurahman Abdullahi, "Tribalism and Islam: The Basics of Somaliness." In *Variations on the Theme of Somaliness*, edited by

The military regime had continued the three nationalist approaches to check clannism, which are proportional representation, legislation against clannism, and the indoctrination of people with Somali nationalism, with more radical approaches. They introduced harsh legislations and conducted intensive ideological propaganda against clannism. A number of laws were enacted to liquidate *dabargoynta* clannism, for example, the traditional Diya system rooted in the Islamic Sharia was replaced with the death sentence, and the tribal chiefs were renamed as peacemakers (*Nabadoon)* and *Afminsharism* (political propaganda and clan gossip) were outlawed.[120] In the urban areas, clan solidarity was undermined by state programs such as the public coverage of funeral expenses in the cases where the deceased individuals had no immediate family members and compulsory insurance for auto vehicles. Above all, the adoption of scientific socialism as the official state ideology produced a well-orchestrated campaign against clannism.[121] Although the clan eradication policy of the military regime had some ephemeral effects, it had epitomized the utopian, populist and hypocritical approach of Somali nationalists that lacks substance and realistic process.

Furthermore, the government excessively abused the policy of curbing clannism, that is, proportional representation. Ironically, while the government had initiated campaigns against clan affiliation, nepotism, and clannism, the President surrounded himself with the kinsmen of three particular clan-families: his own Marehan clan, his mother's Ogaden clan, and his son-in-law's Dhulbahante clan.[122] Moreover, the personality of President Mohamed S. Barre was elevated to the status of a "Maoist cult" figure, honored with the title "The Father of the Nation" *Aabihi Ummada.*[123] As the father, the President expected every person to

---

Muddle Suzanne Lilius. Turku, Finland: Centre of Continuing Education, Abo University, 2001: 227-24.

[120]   Samatar, *Socialist Somalia*, 108.

[121]   Mohamed Haji Ingiriis, *The Suicidal State in Somalia: The Rise and Fall of the Siad Barre Regime* (University Press of America, 2016), 166.

[122]   Laitin and Samatar, Somalia: Nation in Search of a State (Boulder: Westview, 1987), 156.

[123]   There are numerous Somali songs referring to the president as the father of the nation, the father of the knowledge, and the father of the revolution. See Lewis, "The Ogaden and the Fragility of Somali Segmentary Nationalism", Horn of Africa, 1&2 (1990),55. Also, Abdi Sheikh Abdi, "Ideology and Leadership in

accept their status as his children. Paradoxically, while the "The Father" attacked clan solidarity among his children, he favored and covertly relied on the specific clans from whom he constructed his inner political power base. At the same time, the elite from the Hawiye, Isaq, and Majeerteen were gradually purged from the administrations. Since these elites could not express their grievances or voice their resentment peacefully due to the curtailment of democratic rights, they opted for armed struggle. It is hard to speculate why and when the President initiated these particular clan alliances. It may have been due to security concerns after the attempted coup of General Mohamed Ainanshe, General Salad Gaverere, and Colonel Abdulkadir Dheel in 1971, who belonged to the former dominant clans of Isaq, Hawiye, and Majeerteen, respectively. Otherwise, it may have represented an initial move on the part of the president to prepare the grounds for his absolute rule.[124] Whatever the reasons may be, the Mohamed Siyad government's clan alliance undermined the role of the proportional representation, destroyed the traditional leadership, and threw the whole social order upside down.

The Horn of the African political landscape had changed in 1974 when the Emperor Hele Selassie was overthrown and the Military junta (the Derg), which had taken power in Ethiopia, and proclaimed socialist orientation. It was the time of internal strife in Ethiopia, and its military capability was greatly weakened. Having in mind its Greater Somalia project, Somalia took advantage of the volatile Ethiopian situation and began to destabilize the Ogaden region. The Western Liberation Front (WLF), with the support of the Somali military, intensified insurgence operations which finally escalated into a full war between the two countries in 1977-1978.[125] Somalia was at war with Ethiopia in pursuit of

---

Somalia." The Journal of Modern African Studies. 19, 1(1981), 169.

[124] Before the coup of 1969, these three clans had provided two presidents and three prime ministers.

[125] See Joseph K. Nkaisserry, "The Ogaden War: An Analysis of its Cause and its Impact on Regional Peace on the Horn of Africa." A thesis submitted to U.S. Army War College, Carlisle Barracks, Pennsylvania, 1997. Also, David Laitin, The war in the Ogaden: implications for Siyaad's role in Somali history. Journal of Modern African Studies 17(1), 1979, 95-115. On the role of the foreign powers in the war refer to Adam Lockyer, Opposing Foreign Intervention's Impact on the Course of Civil Wars: The Ethiopian-Ogaden Civil War 1976-1980. A paper presented to the Australian Political Science Association Conference, September, 2006. Available from (accessed on Jan. 26, 2017).

the Greater Somalia project at a time when its social cohesion was faltering and elite grievances were mounting. The opposition to the regime was growing after the execution of the Islamic scholars and members of the Revolutionary Council. What is more, the establishment of the Socialist party in 1977 deepened clannism and grievances since majority of the central committee members were selected from the clans who are the power base of the President. Moreover, the war with Ethiopia in 1977-78 and the defeat of the Somali Army became the second turning point towards the weakening of pan-Somalism and the downfall of the state.[126] The political situation of 1978 was very much similar to the political situation of 1969 when a one-party regime was established and political grievances were not addressed but rather exacerbated. The army that saved the state from failing in 1969 and had previously been in power is now fragmented, and its command structure had lost its independence and professionalism, thus becoming an inseparable part of the ruling political clique. This is why the third attempted coup in the history of Somalia was easily foiled on 9 April 1978, resulting in the execution of 18 army officers and the detention of hundreds more. Nonetheless, some of the coup plotters succeeded in escaping, formed armed oppositions, and received a welcoming hand from their hostile neighbors, particularly Ethiopia. After the attempted coup, the regime was terrified and adopted a policy of extreme security measures pitting friendly clans against other clans that were labeled the enemies of the Somali nation, known as *"Sama-diid* and *Qaran-Dumis"* (rejecters of the goodness and destroyers of the state).

The military governments' clan politics led to the radicalization of the disaffected clans and their eruption into armed opposition. The first armed opposition against the regime began after the defeat of the Somali army in the war of 1977- 1978, and the failure of the coup attempt on 9 April 1978. The defeat of the Somali army was, in addition to the devastating human and economic consequences, a severe humiliation for the "Father of the Nation" and his regime. Thus, the politics of factionalism actually began in 1978. However, in the withering economic capacity of the state, and regime's resistance to real political and economic reforms, the era of clannish factionalism was set in motion and

---

[126] Relations between Somalia and the Soviets had deteriorated and Soviet experts were expelled from Somalia on 13 November, 1977. The author of this article was also among the expelled Somali military officers from the USSR reciprocally.

the genie was out of the bottle. After that, a new chapter of Somali history began, which could be characterized as a new stage of terror, exclusionism, cronyism, and an emergence of antithetical originations.

The Radical Nationalist Approaches and the Collapse of the State

The failure to curb clannism, in addition to the defeat of Somali army failing to realize the objectives of Greater Somalia, had put great challenges on the military regime. The regime undertook aggressive policies and did not opt for negotiation and peaceful conflict resolution. Instead, military option and suppression of the oppositions was his official policy. Therefore, oppositions were radicalized even more, and Ethiopian sponsorship, hitherto considered treason, was accepted by all armed factions. The first opposition movement was the Somali Salvation Front (SSF) which emerged in 1979. It was stationed in Ethiopia and its members were predominantly from the Majeerteen clan. The SSF was transformed into the Somali Democratic Salvation Front (SSDF) after two opposition parties had merged with it.[127] The second opposition movement was the Somali National movement (SNM), founded in London in April 1981 by Isaq exiles and was based in Ethiopia. Despite the serious efforts of the SSDF and SNM to form a unified national opposition front, they did remain predominantly Majeerteen and Isaq parties. The government reacted against the two movements with a brutal military campaign based on a "scorched earth policy." Ali Khalif Galaydh noted that "gross violation of human rights was not new, but what was new, disturbing and monstrous was the targeting of an entire clan or sub-clan as enemies of the regime."[128] The scorched earth policy, experimented in Mudug region against the Majeerteen clan, was applied fully in the northern regions against the Isaq clan family. The political reaction of the regime was also bent on the elimination of the political support from the opposition movements. Therefore, on 4 April 1988, the regime signed peace accord with Ethiopia in Djibouti and withdrew

---

[127] "In October, 1981, the provisional eleven members of the executive committee included two Isaqs, one Dhulbahante, and one Hawiye. However, in 1983, only four out of 24 executive committees were from non-Majeerteen clans. See, Daniel Compagnon. "The Somali Opposition Fronts: some comments and questions", Horn of Africa, 1 & 2 (1990), 29.

[128] Ali Kkalif Galaydh, "Notes on the State of the Somali State." Horn of Africa 13: 1 & 2 (April/June, 1990): 1-28.

its support from the Western Somali Liberation Movement (WSLF) in a bid to eliminate Ethiopian support for all armed oppositions, particularly for SNM.[129] In this historical moment, it is noteworthy that Somali elites (the government and oppositions), instead of talking to each other, sought Ethiopian support to destroy each other. However, the agreement with Ethiopia offered a disastrous impact when SNM fighters left their bases in Ethiopia and launched surprising attack on the major cities in the north like Hargeisa and Burao on May 27, 1988, occupying them temporarily.[130] The ensuing bloody and brutal confrontations caused a death toll of more than 50,000 and turning to refugees most populations in these cities. Other clan opposition movement, namely the Hawiye-dominated United Somali Congress (USC) and the Ogaden-dominated Somali Patriotic Movement (SPM), both based in Ethiopia, emerged in 1989. If the establishment of the USC signified the reemergence of the former dominant clans, the SPM represented the breakdown of pro-regime clan alliances.

In the period of 30 years, Somali nationalists undertook the big task of eradicating deep-rooted clannism and in the pursuit of Greater Somalia. However, a blocked democratic process, a despotic military regime, and the radicalization of the approaches in realizing national agendas have contributed to the waning of Somali nationalism. The last trial to save Somalia from collapsing was undertaken by Somali elder statesmen in May 1990, who signed a *Manifesto* calling for Siyad Barre's resignation, the establishment of an interim government representing opposition movements, and a timetable for multiparty elections.[131] Nevertheless, Siyad Barre ordered the arrest of the 114 signatories, even though they were released due to foreign pressures, thus aborting their plan.[132] The following table (5) demonstrates a comparative analysis of

---

[129] Lewis, "The Ogaden and Fragility", 59

[130] Peter J. Schraeder, "From Irredentism to Secession: Decline of Pan-Somali Nationalism", In *After Independence: Making and Protecting the Nation in Postcolonial and Post-Communist States* edited by Lowell W. Barrington (The University of Michigan Press, 2006), 124-25.

[131] Mohamed Haji Ingiriis, *The Suicidal State in Somalia, 211.*

[132] Moshe Terdman, *Somalia at War – Between Radical Islam and Tribal Politics*, The S. Daniel Abraham Center for International and Regional Studies, Tel Aviv University, Research Paper No. 2, 2008, 23.

the political parties of 1960 and armed factions of 1991. It shows how far political development was blocked and previous political parties recycled themselves in the form of armed factions. It also shows the disintegration of the SYL party failing the institutional expression of Somali nationalism.

Parties 1960	SNL	HDMS	SYL+GSL	SYL+PLGS	SYL	USP	USP	SYL
Factions 1991	SNM	SDM	SSDF	USC	SPM	USF	SDA	SNF
Clans	Isaq	Digil& Mirifle	Majeerteen	Hawiye	Ogaden	Isse	Samaro on	Marcehan

Fig. 7. Political parties of 1960 compared with factions of 1991

On 26 January 1991, President Mohamed Siyad Barre fled Villa Somalia, the presidential palace, and retreated with his supporters into the southern Somali regions. The conflict between the regime and the armed oppositions transformed into warfare between the two clan families: Darood and Hawiye. At the same time, the capital city was engulfed in utter mayhem as unbridled militias engaged in the plundering, looting, and killing civilian residents. On January 28, a provisional government was announced, and Ali Mahdi Mohamed was designated as the interim president. General Aidid opposed the hazy presidential appointment, further polarizing the previously divided USC into two antagonistic armed camps which was mobilized along clan lines: the Ali Mahdi camp and the General Aidid camp. At the same time, the SPM and SSDF formed a new coalition of Darood and allied with Mohamed Siyad Barre's supporters in Gedo and Kismayo. Meanwhile, in northern Somalia, the Somali National Movement (SNM) unilaterally revoked the act of Union of 1960 and declared the independent state of Somaliland on 18 May 1991. The appointment of the interim government triggered a bitter feud between the rival Hawiye clan factions who had been fighting for about 100 days, causing an estimated 20,000 to 30,000 deaths. The United Nations (UN) mediated a cease-fire agreement in March 1992 and reduced the magnitude of the conflict to some extent. Moreover, the fight between the Somali National Front (SNF) and the USC faction of General Mohamed Farah Aidid devastated inter-riverine communities, causing approximately 300,000 deaths. As a result, US forces landed in Mogadishu in December 1992 leading multinational forces consisting of more than 37,000 troops from 22 nations. However, the mission was aborted on October 3–4 1993 when a fight erupted between peacekeepers and General Aidid's militia.[133] The UN withdrew from Somalia on March 3, 1995. The UN mission relieved famine, weakened the warlords, promoted civil society organizations, and encouraged business ventures in the private sector. The culmination of these developments was a change in national reconciliation strategy, which recognized a greater role for civilian leadership. One outcome was the National Reconciliation Conference, held in Arta, Djibouti in 2000, which incorporated a wide spectrum of civil society actors after 10 years of failed, warlord-driven conferences. The Arta Peace conference produced the Transitional National Government (TNG), which gave some hope of restoring civilian governance in Somalia and reconciling the warring factions. The new era of reviving Somali nationalism began with a totally modest vision and agenda thereby resuscitating the Somali Republic and the reunification of the two Somali territories: former British Somaliland and Former Italian Somalia.

Conclusion

The Somali nationalism has emerged as anti-colonial and cultural nationalism that has gone through three phases: romantic, strong, and weak. Its beginning was romantic and ambitious, aiming for the liberation of the Somali people under the rule of multiple colonial powers and uniting them in one Greater Somalia state. It was also a modernizing project against tradition, which aimed to reform segmented clannish society by diminishing its role, marginalizing its leadership, and alleviating local clannism to the higher level of super-clannism, Somali nationalism. Thus, the idea of Somali nationalism perfectly matches the European conception of nationalism founded on the rights of colonized nations for self-determination and to constitute their nation-states. Since Somalis constituted one cultural nation united in their common language,

---

[133] This conflict resulted in the death of 24 Pakistanis, 19 US soldiers, and 500–1,000 Somalis.

the religion of Islam, and history; Somali nationalists undertook the great task of transforming their cultural nation into a political nation. This viewpoint was encouraged by the wind of liberation movements, the global wave of decolonization, and foreign interested countries. Moreover, it was strengthened with the emergence of educated elites, improved economic conditions, and a drive for independence. The first triumph of Somali nationalism was celebrated when the Somaliland Protectorate and Italian Somalia joining and proclaiming the Somali Republic on the first July,1960. But, as they claimed, Somali nationalists would not rest until all of the "Missing Three" are freed and join the unity.

The formative period of Somali nationalism coincided with the poisonous atmosphere of the Cold War after WWII and was implicated by the competing super powers and regional states interested in the Somali strategic geographic location. Moreover, following independence, the colonial powers left behind frail state institutions, an unsustainable economy, and continued conflict with Somalia's neighbors. Moreover, the inherited political system nurtured and regenerated political clannism and elite culture that prioritized power sharing and indulged in a corrupt democracy. The promotion of citizenship, rule of law, transparency and economic development was not given enough attention, and dependence on Foreign Aid was pursued. The two main tasks of nationalism; curbing clannism, and the Greater Somalia projects, were subsequently approached in moderation and radicalism. The civilian and quasi-democratic governments (1960-69) opted for moderation in two levels (aggressive and entente) while the military regime (1969-1991) favoured radical approaches. In both periods, emotionalism was tactfully employed and strengthened through systematic propagation via mass communication, songs, poetry, arts, folklore, education systems, symbolism of national heroes, etc. Further, the homogeneity of the people, religion, and culture and the right for self-determination were the hallmark of the nationalist discourse and narratives.

The radical approach of the military regime embarked on implementing the unfeasible projects of rapid eradication of clannism, countering growing Islamism and fulfilling the Greater Somali project. This approach generated negative implications in weakening the very idea it aimed to foster, the Somali nationalism. For example, the radical approach enfeebled social cohesion and provoked resentment expressed in the language of clannism and Islamism. Moreover, the radicalization of

Somali nationalism premeditated the military conflict with Ethiopia in the war of 1977-78. This war had attracted international military intervention from the Ethiopian side and Somalia was badly beaten after its earlier victories and was isolated, weakened, and finally defeated by the alliance forces. The war with Ethiopia was suicidal and marked the beginning of the downfall and the ruinations of the first fruits of Somali nationalism, the Somali state. Hence, Somali nationalism suffered an enormous blow in 1977-1978 with the independence of Djibouti without joining Somalia, defeat in the war with Ethiopia, and the establishment of armed oppositions hosted by Ethiopia. The dictatorial regime's policy towards armed oppositions had further aggravated the situation. This policy was based on the clannization of the state apparatus, the militaristic approach to the armed insurgencies, and the blockade of all avenues of peaceful settlement. Consequently, the national goal of uniting all Somalis dwindled and its iconic state was totally collapsed in 1991. Thus, the centrifugal forces of Somali clannish particularism overwhelmed the centripetal forces of nationalism, witnessing its weakness and shallowness.

Even so, Somali nationalism did not die but suffered great losses as a result of the flawed emotional approaches and elite competition for political power. It possesses natural and organic ingredients that sustain its viability and rejuvenate its identity, such as in Somalia's ethnic and linguistic homogeneity and common Islamic faith. Therefore, Somalis everywhere are disillusioned with their clannish conditions in the diaspora, in the refugee camps, and inside the country; hence, a new brand of Somali nationalism with cultural sensitivities is in the rise. This form of nationalism uses social media and assertively criticizes the past and present, while it explores innovative approaches for reviving the idea of nationalism. In conclusion, Somali nationalism could be salvaged in pursuing proper state-building and nation-building strategies, economic development and socio-cultural advancement, thus altering the conception of Greater Somalia from political unity to cultural and economic integration. This approach will be possible only through fostering democracy, social cohesion, promoting peace, and regional cooperation.

Further Readings

Abdi, Sheikh Abdi. Divine Madness: Mohammed Abdulle Hassan (1856-1920. Zed Books, 1993.

Barnes, Cedric. "The Somali Youth League, Ethiopian Somalis and the Greater Somalia Idea, 1946-48." Journal of Eastern African Studies Vol. 1, No. 2, 277-291, 2007.

Hobesbawn, Eric. Nations and Nationalism since 1780: Programme, Myth, Reality second Edition. Cambridge: Cambridge University Press, 1992.

Kohn, Hans. The Idea of Nationalism: A Study in its Origins and Background. New York: the Macmillan Company, 1956.

Laitin, David and Samatar, Said. Somalia: Nation in Search of a State. Boulder: Westview, 1987.

Lewis, I. M. A Modern History of Somalia: Nation and State in the Horn of Africa. London: Longmans, 1980.

Touval, Saadia. Somali Nationalism: International Politics and the Drive for Unity in the Horn of Africa. Harvard: Harvard University Press, 1963.

CHAPTER FIVE

THE COLLAPSE OF THE SOMALI STATE: THEORETICAL FRAMEWORK AND PERSPECTIVES

Whatever misfortune happens to you, is because of the things your hands have wrought, and for many (of them) he grants forgiveness.
(Qur'an 4:30)

America will never be destroyed from outside.
If we falter and lose our freedom, it will be because we destroyed our selves
- Abraham Lincoln.

The total collapse of the Somali State in 1991 caught scholars, policy makers, and Somali people by profound surprise and puzzlement, being antithetical of what had been taken as a fact in the preceding decades. Somalia has typically been depicted as an organic nation and an impeccable blueprint for postcolonial state-building in Africa.[1] It represented one of the most homogeneous nation-states and early democracies in Africa.[2] Its people share the same language, the Islamic faith, and belong mainly to one ethnic group. Also, because of the multi-colonial legacies, the people of the Somali ethnicity are citizens of four countries in the Horn of Africa: the Somali Republic, Djibouti, Ethiopia, and Kenya. Moreover, as a result of their massive migration since the collapse of the state in 1991, many Somalis have acquired citizenship of many states in all continents.[3]

To accurately explain the failure and collapse of Somalia, the simple answer points to the postcolonial state and its leaders which was built on frail and shaky foundation in its ideology, together with its structures, institutions, and policies. Such failure should not be associated with the

---

[1] "Organic nation" is a new terminology coined by the author, meaning inseparable, biologically-related, and with the culture of a nomadic lifestyle with territorial or spatial livelihood that is ever-expanding.

[2] Abdi Ismail Samatar, *Africa's First Democrats: Somalia's Aden A. Osman and Abdirizak H. Hussen* (Indiana University Press, 2016).

[3] UNDP-Somalia, *Somalia's Missing Million; The Somali Diaspora and Its Role in Development* (UNDP-Somalia, 2009).

people of Somalia and its social institutions, who have been alienated, marginalized, and victimized as a result of the state policies, conflicts, and collapse.[4] The nature of the Somali state, much like other colonized nations, is the derived state which received its impulse not from within but from without.[5] Thus, its collapse should be studied in the context of its tenacious challenges, such as its dismal capacities, fuddled ideologies, and unrelenting external pressures. The three core challenges of the Somali state formation, the consequence which led to the failure and collapse of the state is due to geographic reasons, and being a divided nation aspiring for unity, and state-society conflict. The geographical challenge is the God-given natural one because of Somalia's strategic location that connects Asia, Europe, and Africa. This strategic crossroads attracted, during the European scramble for Africa, multi-colonial competition and domination. It became the theater of WWII, which was fought on Somali soil, with Somali people participating on all fighting sides. Also, being part of the Suez Canal and oil-rich Gulf region geopolitics, the Somali Peninsula was incorporated into the Cold War Theater of operations. What is more, Somalia was drawn into regional conflicts because of geopolitical tensions between Egypt and Ethiopia involving the Nile River politics.[6] Additionally, due to geographical implications, Somalia became a place where the double identity of "Arabness" and "Africanness" compete and conflict each other.[7] It is also where the Christian-Muslim borders are drawn, with Somalia championing the Muslim cause in the Horn of Africa, conflicted with Ethiopia and Kenya, where Christianity is dominant.[8]

---

[4] Chinuwa Achebe, *The Trouble with Nigeria* (Heinemann, 1984).

[5] Formation of the states can be classified into original historical formation, secondary formation and derived formation. All postcolonial states are derivative states that inherited a certain structure, legal framework, political and economic system, and infrastructure.

[6] Osman Abdullahi, "The Role of Egypt, Ethiopia the Blue Nile in the Failure of the Somali Conflict Resolutions: A Zero-Sum Game" (paper presented at the annual meeting of the International Studies Association, Hilton Hawaiian Village, Honolulu, Hawaii, March, 2005).

[7] Osman Abdullahi, "The Role of Egypt, Ethiopia the Blue Nile in the Failure of the Somali Conflict Resolutions: A Zero-Sum Game" (paper presented at the annual meeting of the International Studies Association, Hilton Hawaiian Village, Honolulu, Hawaii, March, 2005).

[8] Ibrahim Farah, "Foreign Policy and Conflict in Somalia, 1960-1990" (PhD diss., University of Nairobi, 2009), 187.

The second challenge is the divided nation and unfinished state project, as envisioned by the Somali nationalists aspiring to a Greater Somalia. The people of Somalia and its territories were cut apart into five enclaves among four colonial powers: France, Britain, Italy, and Ethiopia. As a result, Somali nationalists advocated the legitimate aspiration of its people to liberate all colonized territories and to unite them under the umbrella of one state. However, this venture was frustrated by the super power politics in the early years of the struggle for the independence, positioning Somalia, after the independence, on collision course with the international conventions on colonially-inherited borders.[9] It also situated Somalia in undesired and destructive conflict with its African neighbours.

The third challenge is the state-society conflict of the post-colonial state founded on secular ideology and a centralized system of governance. This form of the state has alienated traditional society, which is based on a clan system, and Islamic faith and culture.[10] The mismatch between the state and society, combined with the postcolonial, pervasive penetration of the state in the society affairs ineptly collided with the clan system and Islamic faith. This prompted the emergence of three conflicting and competing ideologies: clannism, Islamism, and nationalism, at times overlapping and cross-cutting.[11] The initial radicalization of the nationalist approach during the military regime and its clumsy relations with the basics of Somaliness: Islam and clan reactively led to their mutual radicalization, thereby exacerbating clashes and conflicts.

---

[9] Somalia did not endorse the declaration of the Organization of African Unity on the sanctity of the borders in Cairo, 1964. See Saadia Touval, "The organization of African Unity and Borders," International Organization 21, no. 1 (1967): 102-127. Also, see the Organization of African Unity, "Resolutions adopted by the first ordinary session of the assembly of the heads of the state and government," Cairo, UAR, from 17 to 21 July, 1964

[10] State-society relations can be described in six possible scenarios ranging from extreme cooperation to extreme conflict: 1) mutual collaboration; 2) mutual engagement; 3) conflictual engagement; 4) mutual disengagement; 5) enforced disengagement; and finally, 6) resistance-revolutionary disengagement. See Tracy Kup erus, Frameworks of State Society Relations, available fromhttp://www.acdis.uiuc.edu/Re search/S&Ps/1994Su/S&P_VIII4/state_society_relations.html (accessed on February 14, 2011)

[11] Abdurahman Abdullahi, "Tribalism, Nationalism and Islam: The Crisis of Political Loyalties in Somalia." A MA thesis submitted to The Islamic Institute, McGill University, 1992.

To explore the causes of the Somali state collapse, this subject matter attracted immense academic interest in the last three decades. However, the bulk of these studies have focused on the topics of practical relevance in formulating options of intervention for the international community. Moreover, existing studies have reflected on descriptions of human suffering and agony as consequences of state collapse, civil wars, piracy, extremism in the name of Islam, and terrorism. Therefore, major themes of the works presented initially focused on the situational analysis of the civil war and humanitarian disaster, the coping mechanisms of the Somalis both inside Somalia and in the Diaspora, international humanitarian intervention, and recently, international terrorism and security issues.[12] Moreover, global studies on state collapse were growing throughout academic circles and Somalia was exposed as an emblem of a classic example of state collapse.[13] However, most of the produced works are in the form of articles and occasional academic papers.[14] Obviously, these writings look at the Somali state failure and collapse from different theoretical perspectives, and most of the time, a comprehensive picture of the causes of the collapse are not drawn. Moreover, the analysis of a number of researchers has focused on the operational and proximate causes, thus leaving the genesis of the state collapse as marginal. Filling this lacuna in the academic literature, this chapter intends to investigate, sift, and regroup the perspectives of the various academic fields into

---

[12] Somalia is projected as a safe haven for terrorist groups after the events of 9/11 and a number of institutions were closed and groups identified as having terrorist links.

[13] Examples may be Harvard University's "Failed State Project" of the Failed States under the auspices of the World Peace Foundation and "Failed State Project" at Perdue University. These two projects have produced considerable literature and research papers on this topic.

[14] Terrence Lyons and Ahmed Samatar, Somalia: State Collapse, Multilateral intervention, and Strategies for Political Reconstruction (*Washington:* The Brooking Institution Occasional Paper, 1995); Ahmed Samatar (ed.), The Somali Challenge: From Catastrophe to Renewal? *(Lynne Rienner Publishers, 1994;*, Hussein M. Adam, "Somalia: A Terrible Beauty Being Born?" In I. William Zartman (ed.),Collapsed States: The Disintegration and Restoration of Legitimate Authority(*London:* Lynne Reinne, 1995); Walter S. Clarke, "Somalia: Can a Collapsed State Reconstitute itself?" In Robert I. Rotberg (ed.), State Failure and State Weakness in a Time of Terror (Washington: Brooking Institution Press, 2000); Brons, Maria, "The Civil War in Somalia: Its Genesis and Dynamics" Current African Issues, *(11,* Uppsala, Nordiska Africainstitutet, 1991); Virginia Luling, "Come back Somalia? Questioning a Collapsed State" Third World Quarterly, 18:2 (1997), 287-302.

major themes to identify the main factors and build a comprehensive picture of what contributed to the collapse of the Somali state. To do so, firstly, an overview of the rise and fall of the Somali state is recaptured (details are in chapter four). Secondly, theories of state capabilities, conflicts, and impacts are briefly produced. Thirdly, major academic perspectives of the Somali state collapse are recollected, analyzed, and classified into genesis, operational, and proximate causes. Finally, conclusions will be drawn and recommendations are offered.

An Overview of the Rise and Fall of the Somali State

The first serious attempt to establish the modern state of Somalia began with the UN trusteeship Mandate to Italy on November 21, 1949, to administer its former colony, which was seized by Britain during WWII in 1941. The Trusteeship Agreement for the Somalia was approved by the UN Trusteeship Council on 27 January, 1950. The preamble of this agreement state, "the territory [Somalia] shall be an independent and sovereign state; that its independence shall become effective at the end of ten years from the date of approval of the trusteeship agreement by the [UN] general assembly."[15] Italy was mandated as the administering authority and representatives of Colombia, Egypt, and the Philippines were given the role of the Advisory Council representing UN Trusteeship Council in Somalia. Moreover, the agreement outlines the major tasks that Italy has to accomplish within 10 years, such as establishing a democratic system of governance, economic development and provision of social services such as building education and health institutions, building security apparatus, and preparing the territory to become an independent sovereign state by 1960.

As mandated by the UN, Italy took over the administration of territory (AFIS) from the British Military Administration (BMA) on April 1, 1950. Even though the return of Italy was not welcomed by the Somali Youth League (SYL), the major nationalist party, AFIS began offering Somalis more administrative responsibilities in a progressive manner, such as forming a Territorial Council and the election of the municipal councils by 1954. Moreover, modest socio-economic development

---

[15] See Draft Trusteeship Agreement for the Territory of Somaliland under Italian Administration as approved on 27 January, 1950 by the trusteeship Council at the eighth meeting of sixth session.

programs were undertaken. The trend of precipitating the "Somalization" program continued in consideration of the already-constrained budget of AFIS and the limited timeframe for the independence. As such, many under trained and under paid Somalis were given hastily administrative responsibilities hitherto held by the Italians. Furthering the democratization trend, the first general election was conducted in 1956, in which SYL achieved a landslide victory, forming the first Somali government "Affare Interno" with limited power and coached by the AFIS administrative apparatus.[16] Moreover, the universal suffrage election of the 90-seat parliament was conducted in 1959 and the Somali Constitution was drafted.[17] On the other hand, in British Somaliland, "in 1957 the first Legislative Council of Somaliland was formed and Somalis began to replace expatriate officials in government."[18] Moreover, the hasty process of preparing the protectorate to independence was at pace and the first election was conducted in February 1960 with the national assembly consisting of 33 seats. Britain agreed to grant independence to Somaliland after two months, which was ratified by The Council of Elders on 19 May, 1960.[19] Therefore, Somaliland celebrated its independence on June 26, 1960, five days before the Independence of UN Trust Territory of Somalia, which was dated to take place on July 1, 1960. At the time, nationalist fervour was very high and after a number of meetings, the nationalist parties in the UN Trust Territory and British Somaliland signed a historic accord of creating a unified and centralized state of the Somali Republic on July 1, 1960.

Although Somali people and their nationalist elites celebrated with fanfare and high hope with the dawn of freedom and self-governance, the inherited state was in a horrible condition in every aspect. Just to mention a few, its human resources were deficient, the political culture was clannized, economic development was in a shamble, neighbour-state borders were not demarcated, and the integration of the two systems of administrations was challenging. The newly established Somali state, like any other postcolonial state, was expected to be responsible for the accumulation of physical capital, the creation of infrastructure, the

---

[16] The Legislative Assembly of 70 seats, 60 for the Somalis, 4 for the Italian community, 4 for the Arab community, and 2 for the Indian and Pakistani communities. See Poalo Tripodi, The Colonial Legacy in Somalia..., 80.

[17] Ibid., 82-84.

[18] Mark Bradbury, *Becoming Somaliland* (Progresso, 2008), 32.

[19] Ibid.

development of agriculture, the absorption of labour supply, and the provision of education and health services. With all these difficult challenges and high expectations, the new republic was operating in an unbearable environment and its political agenda was highly ambitious and progressive. For instance, two parliamentary and presidential elections were held. Yet, the hasty application of the alien model of democracy in a tradition-bound society had brought negative consequences, such as clan conflict, political anarchy, and immeasurable political turmoil. The Somali nationalist elite had attested their lack of expertise and experience in achieving a successful reformation of the state institutions, economy, and society, which commensurate the challenges they were facing. The administrative culture inherited from the colonial setting had long been in a state of decay and had exhausted all its inertial energy by 1969. Therefore, at this point, the country had reached the verge of collapse, which culminated during the corrupted election of 1969, where the democratic experience of the early years was perverted and SYL dictatorship was in gestation.[20] The situation of the country was catastrophic in all aspects and the public grievances were mounting, as expressed in the tragic assassination of the president Abdirashid A. Sharmake on October 15, 1969. Therefore, the year of 1969 could be considered as the first milestone towards the failing of the Somali state.

To save the state from falling apart, the Somali National Army launched a bloodless coup on 21 October, 1969, with the Somali people enthusiastically offering overwhelming support. The first decade of the postcolonial states in Africa failed to deliver their post-independence promises, as well as failing to fulfill the high expectations of the people. Thus, military institutions undertook alternative approaches, shifting the paradigm from the colonially inherited model to a socialist orientation.[21] The Somali public did not have any imagination of what military regime

---

[20]   In the elections of March, 1969, 1002 parliamentary candidates from 62 political parties competed for 123 seats, with an average of 8 candidates for each seat. Bradbury, Becoming Somaliland, 35. Moreover, the level of corruption was so high that some candidates paid about $30,000. See Lewis, A History, 1976, 296.

[21]   Pat McGowan; Thomas H. Johnson, "African Military Coups d'état and Underdevelopment: A Quantitative Historical Analysis. The Journal of Modern African Studies, Vol. 22, No. 4. (Dec., 1984), 633-666. Also, EU Institute for Security Studies, Understanding Africa Armies, Report no. 27 (Published by the EU Institute for Security Studies and printed in France, 2016), 25-31.

might bring, though they were desperately yearning for change. On the other hand, the military regime wrongly assumed the role of the state in traditional society, lacking the necessary knowledge and capacity for managing elite power-sharing that failed the previous regimes. Thus, the new regime proclaimed rigorous socialist and nationalist programs, developed closer relations with the Soviet Union (USSR) and initiated the application of socialist programs. Moreover, the regime gained considerable support and respect from the public due to improved economic performance, expanding social services, generating employment opportunities, and introducing a better culture of governance. Nevertheless, after the first few years of socialist rhetoric campaigns, the real nature of the dictatorial regime was exposed and oppositions began to surface. The first opposition to the regime stemmed from within the Revolutionary Council (RC) when some prominent officers who were members of the RC, organized a failed coup d'état as early as 1971, resulting in the public execution of their leaders.[22] The second voice of opposition came from the Islamic scholars who declared their disapproval with respect to the regime's interference with the Islamic family law. The reaction of the regime to the peacefully protesting scholars was imprudent and barbarous in the execution of 10 leading scholars on 23 January 1975 together with the prosecution of hundreds more.[23]

The execution of the leaders of the coup plotters and religious scholars mark another milestone that hastened the collapse of the Somali state. The consequences of the execution of the attempted coup leaders in the course of Somali history was disastrous, marking the beginning of the re-emergence of clannish sentiments that grew drastically afterward. On the other hand, following the execution of the Islamic scholars, the embryonic Islamic movements took new momentum and underground

---

[22] The three executed officers were General Ainanshe, General Salad Gavere, and Col. Abdulqadir Dheel.

[23] Ali Sheikh Abukar, *Judur Al-Ma'sat Al-Rahina* (Bairut: Dar Ibn Hazm. 1992), 181-185; also, see the complete text of the agreement of cooperation and friendship between Somalia and Soviet Union in the attachment, 247. The executed officers belonged to the Isaq, Majertain, and Abgal clans. From then, their close relatives and sub-lineages were targeted and dealt with as ant-revolutionaries. See a complete and firsthand account of the campaign of the military regime against Islam in Ali Sheikh, *Judur Al-Ma'sat*, 109-137.

organizations spread in every corner in defense of the faith against the *"godless socialists"*. From this historical crossroad, the Islamic movements formulated their ideological foundation and launched socio-political programs. Gradually, these two forces, stemming from the local ideologies of clannism and Islamism, had engaged in the active subversion of the regime. Moreover, the military regime's policies in establishing the Somali Socialist Revolutionary Party (SSRP) in 1977 further alienated clan power sharing. Furthermore, the war with Ethiopia in 1977-78, when Somalia was defeated by the allied forces organized by the USSR, together with Cuba, South Yemen, and other countries, became the second turning point towards the downfall of the state.[24]The defeat in the war produced a national mood of depression and frustrated the idea of Somali nationalism.

The Somali political condition in 1978 was very much similar to the political atmosphere of 1969, when a one-party regime was established and political grievances exacerbated, thus leading to the military take-over. Regrettably, the army who saved the state from failing in 1969 was now in power and had become fragmented. Also, its command structure had lost its independence and professionalism and became an inseparable part of the ruling party and the regime.[25] Therefore, the attempted coup d'état of April 9, 1978 was easily foiled, resulting in the execution of 18 army officers and the detention of hundred officers. The coup d'état, even though did not succeed in immediately toppling the regime, it nonetheless set the stage for the demise of the regime. The officers of the coup plotters who succeeded in escaping formed armed oppositions and received a welcoming hand from the hostile countries, particularly Ethiopia.[26]As a reaction, the frightened regime intensified political repression, summary executions of dissidents, and the collective

---

[24] Relations between Somalia and Soviets had deteriorated and Soviet experts were expelled from Somalia on 13 November, 1977. The author of this article was also among expelled Somali military officers from USSR reciprocally.

[25] The ruling political party, the Somali Socialist Revolutionary Party, incorporated higher ranking officers in its central committee and officers trained as political cadres who were party members were attached to all military units to indoctrinate military personnel.

[26] During this period, both Somalia and Ethiopia were supporting each other's armed oppositions. Somalia was supporting the current leaders of Ethiopia and Eritrea, while the Ethiopian regime was supporting Somali clan-based factions that toppled the Siyad Barre regime; nevertheless, they failed to re-establish the Somali nation-state.

punishment of clans thought to have supported armed insurgences. Thus, the era of clannish factionalism was in tumult, and the proverbial genie that collapsed the Somalia state had now been released. Throughout the difficult decade of the 1980s, clannish armed factions had established bases in Ethiopia one after another. These factions were the Somali Salvation Democratic Front (SSDF) (1978),[27] the Somali National Movement (SNM) (1981), the United Somali Congress (USC) (1989), and the Somali Patriotic Movement (SPM) (1988). These armed factions lacked organizational capacity and national vision, and thus, fought the regime without coordination. Finally, the USC forces overran the presidential palace of Villa Somalia in Mogadishu on January 26, 1991, and the military regime came to a disgraced conclusion. Other factions like the SNM took over the northern cities, whilst the SPM was controlling major cities in southern Somalia. Concluding this section, the collapse of the Somali state went through three stages: the first stage was before the military takeover of the state power in 1969. The second stage was after the defeat of Somalia in the war with Ethiopia in 1978, after which the attempted coup was aborted. From 1978, the trajectory of state collapse was rolling towards the complete breaking point of January 26, 1991, which is the third and final stage. In this historical juncture, scholars began to puzzle and to seek answers to the difficult equations behind the Somali state collapse. The following section delves into the theories of the state collapse and conflict to lay the theoretical foundation to the perspectives put forth by these scholars.

1969	The First Failure of the State: • Rigged elections of 1969 • Assassination of President Sharmarke • Military coup d'état
1978	The Second Failure of the State: • Defeat in the war with Ethiopia (1977/78) • Foiled coup d'état of April 9, 1978 • Establishment of the first armed opposition (SDF) in September 1978
1990-91	The final collapse of the state in January 1991 and escalation of the civil war

Fig. 8. Periods of the Somali state failures and collapse

---

[27] The SSDF merged with Somali Democratic Action Front (SODAF) and the Somali Salvation Front (SSF) in 1981.

Theories of State Capabilities and Conflict

Studies on the state collapse have been conducted in the field of state capacities in the comparative political analysis.[28] Scholar Joel Migdal provided a set of theories on state capabilities in examining weak and strong states and weak and strong societies. Migdal argues that states have to provide a single political status of citizenship to all its members in its jurisdiction and exercise hegemonic control over the society. Moreover, in order for a state to survive, a number of factors need to be present. These include; the organizational capabilities of its leaders, population size, potential material and human resources available, and larger international configurations."[29] States that are capable of performing functions of a state are called empirical states and are expected to be "an independent political structure of sufficient authority and power to govern a defined territory and its population."[30] On the other hand, when a state is recognized by other states as a legal entity but is unable to perform the functions of a state, it is then referred to as a juridical state "de jure", which means that no other state can intervene in its affairs without their consent. The capability of the state is measured by its capacity to "penetrate society, regulate social relationships, extract resources, and appropriate or use resources in determined ways."[31] Strong states normally perform these tasks effectively, and to the contrary, weak states perform poorly in these four elements. Based on that classification, comparative state capacities are calculated relative to their governance capabilities. The measurable indicator is state performance in delivering the most fundamental "political goods", which means the effective supply of security to its citizens and inhabitants within its state borders. It is the prime responsibility of the state to

---

[28] States may be classified in accordance with their status with the international system, economic capabilities, or their leadership. As such, they are classified as weak and powerful, radical and conservative, patron and client, modern and traditional, and developed and developing. see Kamrava, Mehran, *Understanding Comparative Politics: A Framework for Analysis*. Routledge, 1996,72.

[29] Joel S. Migdal, *Strong Societies and Weak States: State-Society Relations and State Capabilities in the Third World* (Princeton University Press, 1988), 21.

[30] R.H. Jackson & C.G. Rosberg, 'Sovereignty and Underdevelopment: Juridical Statehood in the African Crisis'. The Journal of Modern African Studies, vol. 24 (1), 1986, p. 1-31.

[31] Joel S. Migdal, *Strong Societies and Weak states: State-Society Relations and State Capabilities in the Third World* (Princeton: Princeton University press, 1988), 4

thwart external threats beyond national borders, as well as check and diminish domestic threats such as insurgencies, rebels, and different kinds of crime related activities endangering human life and properties. The second in the hierarchy of "political goods" is to set up a system for arbitrating disputes and an effective judicial system to maintain law and order. The third in the hierarchy of "political goods" is to deliver essential social services such as medical and health care; schools, and the protection of the environment. Moreover, states are expected to provide basic infrastructures such as roads, railways, harbours, etc. Fourth, states have to supply and protect arteries of commerce, including currency and banking in addition to offering a space for civil society[32].

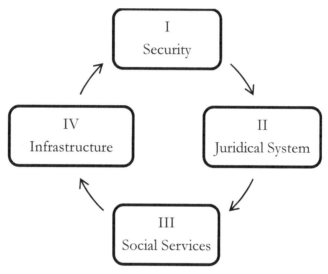

Fig.9. The four fundamental political goods of the state

Theory of State Capabilities

According to state capability and performance in developmental and security studies, states are placed in a developmental continuum, classifying them as "strong", "weak", "failed" or "collapsed". Strong states are described as those states that effectively "control their territories and deliver a full range and a high quality of political goods to

---

[32] Robert I. Rotberg, *State Failure and State Weakness in a Time of Terror* (The World Peace Foundation: Brooking Institution Press, 2003), 2-4.

their citizens".[33] Their high performance could be detected through recognized indicators such as their "per capita GDP, the UNDP Human Development Index, Transparency International's Corruption Perceptions Index, and Freedom House's Freedom of the World Report".[34] Strong states also tend to show higher marks on the 8 major characteristics of good governance, which are stated as thus: participatory, consensus oriented, accountability, transparent, responsive, effective and efficient, equitable and inclusive, and following the rule of law. Good governance also assures that corruption is minimized, that the views of minorities are taken into account, and that the voices of the most vulnerable in the society are heard in decision-making. Moreover, good governance should also be responsive to the present and future needs of the society.

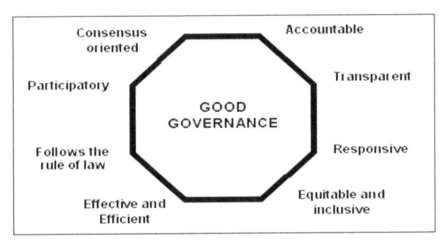

Fig. 10. Elements of good governance

Weak states are classified into weak states that develop a positive direction of strength, and weak states that move down to the negative direction of failing stage. Those moving towards failure comprise states that may be weak for a variety of objective reasons, for example, geographical, physical, and economic constraints; in addition, weakness

---

33 Robert I. Rotberg, *Nation-state failure: A recurrence Phenomenon?* (www.cia.gov/nic/PDF_GIF_2020_Support/ 2003_11_06_papers/panel2_nov6.pdf), 3-5

34 Ibid., 2

may be due to a lack of internal cohesion and absence of an adequate political system and leadership. These weak states, in general, fail to solve ethnic, religious, linguistic, or any other grievances that culminate in creating tensions and conflict. The capability of the state to provide satisfactory basic "political goods" is low. Erosion of the physical infrastructure, such as roads, schools, and hospitals is wide spread. Most of the indicators are falling, such as per capita GDP; meanwhile, corruption is escalating, the rule of law is diminished, civil society is harassed, and despots rule.[35] Some of the weak states, which are ruled by an autocracy, have shown high levels of security despite providing few other political goods.[36]

Failed States can be found at either end of two extremes. The first extreme is when a state is no longer capable of functioning; the second is when the state becomes "too effective", too intrusive into the private realms of its citizens, and constantly harasses its people. This could be equated with high blood pressure and low blood pressure: both are unhealthy symptoms that require medication. The first form of state failure is characterized by the limited ability to provide essential political goods; gradually, the state gives up its control and relegates it to warlords and other non-state actors. Most of the institutions of the failed state are defective and dysfunctional; its polity is unable to perform the fundamental tasks of the state. Moreover, its legislatures are merely a rubber stamp for the strong executive, whereas its judiciary has lost credibility in the eyes of its citizens, who withdraw their trust from the court system, with litigations solved in the localized system of justice. In addition, state bureaucracy becomes unaccountable and unresponsive to the public they aim to serve. The state also loses their professional responsibility and exploits their public office for personal gains. As a result, the infrastructure of the failed states is damaged. National utilities such as communication, water, and the supply of electricity are in a shamble. Moreover, social service facilities such as schools and hospitals

---

[35] The new definitions and explanations contained in this paper are elaborated upon at much greater length in Robert I. Rotberg, "The Failure and Collapse of Nation-States: Breakdown, Prevention, and Repair," in Robert I. Rotberg (ed.), *Why States Fail:Causes and Consequences* (Princeton, 2004), 1-45.

[36] Somalia under Siyad Barre, Cambodia under Pol Pot, Iraq under Saddam Hussein, Libya under Qadaffi, and North Korea all fit this rubric.

are not renovated and crumble, causing national literacy rates to fall and infant mortality rates to rise. On top of this, most of the industrial projects do not function properly due to their lack of competitiveness; as a result, unemployment becomes rampant, and the vulnerability of the population increases in turn. Agricultural farms then decline as local economic production falls. Consequently, the masses become dissatisfied with state performance and lose hope. International investors shy away, inflation skyrockets and local currency loses its value. Security forces cooperate with the criminals and collect illegal taxations. The middle class shrinks and migrates. Therefore, loyalty to the state diminishes and patriotism/nationalism fades away to sub-cultural loyalty. Failed states offer enormous economic opportunities for a privileged few, who, through a patronage system, use the prevailing scarcity to enrich themselves through corruption.

A Collapsed State is considered an extreme form of a failed state. States collapse when their structure, political authority, legitimate power, and law and order fall apart and the country lacks an alternative political force capable of filling the vacuum. The demise of a state is attributed to a breakdown of social coherence on an extensive level, as civil society can no longer create, aggregate, and articulate the support and demands that are the foundation of the state. States do not break up overnight; it is a long cumulative and incremental process similar to degenerative diseases. It passes through stages of weakness and failure until it collapses. Therefore, in due course, it could be rectified and reverted from failing to weakness and strength. For instance, governments lose the ability to exert legitimate authority over a certain territory of its jurisdiction, and as a result, certain regions fall away from the control of the state apparatus. Subsequently, communities realign in the form of ethnic, kinship, and cultural attachments. Security becomes the rule of the strong, and in the Somali case, belongs to the armed clans. Sub-state actors of particular ethnic or clan-like business groups, religious leaders, and clan elders take over and try to restore some form of functionality to the parts of the collapsed state. However, recovering the original state requires strong external support.[37]

---

[37] Collapsed states could recover by returning it into the status of failed if sufficient security is restored to rebuild the institutions and strengthen the legitimacy of the resuscitated state. Lebanon did so thanks to Syrian security, Tajikistan because of Russia, Afghanistan because of the U. S. led invasion, and Sierra Leone because of

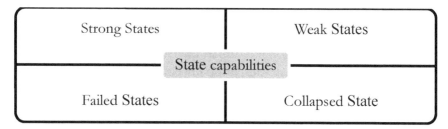

Fig.11. Classification of state capabilities

Theories of Social Conflict

States do not collapse without conflict, the causes of which can be divided into original causes or genesis, operational causes, and proximate efficient causes. The original causes consist of those long-term, deeply rooted conditions that date back to the very formation of the society or the state. They constitute the objective factors employable for initiating conflict in case of subjective factors. The scales of the operational causes that nurture the conflict and deepen its probabilities depend on the magnitude and pervasiveness of these original causes. Moreover, proximate and efficient causes serve as trigger mechanisms for the outbreak of the intrastate conflict and civil strife. Many theories consider the primordial, class, and eclectic theories as the prime causes of conflicts.

There is no consensus on the definition and description of conflicts among scholars. Conflict is normally understood as a social phenomenon which results from the differences in the social circumstances and/or disparate interests of at least two parties (individuals, groups, states, etc).[38] Studies of the root cause of the conflict put forth various types of conflict. Kieh and Mukenge define civil conflict as "a dispute between domestic actors – government and private groups – over economic, political, social, cultural or any combination of these issues." In their

---

British intervention. Somalia is in the process of recovery under African Union Mission for Somalia (AMISOM). See Robert I. Rotberg. *Nation-state failure: A recurrence Phenomenon?*

[38] Woo Idowu, Citizenship, alienation and conflict in Nigeria, Africa Development, Vol. 24, No. 1/2, 1999, 31-55, 34.

research, the authors identified three major theoretical frameworks on the causes of civil conflicts: primordial, class, and eclectic theories.[39]

Primordial theory, which is based on the premise that identity of a primordial group, such as a clan, sub-clan, or racial group, is something that people are either born with, or that gradually shapes their identity through deep psychological processes, over which politics and society have little effect. The ramifications of this view are that these identities cannot be changed, and that individual choices are permanently defined by these identities. Accordingly, in a nation of clans like Somalia, when conflicts occur, people are organized by their primordial attachments. Moreover, in line with this theory, a hegemonic pattern of relations exists in which one group controls others in political and/or economic power. George Kaly Kieth and Ida Rousseau Mukenge explained perfectly how a hegemonic pattern functions within post-colonial nation-states. In particular, the Somali case is a classical one, where specific clans dominated political power and were instrumented to gain economic privileges. Consequently, elites belonging to the marginalized clans (civil/military) formed armed insurgencies.[40] According to a World Bank study, "nearly all armed conflicts in contemporary Somalia break out along clan lines. Clan identities are malleable and can be shaped by leaders to pursue control of resources and power. Clan identities are not the basis for conflict; rather, their deliberate manipulation creates and exacerbates divisions. Clan groups can serve as destructive or constructive forces as well as traditional conflict moderators".[41]

Class Conflict Theory is based on the fact that every society has its economic mode of production and that each member of a society bases his or her own relationship to the mode of production, which belongs either to the owning class or to a subaltern one. According to Marxist theory, all conflict arises from the class-based struggle to own the means of production, and the capitalist class would never give up their

---

[39] George Klay and Jr Kieh, "Theories of Conflict and Conflict Resolution, in George Klay Kieh Jr and Ida Rousseau Mukenge (eds), *Zones of Conflict in Africa: Theories and Cases* (Westport, Conn: Praeger, 2002), 3.

[40] George Kaly Kieth, and Ida Rousseau Mukenge, Zones of Conflict in Africa: Theories and Cases. (Praeger, 2002), 10.

[41] The World Bank, "Conflict in Somalia: Drivers and dynamics", January, 2005, 15. Available from http://siteresources.worldbank.org/INTSOMALIA/Resources/conflictinsomalia. pdf.

privileged place as owners of the means of production. As such, the capitalist class has the power to affect the life of the people and produce irresolvable conflict between them and the working class. This capitalist class controls the major means of production and determines the allocation and distribution of resources and wages. This leads to the exploitation of the working class by the capitalist class, which necessarily produces class conflict. However, the actual eruption of the conflict requires the fulfillment of a set of conditions, the first one being rising consciousness of the exploitation and being organized in a form of movement or political party in order to be able to wage class struggle.[42] In Somalia, analysis of class conflict is not well developed as a conflict driver; however, some recent studies show the existence of such conflict in some areas. Alex de Waal writes,

> We must develop a class analysis of the origins and development of the crisis, locating it in the growth of state-mediated capitalist relations in both agriculture and pastoralism, and the key role that control of the state apparatus played in allowing capital accumulation among certain sections of the capitalist class in the 1980s.[43]

The Eclectic Theory is located between the primordial and class theories, and holds that conflict is the product of a confluence of many factors that are cultural, economic, historical, political, social, and so on. This theory recognizes that a single variable or factor is insufficient to explain the complexity of civil wars. Thus, many interconnected causes of conflict may reinforce each other. For example, poverty is based on individual and regional disparities, repression, the abuse of human rights, the concentration of power at the political center, the willingness of neighbouring states to lend their support to dissident forces in countries, all these play their parts. To resolve conflicts, various means are used, such as peacemaking based on negotiation and mediation, peacekeeping such as the use of military forces, peace observation and humanitarian assistance, and peace enforcement that involves the coercion of parties in conflict seeking their compliance.

---

[42] Jack A. Goldstone, *Revolutions: A Very Short Introduction* (Oxford University Press, 2014), 16-25.

[43] Alex de Waal, Class and Power in a Stateless Somalia A Discussion Paper, August 1996, 1. Available from http://justiceafrica.org/wp-content/uploads/2014/03/DeWaal_ClassandPowerinSomalia.pdf.

Ibn-Khaldun's Theory of Asabiyah

Ibn-Khaldun's theory of Asabiyah answers three main questions related to the theory of social conflict. Like the primordial theory of social conflict, it explains the causes of conflicts, but additionally offers a comprehensive understanding of conflict dynamics in the tribal societies. The theory of Asabiyah explains how conflicts develop in the tribal nomadic societies; what happens after their conquest of the urban centers; and how to mitigate their destructive culture. This theory was developed as a result of empirical studies on the cyclical rise and fall of the medieval states in North Africa in the 14th century. The *Muqaddimah* (prolegomena) to the Universal History, authored by Ibn-Khaldun, delves into the studies of the relations between civilizations and nomadic people. The societies of Ibn-Khaldun's subject of study were clans and tribes, and their religion was Islam. Hence, this theory may be still relevant in similar societies like Somalia. This theory has some shared conceptions with the primordial theory of conflict, but also offers a deeper explanation in terms of explaining the behaviour of the nomads after their conquest of the civilized centers and difficulties of resuscitating the state because nomads do not agree on one leadership, which prolongs the conflict. Thus, Somalia may be the ideal model of Asabiyah in action in collapsing the state in 1991 and sustaining the civil war over three decades.

Rosenthal, the translator of the *Muqaddimah* to the Universal History (*Kitab al-'Ibar*) into English defines the differences between nomadism (*badawa*) and civilization (*hadara*). The *Badawa* is characterized as simplicity of life, courage, violence, and striking power. On the other hand, *Hadara* is defined as a life of urban civilization in which these natural qualities are gradually submerged by the desire for peace and security, ease, luxury, and pleasure.[44] The term Asabiyah is derived from the Arabic root *Asab* (to bind the individuals into a group).[45] Mohamed Al-Jaberi suggests that Asabiyah is "socio-psychological solidarity, conscious and unconscious at the same time, which binds members of a group of people who are related to each other (in blood relations mostly) in a continuous manner; and appears and strengthens when there is a

---

[44] Ervin Rosenthal, *Political Thought in Medieval Islam* (Cambridge University Press, 1962), 90.
[45] See the Qur'anic conception of *Asab* in the verses 12:8, 12:14, 24:11, and 28:76.

common threat towards the group and individuals."[46] Moreover, Ibn-Khaldun connotes Asabiyah as "basically a social force which offers ability for confrontation, whether that confrontation is [political] demands or defends [from threats]".[47] Furthermore, Al-Jaberi argues that the driving force that binds these nomads is primarily the "economic factor." Their primitive political structure is not defined by hierarchy and stratification, a typical element of many modern bureaucratic states. Therefore, the traditional nomadic state is antithetic to the modern concept of statehood.

Besides the primordial and nomadic factors as the causes of social conflicts, here we will produce and analyze two propositions of the theory of Asabiyah which are relevant to our topic of enquiry. The first proposition offers the answer of how the nomads behave when they conquer urban cities. This proposition is that "palaces that succumb to the Arabs [nomads] are quickly ruined."[48] This means when these nomads conquer urban centers, whose way of life is based on luxurious houses and buildings, a different lifestyle form to what they were previously accustomed to, and hence they utilize material elements available in the cities to bolster their previous way of life. They do not shy away from looting and plundering other people's properties, they do not value professionals, they do not respect or abide by laws, and they do not value human lives. Also, they rarely agree on one leader, since everyone among them strives to be the leader and thus, continually struggles for power. Therefore, civilization cyclically rises and falls in places conquered by the nomads.

The second proposition deals with the remedy and how to mitigate the destructive behaviour of the nomads. This theory puts forth that Asabiyah cannot be weakened without the intervention of a religious moral standard that lessens its ferocity and savageness with the teaching of the universal values. Addressing this question, Ibn-Khaldun wrote: "Arabs [nomads] can obtain royal authority only making use of some religious coloring such as prophecy, or sainthood, or some great religious event in general."[49] Further explaining this concept, he wrote,

---

[46] Mohammed Abidi Jabiri, *Fikr Ibn-Khaldum: Al-Asabiyatu wa Dawlah* (Dar al-Nashr al-Maghribiyah, no date), 254.
[47] Ibid., 257.
[48] Ibn-Khaldun, *The Muqaddimah: An Introduction to History* (Princeton University Press, 1980), 302.
[49] Ibid., 305.

But when there is a religion [among them] through prophecy or sainthood, then they have some restraining influence in themselves. The quality of haughtiness and jealousy leaves them. It is, then, easy for them to subordinate themselves and to unite.[50]

This proposition states that evil actions are not in the nature of the nomads but rather a product of their particular ecology. The only remedy for minimizing the savageness of nomads is through religion, which offers a new outlook and the spirituality needed to widen the narrowed tendency of Asabiyah. Instilling a universal outlook, a sense of human brotherhood, equality, the value of human life, and so on, are the only solutions for curtailing the nomads' savageness, according to Ibn-Khaldun. Taking the Asabiyah theory from its narrow historical definition, its conception could be generally understood as a tightly knit organization with a strong, driving ideology focused on realizing a common purpose such as attaining political supremacy or economic gains. In the Somali context, there are three identifiable compounded Asabiyah (loyalties): clan-centered (clannism), national (nationalism), and religion-centered (Islamism).[51] Religious and national Asabiyah often converge in resisting and repulsing external enemies while clan-centered Asabiyah is mainly divisive and causes internal weakness, conflict, and potentially, civil wars. However, these Asabiyah are not isolated from each other in terms of space and time; they may converge at times and create a strong social solidarity. To guarantee such solidarity, an appropriate leadership must be created. The leader should act as the chief of all other chiefs, while the super-chief (head of the state) should exhibit affinity, affection, and administer justice among the clans as equals (citizens). On the other hand, when that actual super-chief favours his particular lineage and attempts to use it to bolster his rule, the angered sub-Asabiyah of the marginalized clans becomes aroused and insurgences are organized in a clannish method. This phenomenon is exactly what

---

50 Ibid.
51 How these three loyalties interact within Somali political culture shaping their world view with propensity for crisis of loyalties is studied in the MA thesis of this author. See Abdurahman Abdullahi, Tribalism, Nationalism and Islam: The Crisis of political Loyalties in Somalia, MA thesis submitted to the Islamic institute, McGill University, 1992.

happened in Somalia during the military regime in the 1980s when armed factions were established to counter the clan-centered government which monopolized power and wealth.

The Asabiyah theory also explains the behaviour of nomads after their dominance of the cities and settled communities where traditional authorities are weakened and where there are no other restraining authorities. As was evident in Somalia, clan militias indiscriminately destroyed everything, both public and private. Towns were looted and plundered, and nothing was spared from destruction. Ibn-Khaldun describing nomadic behaviour, wrote: "It is their nature to plunder whatever other people possess ... They recognize no limits in taking the possessions of other people."[52] Moreover, ibn-Khaldun articulates that "[every Arab] is eager to be a leader. Few militia men would cede his power to another, even to his father, his brother, or the eldest member of his family."[53]

Ibn-Khaldun's Theory of Asabiyah

1. Asabiyah binds members of a group of people who are related to each other, mostly blood relations.
2. Nomadic people ruin civilizations wherever they conquer
3. Nomads rarely agree on one leader and every one strives to be the leader.
4. The driving force of nomads is **primarily** "economic factor."
5. Only religion mitigates haughtiness, jealousy and negative manners of nomads (Islam in the Somali context)

Fig. 12. Summary of Ibn-Khaldun's Theory of Asabiyah

Having seen the theoretical backdrop of the state's capabilities, we can locate the Somali state from its formative period in the 1950s and after its independence, placing it in the category of the weak sstates. The political leadership had the option to steer the country in a positive direction in terms of strength, or to move toward a negative direction of the state failure. Regrettably, due to the absence of an adequate political

---

[52] Lineage segmentation and civil war (www.country-study, Somalia.com/Somalia).
[53] Ibn Khadun, *Muqadimmah*, 304.

system and competent leadership, Somalia was cyclically moving towards the direction of state failure. During the 1980s, the state reached a point where it was no longer capable of functioning and was engaged in internal wars with various armed groups. Obviously, states do not collapse without conflict, and for that reason, we have summarized the theory of conflict and its perspectives, which include primordial, class, and eclectic.

Perspectives of the Somali State Collapse

Having grasped the theories of state capabilities and conflict, let us now explore the nature of the conflict that led to the collapse of the Somali state, which had gradually regressed from being a weak state in 1960 to a failed state in the 1980s, and finally reaching breaking point in 1991. Exploring the theories of the social conflict, this paper has objected to the single factor explanation and opted for eclectic theory, which shares the view that conflicts are the product of a confluence of many factors. Moreover, Ibn-Khaldun's theory of Asabiyah emphasizes the role of primordial attachment as an instrument of the conflict. Additionally, the theory of Asabiyah explains the persistent instability of clan-based states and their cyclical rise and fall. We will now delve into the plethora of perspectives on the collapse of the Somali state. These perspectives will be classified according to their focus to construct a comprehensive model linking all the causes to each other. Scholars looked at Somali state collapse from different perspectives in accordance with their schools of thought and subject matters. These perspectives include the impact of the Cold War and dried foreign aid, Somali irredentism and war with Ethiopia, primordialism, resource overextension, moral degradation, and eclectic factors. Our sequential study is not based on any criteria and we treat them equally until we offer our final conclusions.

The Impact of the Cold War and Dried Foreign Aid

Somalia is situated in the strategic Horn of Africa, which has long attracted competing global powers.[54] The strategic geographical location, which could be an asset for Somalia, has instead become a liability by attracting multiple colonial and Cold War superpower rivalries.[55]After the independence in 1960, there was a competition over Somalia between US and the Soviet Union. However, the Soviets won when Somalia precipitately signed a military agreement worth $30 million in 1963.[56] The Soviet Union outbid the West by agreeing to expand the Somali army from 4,000 to 20,000 in comparison to the provision of $10 million for military aid and training 5,000-6,000 army promised by the USA and its NATO allies. Since then, Soviet influence had grown exponentially, particularly after General Mohamed Siyad Barre overthrew the civilian government in 1969, adopted socialism, and signed a treaty of friendship with the Soviet Union.[57] However, during the Somali-Ethiopian war in 1977-78, the Soviet Union and Somalia ended their cooperation, and Washington offered military and economic aid to Somalia in order to counterbalance the Soviet and Cuban support for Ethiopia. It was estimated that Washington provided $500 million dollars' worth of military aid to Mogadishu in the 1980s. However, when the Soviet Union

---

[54] The Somali coastline, which is about 3,025 km in total, is the longest in mainland Africa and the Middle East. Through its territorial waters passes about 33,000 commercial ships every year. These ships carry 26% of global oil trade and 14-15% of the international trade with the cost of $1.8 trillion annually.

[55] Abdurahman Abdullahi, "Perspectives on the State Collapse in Somalia," in *Somalia at the Crossroads: Challenges and Perspectives in Reconstituting a Failed State*, ed. Abdullahi A. Osman and Issaka K. Soure, London: Adonis & Abbey Publishers Ltd., 2007.

[56] S. Chirumamilla, *U.S intervention in the Horn: Revisiting Ethiopia Somalia dispute*, 2011, 189.
    Available from http://shodhganga.inflibnet.ac.in/bitstream/10603/1861/13/13_c hapter6.pdf (accessed on January 31, 2017).

[57] The Treaty of Friendship between Somalia and the Soviets signed in 1974 was abrogated on Nov. 13, 1977 because of the Soviet Union's collaboration with Ethiopia during the war. As a result, Soviet military and civilian advisers stationed in Somalia would have to leave the country within a week, and that all military facilities granted to the USSR in Somalia were withdrawn with immediate effect. See http://web.stanford.edu/group/tomzgroup/pmwiki/uploads/2069-1978-KS-a-LIZ.pdf (accessed on February 2, 2017).

collapsed in the 1990s and the Cold War ended, foreign aid policy drastically changed. Thus, Somalia lost the advantage of being a "strategic Magnet of the Seventies"[58] and as a Cold War partner for the US. As a result, aid was withdrawn from Barre's regime and the regime was weakened and was easily overthrown by the armed insurgencies.[59]

The Cold War and the withdrawal of foreign assistance as the main factors of state collapse were the focus of a number of scholars, including Terrence Lyons, Walter S. Clarke, Robert Gosende, Ahmed Samatar, Ken Menkhaus, and John Prendergast. For instance, Terrence Lyons ties the Somali state collapse with the withdrawal of external assistance and increased local demand for improved political goods. He notes that the Somali state collapsed when "external support was withdrawn and societal demand for economic advancement and better governance increased."[60] Walter S. Clarke and Robert Gosende agree with Terrence Lyons in attributing the failure to the shortage of external assistance, but not exclusively. They wrote that "Somalia's failure may be only partially related to the end of the Cold War."[61] Ahmed Samatar relates the collapse to a triple burden, which includes defeat in the war and low economic performance (Aid/domestic). He notes"Bearing the triple burden of defeat in the war and accompanying humiliation, an economy on the skids and a lack of superpower patronage, Somali politics turns inward. The national focus became the regime and the state, which were caught in an enveloping atmosphere of acridity and suspension."[62] Ken Menkhaus expresses even further, seemingly over-

---

[58] J. Bowyer Bell, *The Horn of Africa: Strategic Magnet in the Seventies* (New York: Crane, Russak 1973)

[59] Alena Hrušková, Comparison of US Foreign Aid Towards Somalia During and After the Cold War, 33. Available from http://www.unob.cz/eam/Documents/Archiv/EaM_1_2014/Hruskova.pdf (accessed on February 2, 2017)

[60] Terrence Lyons and Ahmed Samatar, *Somalia: State Collapse, Multilateral intervention, and Strategies for Political Reconstruction*(Washington: The Brooking Institution Occasional Paper, 1995), 1

[61] Walter S. Clarke and Robert Gosende, "Somalia: Can a Collapsed State Reconstitute itself"? In Robert I. Rotberg (ed.), *State Failure and State Weakness in a Time of Terror* (Washington: Brooking Institution Press, 2000), 129-158.

[62] Ahmed Samatar, "The Curse of Allah: Civic Disembowelment and the collapse of the State in Somalia" in in Ahmed Samatar (ed.), *The Somali Challenge: From Catastrophe to Renewal?* (Lynne Rienner Publishers, 1994), 117.

emphasizing external assistance. He wrote, "It may be an exaggeration to claim that the Somali state is a creation of external assistance, but it is indisputable that the state has never been remotely sustainable by domestic sources of revenue. As far back as the 1950s, observers worried that an independent Somali state would not be economically viable."[63] Moreover, Ken Menkhaus and John Prendergast even went further. They noted, "There was never in Somalia's history a sustainable basis for a viable central state authority. In the past, the Somali state was funded almost entirely by Cold War driven foreign aid, leading to a bloated and artificial structure which collapsed soon after that aid was frozen in the late 1980s."[64]

Somali Irredentism and War with Ethiopia

Somali Irredentism is rooted in the historical fact that the Somali-inhabited territories in the Horn of Africa were occupied and divided among four foreign powers during the European scramble for Africa. These powers were Italy, Britain, France, and the Ethiopian Empire. Encouraged by the Bevin Plan, Somali nationalists grasped the concept of "Greater Somalia", founded on the vision of reunifying Somali populations living in five different regions, as represented by the Somali flag's five pointed white star. In two of these regions, Somali territory mandated to Italian administration under UN trusteeship, and British Somaliland became independent and united to become an independent Somali Republic in 1960. The other "missing territories" include the Somali-inhabited areas in the current Republic of Djibouti, Region Five or the Somali Region in Ethiopia, and the Northern Frontier District (NFD) in Kenya. Pursuing the vision of "Greater Somalia", the newly independent state of Somalia was encouraged, manipulated, and absorbed into the Cold War by the two superpowers competing for the supremacy of the strategic Horn of Africa. Thus, many scholars portray Somalia as a "pawn" of the Cold War, as the United States and the Soviet Union competed for global influence.[65] As a result, Somalia was induced through military assistance to quench its aspiration for "Greater

---

63   Ken Menkhaus, "US Foreign Assistance Somalia: Phoenix from the Ashes?" Middle Eastern Policy, 1:5, 1997, 126
64   Ken Menkhaus and John Prendergast, "Governance and Economic Survival in Post-intervention Somalia" in CSIS Africa Note, No.172 (May 1995).
65   John T. Fishel, *Civil Military Operations in the New World* (Praeger, 1997), 189

Somalia." This hostile environment with its neighbours had created the condition that Somalia had fought two wars with Ethiopia in 1964, and 1977-78. The Somali-Ethiopian war of 1977-78 was internationalized and concluded with a disastrous defeat of Somalia, leaving behind severe consequences on the regional peace on the Horn of Africa.[66]

Somali irredentism and war with Ethiopia as the main factor for the collapse of the state was the focus of Terrence Lyons, Jeffrey A. Lefebvre, and Peter Woodward. Again, Lyons emphasizes the historicity of the causes of the collapse. She points to the Somali national aspiration for unity and its neighbour's unwillingness to cede the disputed territory due to different perceptions of the state-territorial versus cultural. She writes,

> "The point here is that [nationalism] as an ideology; it encouraged leaders in Mogadishu to pursue foreign policies that inherently led the state into conflict with neighbours that had rival claims to the Somali-inhabited territories. Somalia's arguments under the principle of Greater Somalia were antithetical to Ethiopia, Kenya and Djibouti's insistence on the principle of territorial integrity and sanctity of colonial border, principles these states were prepared to defend by force if necessary."[67]

Jeffrey A. Lefebvre observed more clearly and wrote: "Ironically, Siad's demise and the disintegration of the Somali state were not only a consequence of clan politics but also attributable in part, to Somalia's irredentist foreign policy, principally the aspect of it aimed at Ethiopia."[68] On the other hand, Peter Woodward relates state failure to domestic factors and also recognizes border permeability as a part of the problem. He notes: "While the destruction of Somalia state as constituted from

---

[66] Joseph K. Nkaisserry, The Ogaden War: An Analysis of Its Causes and Its Impact on Regional Peace and on the Horn of Africa. USAWC Strategic Research Project, US Army War College Carlisle Barracks, Pennsylvania, 1997. Available from file:///C:/Users/Abdurahman/Downloads/ADA326941%20(1).pdf (accessed on February 2, 2017)

[67] Terrence Lyons. "Crises on Multiple Levels: Somalia and the Horn of Africa" in Ahmed Samatar (ed.), *The Somali Challenge: From Catastrophe to Renewal?* (Lynne Rienner Publishers, 1994), 193

[68] Jeffrey A. Lefebvre, "The US Military in Somalia: A hidden Agenda?" Middle Eastern Policy, 1:2 (1993), 47.

1960 was primarily due to domestic factors, the issue of the permeability of the state's border was also relevant." Moreover, he argues "border permeability was to work against Somalia from 1978 as Ethiopia hosted Siyad Barre's growing number of opponents."[69] Furthermore, he acknowledges that the opposition's struggle to overthrow the regime developed into the destruction of the state. He remarks,

> In terms of state collapse, Somalia appears to be the most complete experience in the Horn. The building of Somali socialism in the 1970s contributed much to making state and regime increase synonymously; the reverse of that coin was the long political narrowing of the regime after the 1977-78 war with Ethiopia, which finally brought the destruction of the state with the overthrow of the regime.[70]

Primordial Political Culture

Somalia is a nation of clans in search of a state, and clan system can be used negatively or positively in nation-building. It can be used as a conflict tool or a peace and conflict resolution mechanism. However, according to the early modernization theory, traditional societies can be brought to development in the same manner as more developed countries. This means traditional religious beliefs and cultural traits usually become less important as they are marginalized and modernization takes hold. Somali nationalists represented by the founding fathers of Somali Youth Leagues (SYL) followed such conception of modernization and emphasized the denial of clan attachments by its members. The members of SYL were obliged "to take the oath which bound the members not to reveal clan affiliation, but to admit only to being Somali."[71] However, with the emergence of more political parties by 1950s, clan divide and primordial attachments were used as political tool facilitated by the adopted Italian political system.[72]

---

[69]   Peter Woodward, *The Horn of Africa: State Politics and International Relations* (New York: Tauris Academic Studies, 1996), 82

[70]   Ibid., p.81

[71]   Cedric Barnes, "The Somali Youth League, Ethiopian Somalis and the Greater Somalia Idea, c.1946–48". Journal of Eastern African Studies, 1:2, 277-291, 2007, 281.   http://www.tandfonline.com/doi/pdf/10.1080/17531050701452564 (accessed on February 2, 2017)

[72]   Paolo Tripodi, *The Colonial Legacy in Somalia: Rome and Mogadishu: from Colonial Administration to Operation Restore Hope* (Macmillan Press, 1999), 82-84.

With all the attempts to curb clannism through legal means and state policies, it remained adamant and robust against the idealistic and rhetoric campaigns of nationalism. The final blow to the Somali state was carried out through primordial conception and political wrangling taking the form of clan conflict between armed insurgencies and government forces.

Based on the aforementioned comprehension, the anthropological school focuses on the primordial factor as a causative factor in the collapsing Somali state. Proponents of this perspective are I.M. Lewis, Said Samatar, Anna Simons, and Okbazghi Yohannes. This traditionalist approach, spearheaded by I.M. Lewis, is based on the Segmentary lineage social system that is antithetical to the nature of the state. Lewis wrote, "The collapse of the colonially created state technically represents a triumph for the Segmentary lineage system and political power of kinship."[73] Said Samatar stretches the clan factor to a single overriding factor. He remarks, "Somali polity is shaped by a single, central principle that overrides all others, namely the phenomenon that social anthropologists call 'the Segmentary lineage system'."[74]Okbazghi Yohannes stretches further the concept of primordialism to the end. In his view,

> In the first place, there has never been a state in Somalia in the strictest sense of the term. Somalia is a country of clans where the beginnings of a modern state have been only in the making in the midst of capricious forces of history within the context of a unitary capitalist order and yet politically compartmentalized system. Ideally, the utter destruction of pre-capitalist decentralization and primordial traditions in Somalia and the concomitant convergence of basic institutions around the market exchange of historic necessity in order for the Somali State to complete its evolution.[75]

---

[73]I. M. Lewis, *Blood and Bone: The Call of Kinship in Somali Society* (Lawrenceville, Nj: Red Sea Pres, 1994), 233.

[74] Said S. Samatar, "Unhappy Masses and the Challenges of Political Islam in the Horn of Africa." Available from www. wardheernews.com/March_05/05 (accessed on February 2, 2017)

[75] Okbazghi Yohannes, *The United States and the Horn of Africa: An Analytical Study of Pattern and Process* (Westview Press, 1997), 225.

Resource Overextension

The Italian administration, during its 10 years UN trusteeship (1950-1960), failed to create an economic foundation for Somalia. It offered independence to the country in conflict with its neighbours and incapable to pay the salary of its employees. In order to survive, Somalia depended on foreign assistance and relied on Italian and British budgetary support of about 31% in the first three years of the independence. Exclusively, all development funds were either loans or grants from Western countries or from the Eastern bloc.[76] Moreover, trained human resources were very small. According to UN report on Somalia, "Three years prior to independence, there was not a single Somali medical doctor, professional pharmacist, engineer, or high school teacher in Somalia."[77] However, there were only 37 Somali students in the Italian universities in 1957-58, among whom 27 were expected to graduate in 1960.[78] Surprisingly, the leadership of the country, aware of their country's low capacity in terms of human and material resources, have made their priority to realize the "Greater Somalia Project", mobilizing scanty resources in achieving this objective. Ambassador Mohamed Osman was the only scholar who addressed the factor of the overextension of meagre resources. He examined leadership policy guidelines towards Somali unity and respectfully criticized them on their prioritization plan of national goals. He sees overextension as reducing the capacity of the state by undertaking too many tasks to be implemented too quickly. Osman asks the question of what should be the priority for the new Somali state, either consolidating the state or focusing on recovering the "missing three." He courageously writes that building domestic institutions should be the priority, without which all other plans falter. "Perhaps," He wrote,

> We devoted too much of our attention and resources to overcoming the disabilities, problems, and disputes which we inherited from our colonial masters and which, naturally, led us to involvement in external

---

[76] CIA World fact book, Somalia economic Development, 1960-1969. Available from http://www.photius.com/countries/somalia/economy/somalia_economy_econom ic_development~1607.html (accessed on January 25, 2017).

[77] Abdirahman Ahmed Noor,"Arabic Language and Script in Somalia: History, attitudes and prospects." PhD diss., Georgetown University, 1999, 52.

[78] Mohamed Osman Omar, *The Road to Zero: Somalia's self destruction* (HAAN associates, 1992), 45.

struggle, giving us no time to consolidate the gains of our national freedom by creating and development of the institutions without which no nation in modern times can survive.[79]

Injustice and Moral Degradation

Human history has evinced that when a society becomes morally corrupt, greed and selfishness prevail, the society becomes volatile, and inescapably the nation slides towards collapse. Morality is simply related to the principles of right and wrong behaviour and the goodness or badness of human character. Islamic perspective of rise and fall of the states and civilizations may be summarized in the following: Injustice (*Zulm*) which creates discord (*Khilaf*); and lack of rectification mechanism to prevent evil and command goodness (*Al-amr bil al-ma'ruf wa nahyi ani al-munkar*), which produces personal and social moral degradation (*Fasad*).[80] In the modern state context, injustice is prevented by the application of the rule of law and establishment of equal opportunity for all citizens of the state without discriminating them in faith, race, ethnicity, clan and gender. Then, application of justice promotes cohesion and prevents discords and social conflicts. Moreover, any disagreements are accepted and allowed to be debated and discussed through freedom of public speech and institutions of civil society and political parties. As such, following the constitution of the land which is, in the Somali context, compliant with the Islamic sharia, is considered good to be followed. The whimsical deviation from the Constitution should be seen as evil to be prevented by all individuals and society through various means. Corruption is a form of dishonest or unethical conduct by a person entrusted with a position of authority, often to acquire personal benefit. Corruption may include many activities

---

[79] Mohamed Osman, *The Road to Zero: Somalia's self destruction* (Haan Associates, 1992).

[80] There many verses in the Qur'an and many Hadith Narrations regarding injustice. For instance, "We sent aforetime our apostles with Clear Signs and sent down with them the Book and the Balance (of right and wrong), that men may stand forth in justice." - Surah Al Hadid (57), Aayah 25. (Qist, Adl)Surah Al Nahl (16), Aayah 90 says: God commands justice, the doing of good and liberality to kith and kin, and He forbids all shameful deeds, and injustice and rebellion: He instructs you that ye may receive admonition. Qudsi Hadith, "O My servant, I have forbidden injustice for Myself and forbade it also for you. So avoid being unjust to one another." [Muslim]

including bribery and embezzlement, abuse of public power or resources, extortion, soliciting or offering bribes, and purchasing votes. Moral corruption in Islam encompasses all forms of corruption that is forbidden in the Islamic Sharia. Few scholars, in the examined English written literature, focused on this factor. However, this concept is widely held by Somali Islamic scholars who trace all of the socio-political malady of the Somali state to moral degradation and the unprincipled expediency of the leaders. However, very recently others have appeared to voice the cultural dimension of the state's collapse. For instance, Ahmed Samatar wrote, "It is one of later arguments that at the heart of the Somali catastrophe is a full breakdown of culture (e.g., Heer, Islam)."[81] Of course, when Islam is mentioned, it means abiding by the transcendental law and morality that prevents transgression and all forms of corruption. Islam promotes social justice, equality, democratic values, and good governance. This author persistently explains how the indigenous ideologies – Islam and clan- were suppressed, perverted, and radicalized in the late 1970s. Therefore, he concludes that "Only Islam possesses the essential ingredients for successfully integrating the various elements of Somali society [Islam, clan, and the state] and providing a stable government capable of meeting the urgent social, political and economic needs of the country."[82] Moreover, he noted, "In the Somali situation, immoral state policies, including not offering enough weight to the Islamic factor, had finally produced the collapse of the state institutions."[83] Mark Huband also remarks that,

> Throughout the civil war, Somalia's religious leaders have argued that application of the Sharia as the sole route by which social order can be restored; they contend that the clan-based political structure, which endured colonialism and dictatorship, has failed to achieve a political resolution on a national level.[84]

The conception of morality and ethics, from an Islamic perspective, is not confined to individual spheres; it practically captures everything

---

[81] Ahmed Samatar, 129. Heer means Somali traditional laws on which social order is based.

[82] Abdullahi, *Tribalism, Nationalism and Islam*, 122.

[83] Abdurahman M. Abdullahi, "Recovering the Somali State: The Islamic Factor," *Somalia: Diaspora and State Reconstitution in the Horn of Africa*, eds. A. Osman Farah, Mammo Muchie, and Joakim Gundel (London: Adonis & Abbey, 2007), 196-221.

[84] Mark Huband, *Warriors of the prophet: the struggle for Islam* (Westview Press. 1998), 33.

that leads to the welfare of the individual or the society. For instance, in the social dimension, breaking the Islamic compliant Constitution of the land, usurpation of power and preying on the coffers of the state, and all forms of injustices are immoral and obnoxious. Conversely, all elements of good governance and social benevolence, establishing institutions that safeguard the security and welfare of the people are the highest moral values in Islam.

Eclectic Factors of the Collapse

Eclectic factors are based upon the fact that a single variable or factor is insufficient to cause the total collapse of the state. Thus, many factors had collectively contributed to the demise of the Somali state. Proponents of this position are many and include Bradbury, Geoge Kaly Kieth, Ida Rousseau Mukende, Ahmed Samatar, and Hussein Adam. When asked why Somalia collapsed so completely in relation to its neighbours, Bradbury answered,

> There is little value in identifying single, causal explanations for war and state collapse in Somalia. To focus solely on the contradictions between a foreign-imposed colonial system of government and an indigenous political system would be to overlook the impact of the oppressive, corrupt, and violent system of political patronage that marked the 21 year military rule of Mohamed Siad Barre (1969-1991), the influence of Cold War and post-Cold War politics in the region, the impact of structural adjustment and economic liberalization policies in the 1980s, and the character of the armed movements in Somalia.[85]

George Kaly Kieth and Ida Rousseau Mukenge articulated the complex causes of the collapse. They wrote,

> The Somali civil war is the product of the synergy of contingent and proximate factors. In the case of the former, the factors are the evolution of the Somali state, its incorporation into the global capitalist system, and the failure of the first experiment at state-building by the Somali compradors, who assumed the reins of

---

[85]   Stacy Feldman and Brian Slattery, "Living without a Government in Somalia: An Interview with Mark Bradbury Development Process in Somalia exist Not as a Result of Official Development Assistance, but in spite of it", Journal of International Affairs, 57, 2003

power when "flag independence" was granted. The latter factors are the repression, exploitation, economic deprivation, social malaise, and manipulation of primordial identities visited on Somalia by the dictatorial regime of General Mohammed Siad Barre.[86]

Hussein M. Adam criticized single factor analysis. He wrote,

> However, one cannot satisfactorily explain problems of political disorder by using an anthropologically determinist approach.... Recently, perhaps angered by this emphasis on primordial sentiment, some scholars have turned to class analysis within the context of global development and under development but have tended to fall into another form of single-factor analysis.[87]

Therefore, he advocates that Somalia collapsed because of "personal rule, military rule, clan rule, poisoning clan relations, urban state terror, neo-fascist campaigns against the north and dwindled international aid."[88] Professor Ahmed Samatar also organized causes for the collapse of the Somali state as follows, "A dictatorial regime which created a bad culture of governance, a lack of national leadership as a result of prolonged dictatorial rule, and low education and the poverty of the population as a result of the failed developmental programs."[89] Finally, David Rawson emphasizes the internal factors and Somali responsibilities for the state collapse citing following three causes: the internal dynamics of elite competition, the militarization of state institutions, and despotism of the regime.[90]

---

[86] George Kaly Kieth, and Ida Rousseau Mukenge, *Zones of Conflict in Africa: Theories and Cases* (Praeger, 2002), 124.

[87] Hussein M. Adam, "Somalia: Militarism, Warlordism or Democracy?" Review of African Political Economy, 54 (1992): 11-26.

[88] Hussein M. Adan, "Somalia: A Terrible Beauty Being Born?" In I. William Zartman (ed.), *Collapsed States: The Disintegration and Restoration of Legitimate Authority* (London: Lynne Reinne, 1995), 69-89.

[89] See the interview of Khalid Mao of professor Samatar in London in the last days of 2004 and published in the website http://www.kasmo.info/WareysiProfSamatar.php (accessed on January 2017)

[90] Divid Rawson, "Dealing with Disintegration: US Assistance and Somali State' in The Somali Challenge: From Catastrophe to Renewal? Edited by Ahmed Samatar London: Lyne Rienner Publisher, 19994), 147-178, 150.

Mapping Perspectives of the Somali State Collapse

The above perspectives could be organized in a number of related themes. It is noteworthy to mention here that although most scholars focused on one or more factors, nevertheless, they did recognize other factors. To reiterate, the major causes for the collapse of the Somali state produced in the perspectives of the scholars investigated above could be summarized as the end of the cold war and withdrawal of foreign aid, colonial division of the Somali people, Somali irredentism and war with Ethiopia, primordialism and rampant political clannism, moral corruption and cultural decay, overextension of resources, and failing to prioritize major objectives and eclectic factors. It could be said that most scholars tend to address the secondary causes of the collapse and they tend to focus on a particular factor based on the objective and circumstance of their research and their field of specializations.

Putting all factors in continuum, we classify them into three categories and each one had shown prominence in three historical periods of Somalia: from colonial incursion to independence of (1888-1960); from the independence to the war with Ethiopia (1960-1978); and from the war with Ethiopia to the state collapse (1978-1991). These categories are interconnected in a web-like way, and some of them have shown continuity in a progressive or regressing pattern. So, we should consider these three categories as a series of interconnected impulses and stages that indicate that the weak Somali state at the time of independence was moving in a negative direction towards a stage of failure. Original Causes or genesis include the colonial division of the Somali territory into five parts, and offering Ethiopia, in particular, a great portion of this territory; a further cause includes the social segmentation of the Somali society into small clan-based mini-states that lacked a unified national institution and collective leadership in their history. These two factors could be considered as the primary objective factors of the collapse of the state by causing the formation of a weak and deformed state. We may add to these two points, economic under development and lack of trained human resources to substitute colonial bureaucracy in running state institutions. The historical period of this condition is prior to and just after gaining independence in 1960.

Operational Causes may be considered the subjective factors that deepened the Somali conflict within itself. These causes include a plethora of factors such as: state policy in achieving national goals of

Somali territorial unity; the effect of the Cold War in the Horn of Africa theatre, which encouraged regional militarism; unresolved conflict with neighbouring countries (Ethiopia in particular); the low capacity of leadership; and socio-political and economic under-development. Moreover, military dictatorship and applications of rhetoric socialism and decadence of social and Islamic values also contributed greatly. These factors led the Somali state to move from a weak state to a failed state. This situation had continued since Somali independence in a variety of degrees until the defeat of Somalia in the war with Ethiopia (1960-1978). Proximate and Efficient Causes are direct causes of the collapse and include the war with Ethiopia and defeat of the Somali army, the end of the cold war and cutting of foreign aid, the continuation of militaristic clan-based dictatorship, the emergence of the armed factions, and lack of foreign patronages. It began with the Somali defeat in the war with Ethiopia, and continued until the total collapse of the Somali state in 1991. The following table shows factors of the Somali state collapse in its three categories and the time frame which each category has developed.

Historical Period and causes of the Collapse	Factors of the State Collapse
Original Causes (1880s-1960)	1. Colonial division of Somali territory into 5 parts 2. Social segmentation of the Somali society into clans 3. Economic under development and lack of trained human resources
Operational Causes (1960-1978)	1. Policy of irredentism (Greater Somalia) 2. Cold War and superpower rivalry in the Horn of Africa 3. Conflict with the neighbors and politics of militarism 4. Economic under-development 5. Injustice, corruption and moral degradation 6. Military dictatorship and political clannism
Proximate Causes (1978-1991)	1. War with Ethiopia and defeat of Somalia 2. Decline of nationalism and emergence of factionalism 3. The end of the Cold War and cutting foreign Aid 4. The civil war and armed factions supported by Ethiopia

Fig. 13. Cumulative factors of Somali state collapse

Conclusion

This chapter tracks the perspectives of the Somali state collapse, its genesis, and its operational and proximate causes. The paper outlines the trajectory of the Somali state formation from statelessness to statelessness, exploring briefly step by step its historical evolution. After that, theories of the state capabilities and conflict were explored, thus laying the theoretical framework of the state collapse. Following this, the chapter expose a number of perspectives expressed by different scholars. To conclude the objective of the chapter, these perspectives are classified and lumped into genesis, operational, and proximate within the chronology of the history of Somali formation. The analysis has shown that the modern Somali state is the product of a deficient system of governance that produced a deficient political, economic, and social system inadequate for the nature of Somali society. The governance system failed to accommodate all elements of Somaliness - Islam and clan culture- within a new hybrid system based on demarcated spaces and responsibilities. As a result, the colonial rulers left behind jubilant and proud Somalis on the day of independence in 1960, but also left a vulnerable society and a very weak state intoxicated with a highly nationalistic fervour and in conflict with its neighbours.

Examining most of the perspectives, it is evident that the collapse of the Somali state occurred in the process of searching its final state identity as perceived by the founding fathers of Somali nationalism. In the process, the meagre national resources were mobilized, and international support was sought to be channelled primarily to the realization of the national aspirations of establishing "Greater Somalia." In that course of action, civilian governments (1960-1969) pursued a moderate strategy in achieving the two Somali nationalist goals: weakening clannism and the Greater Somalia project, while the military regime radicalized its policies. This militaristic policy led to enter a devastating war with Ethiopia in 1977-78.[91] Regrettably, Somalia was not only humiliated in this war but also suffered great strategic defeat. The defeat of the Somali army in the war was indeed the beginning of the downfall of the very idea it was founded upon, that is Somali

---

[91] In the Somali –Ethiopian War of 1977-78, Cuban, East German, Southern Yemen and Russians forces had supported Ethiopian forces to dislodge Somali armed forces who had occupied more than 90% of Somali claimed territory.

nationalism. The impact of the war was catastrophic and instigated inward fighting between the government and the armed Somali oppositions supported by Ethiopia. It could be said that, strategically, Ethiopia succeeded in converting its war with Somalia into an internal Somali civil war that finally caused the breakdown of the Somali State.

In conclusion, the responsibility of the collapse of the Somali state lies primarily on the shoulders of the leadership of Somalia. The causes of the Somali state collapse are primarily due to internal factors, such as elite competition for political power and the harmful political culture of elites, such as despotism, corruption, clannism, and seeking foreign patronage. Seeing the collapsing state, both the ruling regime and the leaders of armed oppositions failed to find ways of preventing the state collapse. The collapse of the Somali state was the beginning of a new chapter in Somali history, being the collapse of the post-colonial state and the death of its constructed identity.

Further Readings

Kaly Kieth, George and Mukenge, Ida Rousseau. Zones of Conflict in Africa: Theories and Cases. Praeger, 2002.

Ibn-Khaldun, The Muqaddimah: An Introduction to History. Princeton University Press, 1980

Migdal, Joel. Strong Societies and weak states: State –society relations and State capabilities in the Third World. Princeton: Princeton University Press, 1988.

Rotberg, Robert I. State Failure and State Weakness in a time of Terror. The World Peace Foundation: Brooking Institution Press, 2003.

Samatar, Ahmed (ed). The Somali Challenge: From Catastrophe to Renewal? Lynne Rienner Publishers, 1994.

Yohannes, Okbazghi. The United State and the Horn of Africa: An analytical Study of Pattern and Process. Westview Press, 1997.

Zartman, William(ed.). Collapsed States: The Disintegration and Restoration of Legitimate Authority. Boulder: Lynne Rienner, 1995.

REFERENCES

Abdi, Sheikh Abdi. Divine Madness: Mohammed Abdulle Hassan (1856-1920. Zed Books, 1993.

Abdi Sheikh Abdi, "Ideology and Leadership in Somalia." The Journal of Modern African Studies. 19, 1, 1981.

Abdi, Sheikh-Abdi, Somali Nationalism: Its origin and Future. The Journal of Modern African Studies, Vol. 15, 7 (1977), 657-665.

Abd al-Qadir, Shiba ad-Din Ahmed bin. Futuh Al-Habasha: The Conquest of Abyssinia, translated by Paul Lester Stenhouse. No date.

Abdo Adou, Abdallah. "The Ethnic Factor in the National Politics of Djibouti." The Oromo Commentary, VOL. II, no.1, 1992.

Abdullahi, Abdurahman. "Recovering the Somali State: The Islamic Factor," Somalia: Diaspora and State Reconstitution in the Horn of Africa, eds. A. Osman Farah, Mammo Muchie, and Joakim Gundel. London: Adonis & Abbey, 2007), 196-221.

Abdullahi, Abdurahman. Tribalism, Nationalism and Islam: The Crisis of Political Loyalties in Somalia. MA thesis submitted to the Institute of the Islamic Studies, McGill University, 1992.

Abdullahi, Abdurahman. The Islamic Movement in Somalia: A Case Study of Islah Movement (1950-2000). Adonis & Abbey, 2015.

Abdullahi, Abdurahman. "Tribalism and Islam: The Basics of Somaliness." In Variations on the Theme of Somaliness, edited by Muddle Suzanne Lilius. Turku, Finland: Centre of Continuing Education, Abo University, 2001, 227-240.

Abdullahi, Abdurahman. Recovering the Somali State: Islam, Islamism and Transitional Justice. Adonis & Abbey, 2016.

Abdullahi, Abdurahman. "Somalia: Historical Phases of the Islamic Movements." Somali Studies Journal. Volume 1 (2016), 19-49.

Abdullahi, Abdurahman. "Non-State Actors in the Failed State of Somalia: Survey of the Civil Society Organizations in Somalia during the Civil War." Darasaat Ifriqiyayyah 31 (2004): 57-87, 65.

Abdullahi, Abdurahman. "Women, Islamists and the Military Regime in Somalia: The new family Law and its Implications." in Markus Hoehne and Virginia Luling (ed.), Milk and Peace,Drought and War: Somali Culture, Society and Politics. London: Hurst&Company, 2010, 137-160.

Abdullahi, Abdurahman. "Perspectives on the State Collapse in Somalia," in Somalia at the Crossroads: Challenges and Perspectives in Reconstituting a Failed State, ed. Abdullahi A. Osman and Issaka K. Soure, London: Adonis & Abbey Publishers Ltd., 2007.

Abdurahman Abdullahi (Baadiyow) and Ibrahim Farah, Reconciling the State and Society in Somalia. Available form https://www.scribd.com/ document/15327358/Reconciling-the-State-and-Society-in-Somalia.

Abdullahi, Mohamed. State Collapse and Post-Conflict Development in Africa: The Case of Somalia (1960-2001). Indiana: Perdue University Press, 2006.

Abdullahi, Osman. "The Role of Egypt, Ethiopia the Blue Nile in the Failure of the Somali Conflict Resolutions: A Zero-Sum Game." paper presented at the annual meeting of the International Studies Association, Hilton Hawaiian Village, Honolulu, Hawaii, March, 2005.

Abstracts in Anthropology, Volume 19. Greenwood Press, 1989.

Abukar, Ali Sheikh Ahmed. Judur Al-Ma'sat Al-Rahina. Bairut: Dar Ibn Hazm. 1992.

Achebe, Chinuwa. The Trouble with Nigeria. Heinemann, 1984.

Adam, Hussein M. "Somalia: A Terrible Beauty Being Born?" In I. William Zartman (ed.), Collapsed States: The Disintegration and Restoration of Legitimate Authority. London: Lynne Reinne, 1995.

Adam, Hussein M. "Somalia: Militarism, Warlordism or Democracy?" Review of African Political Economy, 54 (1992): 11-26.

Adam, Hussein M. "Somalia: A Terrible Beauty Being Born?" In I. William Zartman (ed.), Collapsed States: The Disintegration and Restoration of Legitimate Authority. London: Lynne Reinne, 1995.

Adamthwaite, Anthony. The Making of the Second World War. New York: Routledge, 1992.

Agarwal, Mamta. "Biography of Herodotus: The Father of History." Available from http://www.historydiscussion.net/biography/biography-of-herodotusthe-father-of-history/1389.

Ahmed, Christine Choi. "Finely Etched Chattel: The Invention of Somali Women" in The Invention of Somalia, edited by Jumale Ahmed. Lawrenceville: The Red Sea Press, 1995.

Ahmed, Christine Choi. "God, Anti-Colonialism and Drums: Sheikh Uways and the Uwaysiyya." Ufahamu: A Journal of African Studies, 17(2) 1989, 96-117.

Ahmed, Hussein. "The Historiography of Islam in Ethiopia," Journal of Islamic Studies, 3, 1992.

Ahmed, Zaid. "Muslim Philosophy of History", in edited by Aviezer Tucker, A Companion to the Philosophy of History and Historiography.Published Online, 2009), 437-445. Available from http://onlinelibrary.wiley.com/book/10.1002/9781444304916.

Ali, Abukar."The Land of the Gods: A Brief Study of Somali Etymology and its Historio-linguistic Potential." Available from http://sayidka.blogspot.co.ke/.

Ali, Ismail Mohamed. Somalia Today: General Information. Ministry of Information and National Guidance, Somali Democratic Republic, 1970.

Ali, Mohamed Nuuh. "History in the Horn of Africa, 1000 BC. - 1500 AD: Aspects of Social and Economic Change Between the Rift Valley and the Indian Ocean." A PhD thesis submitted to the University of California, LA, 1975.

Al-Najjar, Abdurahman. Al-Islam fi Al-Somal. Al-Qahira: Madba'at AlAhram Al-Tijariyah, 1973.

Anderson, Benedict. Imagined Communities: Reflections on the Origins and Spread of Nationalism. London: Veso, 1983.

Aram, Ben I. "Somalia's Judeo-Christian Heritage: A Preliminary Survey." Africa Journal of Evangelical Theology 22.2 2003.

Atlantic Charter. Available from file:///C:/Users/Abdurahman/Downloads/Atlantic%20Charter.pdf.

Banitalebi, Masoumeh; Yusoff, Kamaruzaman; and Mohd Nor, Mohd Roslan. "The Impact of Islamic Civilization and Culture in Europe during the Crusades." World Journal of Islamic History and Civilization, 2 (3): 182-187, 2012.

Bakano, Otto. "Grotto galleries show early Somali life", April 24, 2011.

Barbarosa, Duarte. A Description of the Coasts of East Africa and Malabar in the Beginning of Sixteenth Century. London: the Hakaluyt Society, 2008.

Bassey, Magnus O. Western Education and Political Domination in Africa: A Study in Critical and Dialogical Pedagogy. Bergin & Garvey, 1999.

Bebbington, David. Patterns in History: A Christian Perspective on Historical Thought. England: Inter-Varsity Press, 1979.

Bradbury, Mark. Becoming Somaliland. Progresso, 2008.

Barnes, Cedric. "The Somali Youth League, Ethiopian Somalis and the Greater Somalia Idea, 1946-48." Journal of Eastern African Studies Vol. 1, No. 2, 2007, 277-291.

Beevor, Antoby. The WW II. Little, Brown and Company, 2014.

Bell, J. Bowyer. The Horn of Africa: Strategic Magnet in the Seventies. New York: Crane, Russak 1973.

Ben-Dror, Avishai. "The Egyptian Hikimdāriya of Harar and its Hinterland" – Historical Aspects, 1875-1887." A PhD Thesis submitted to the School of History, Tel Aviv University, 2008.

Bertin, G. Bertin. Christianity in Somalia. Muqdisho: Croce del Sud Cathedral. Manuscript, 1983.

Borgwardt, Elizabeth. A new Deal for the World. Harvard University Press, 2007.Borodulina, T. On Historical Materialism (Marx, Engels, Lenin). Progress Publishers in the Union of Soviet Socialist Republics, 1972.

Brandt A. "The Importance of Somalia for understanding African and World prehistory", Proceedings of the First International Congress of Somali Studies in 1992.

Brandt, A. "Early Holocene Mortuary Practices and Hunter-Gatherer Adaptations in Southern Somalia". World Archaeology. 20, 1, 1988.

Briggs, Philip. Somaliland with Addis Ababa with East Ethiopia. Bradt Travel Guides, 2012.

Brons, Maria. "The Civil War in Somalia: Its Genesis and Dynamics" Current African Issues. 11, Uppsala, Nordiska Africainstitutet, 1991.

Brons, Maria. Society, Security Sovereignty and the state of Somalia: From Statelessness to statelessness. International books, 2001.

Brons, Maria. "The Civil War in Somalia: Its Genesis and Dynamics" Current African Issues. 11, Uppsala, Nordiska Africainstitutet, 1991.

Brown, D. J. Latham, "The Ethiopia-Somaliland Frontier Dispute". International and Comparative Law Quarterly, 5 (2): (1956), 245–264.

Bunson, Margaret. The Encyclopedia of Ancient Egypt. Gramercy Books, 1991.

Burton, Richard F. First Footsteps in East Africa. Biblio Bazaar, 2009.

Caqli, Cabdirisaq. Sheikh Madar: Asaasaha Hargeysa. Biographical Work on Sheikh Madar written in Somali Language, no date or publishing house).

Cassanelli, Lee and Abdulkadir, Farah Sheikh. "Somali Education in Transition." Bildhan, vol. 7, 2007, 91-125.

Cassanelli, Lee. The Shaping of Somali Society: Reconstructing the history of the Pastoral People, 1600-1900. Philadelphia: University of Pennsylvania Press, 1982.

Cerulli, E. Documenti Arabi per la Storia dell'Ethiopia. Roma: Memoria della Accademia Nazionale dei Lincei, Vol. 4, No. 2, 1931.

Cerulli, Enrico. Somalia: scritti vari editi ed inediti. Vol.2. Roma: Istituto poligrafico dello Stato, 1957-1964.

Chittick H. "An archaeological reconnaissance of the southern Somali coast", Azania, 4.

CIA World fact book, Somalia economic Development, 1960-1969. Available from http://www.photius.com/countries/somalia/econo my/somalia_economy_economic_development~1607.html.

Chirumamilla, S. U.S intervention in the Horn: Revisiting Ethiopia Somalia dispute, 2011, 189. Available from http://shodhganga.inflibnet.ac.in/bitstream/10603/1861/13/13_ch apter6.pdf

Clark, Grahame. World Prehistory: A New Outline. Cambridge University Press, 1971.

Clarke, Walter S. and Gosende, Robert. "Somalia: Can a Collapsed State Reconstitute itself"? In Robert I. Rotberg (ed.), State Failure and State Weakness in a Time of Terror. Washington: Brooking Institution Press, 2000, 129-158.

Colman, James. "Nationalism in Tropical Africa", In African Politics and Society, (ed.) Irving Markovitz. New York: The Free Press, 1970.

Compagnon, Daniel. "The Somali Opposition Fronts: some comments and questions", Horn of Africa, 1 & 2, 1990.

D, Nohlen; M, Krennerich; and B, Thibaut. Elections in Africa: A data handbook. Oxford University Press, 1999.

Dam, Mensel Longworth (translated and ed.). "The book of Duarte Barbosa: an account of the countries bordering on the Indian Ocean Asian Educational Services, 1989.

Del Boca, Angelo. Italiani in Africa Orientale: La caduta dell'Impero. Roma-Bari: Laterza, 1986.

De laet, S.J. (ed.). History of Humanity: Prehistory and the beginning of Civilization, Vol.1, first edition. Routledge, 1994.

De Waal, Alex. Class and Power in a Stateless Somalia A Discussion Paper, August 1996, 1. Available from http://justiceafrica.org/wp-content/uploads/2014/03/DeWaal_ClassandPowerinSomalia.pdf.

Elby, Omar. Fifty Years, and Fifty Stories: the Mennonite Mission in Somalia, 1953-2003. Herald Press, 2003.

Elper, Edward. "On Critique of the Somali Invention" in Ali Jumale (edt.), The Invention of Somalia. The Red Sea Press, 1995.

Eshetu,Salahadin. "King Nagash of Abyssinia." Available from http://dcbun.tripod.com/id17.html.

Ervin Rosenthal, Ervin. Political Thought in Medieval Islam. Cambridge University Press, 1962.

EU Institute for Security Studies, Understanding Africa Armies, Report no. 27. Published by the EU Institute for Security Studies and printed in France, 2016, 25-31.

Fakhry, Majid. A History of Islamic Philosophy (New York: Colombia University Press, 1983.

Farah, Ibrahim. "Foreign Policy and Conflict in Somalia, 1960-1990." PhD diss., University of Nairobi, 2009.

Finkelstein, Lawrence S. "Somaliland Under Italian Administration: A case Study of in United Feldman, Stacy, and Slattery, Brian. "Living without a Government in Somalia: An Interview with Mark Bradbury Development Process in Somalia exist Not as a Result of Official Development Assistance, but in spite of it", Journal of International Affairs, 57, 2003.

Fishel, John T. Civil Military Operations in the New World. Praeger, 1997.

Furay, Conal and Salevouris, Michael. The Methods and Skills of History: A Practical Guide. Harlan Davidson Incorporated, 1988.

Garner, Judith and Al-Bushra, Judy. Somalia: The Untold Story, the War Though the Eyes of Somali Women. London: Pluto Press, 2004.

Goldstone, Jack. Revolutions: A Very Short Introduction. Oxford University Press, 2014.

Graziosi, Paolo. "L'Eta della Pietra in Somalia: Risultati di una missione di ricerche paletnologiche nella Somalia italiana in 1935. Universitá degli studi di Firenze. Firenze: Sansoni, 1940.

Brereton, George Wynn and Huntingford, The Periplus of the Erythraean Sea.Ashgate Publishing, 1980).

Gutherz, X., Cros, J.-P., & Lesur, J. The discovery of new rock paintings in the Horn of Africa: The rock shelters of Las Geel, Republic of Somaliland. Journal of African Archaeology, 1(2), 2003, 227-236.

Haji, Aweys Osman and Haji, Abdiwahid Osman. Clan, sub-clan and regional representation 1960-1990: Statistical Data and findings. Washington D.C., 1998.

Hassan, Ibrahim Hassan. Intishar al-Islam wa al-Uruba fi ma Yali al-Sahra al-Kubra, Sharq al-Qarra al Ifriqiyyah wa Gharbiha. Cairo: Madba'at Lujnat al-Bayan al-Arabi, 1957.

Healy, Sally. "Reflections on the Somali state: What Went Wrong and why it Might not Matter." In Milk and Peace, Drought and War: Somali Culture, Society and Politics edited by Markus Hoehne and Virginia Luling. London: Hurst&Company, 2010.Hegel, G. W. F. and Leo Rauch, Leo. Introduction to The Philosophy of History: With Selections from The Philosophy of Right. Hackett Publishing, 1988.

Henze, Paul B. Layers of Time: History of Ethiopia. London: Hurst & Company, 2000.

Hersi, Ali Abdirahman. The Arab Factor in Somali History: The Origins and Development of Arab Enterprises and Cultural Influence in the Somali Peninsula. Los Angeles: University of California, 1977.

Hess, Robert. Italian colonialism. University of Chicago Press, 1966.

Hobesbawn, Eric. Nations and Nationalism since 1780: Programme, Myth, Reality second Edition. Cambridge: Cambridge University Press, 1992.

Hodd, Michael. East African Handbook: Trade & Travel Publications. Passport Books, 1994.

Hrušková, Alena. Comparison of US Foreign Aid Towards Somalia During and After the Cold War. Available from http://www.unob.cz /eam/Documents/Archiv/EaM_1_2014/Hruskova.pdf.

Huband, Mark. Warriors of the prophet: the struggle for Islam. Westview Press. 1998.

Huntingford, The Periplus of the Erythraean Sea. Ashgate Publishing, 1980.

Ibn-Khaldun, The Muqaddimah: An Introduction to History. Princeton University Press, 1980.

Ibn Khaldun. An Arab Philosophy of History: Selections from the Prolegomena of Ibn Khaldun of Tunis (1332-1406). Darwin Press, 1987. Idowu, Woo. Citizenship, alienation and conflict in Nigeria, Africa Development, Vol. 24, No. 1/2, 1999, 31-55.

Ilmi, Ahmed Ali. "The History of Social Movements in Somalia through the Eyes of Our Elders within a Diasporic Context." A PhD thesis submitted to Graduate Department of Humanities, Social Sciences and Social Justice Education Ontario Institute for Studies in Education, 2014.

Ingriis, Mohamed Haji. 'Sisters; was this what we struggled for?': The Gendered Rivalry in Power and Politics. Journal of International Women's Studies Vol. 16, No. 2 January 2015.

Ingiriis, Mohamed Haji. The Suicidal State in Somalia: The Rise and Fall of the Siad Barre Regime. University Press of America, 2016.

International Institute of Islamic Thought. The Essence of Islamic Civilization: Volume 21 of occasional papers.International Institute of Islamic Thought, 2013.

Isse, Aw Jama'a Omar. Taariikhdii Daraawiishta iyo Sayid Maxamed Cabdulle Xasan, (1895–1921). Wasaaradda Hiddaha iyo Tacliinta Sare, edited by Akadeemiyaha Dhaqanka, Mogadishu, 1976.

Isse-Salwe, Abdisalam M. The Collapse of the Somali State: The Impact of Colonial. Haan Publishing; 2nd edition (January 1, 1996.

Jabiri,Mohammed Abidi. Fikr Ibn-Khaldum: Al-Asabiyatu wa Dawlah. Dar al-Nashr al-Maghribiyah, no date.

Jackson, R.H. & Rosberg, C.G. 'Sovereignty and Underdevelopment: Juridical Statehood in the African Crisis'. The Journal of Modern African Studies, vol. 24 (1), 1986, 1-31.

Jackson, Peter. "Travels of Ibn Battuta", Journal of the Royal Asiatic Society, 264.

Jackson, Ashley. The British Empire and the WW II. London: Habledon Continuum, 2006.

Jama'a, Ahmed duale. The Origins and Development of Mogadishu AD 1000 to 1850: A Study of urban growth along the Banadir coast of southern Somalia. Repro HSC, Uppsala 1996.

Jama'a, Mohamed. An Introduction to Somali History from 5000 years B.C Down to the Present Times, 1962.

Jardine, Douglas. The Mad Mullah of Somaliland. London: 8vo., 1923.

Jean Strouse, Newsweek, Volume 69, Issues 10-17. Newsweek: 1967.

Jonsson, Sune. "An Archeological site file in Somalia." Proceedings of the Second International Congress of Somali Studies, University of Hamburg, August 1-6, 1983.

Kapteijns, Lidwien, and Maryan Omar Ali. Women's voices in a man's world: women and the pastoral tradition in Northern Somali Orature, c.1899-1980. Portsmouth, NH: Heinemann, 1999.

Kapteijns, Lidwien. "Women and Crisis of Communal Identity: The Cultural Construction of Gender in Somali History," in The Somali Challenge: From Catastrophe to Renewal? ed. Ahmed Samatar. Colorado: Lynne Reinner Publishers, 1994.

Kapteijns, Lidwien. "Ethiopia in the Horn of Africa," in The History of Islam in Africa edited by Levtzion, Nehemia and Pouwels, Randall L. Athens, Ohio: Ohio University Press, 2000.

Kapteijns, Lidwien. "The Disintegration of Somalia: A Historiographical Essay." Bildhaan: An International Journal of Somali Studies, Vol. 1, 2008.

Karp, Mark. Economics of Trusteeship in Somalia. New York University Press, 1960.

Klay.George and Jr Kieh, "Theories of Conflict and Conflict Resolution, in George Klay Kieh Jr and Mukenge, Ida Rousseau (eds). Zones of Conflict in Africa: Theories and Cases.Westport, Conn: Praeger, 2002.

Kaly, Kieth George and Mukenge, Ida Rousseau. Zones of Conflict in Africa: Theories and Cases. Praeger, 2002.

Keesing's Record of World Events (formerly Keesing's Contemporary Archives), Volume 13, November, 1967 Kenya, Somalia, Ethiopia, Kenyan, Somali, Ethiopian, Page 22386.

Kelly, S. Cold War in The Desert: Britain, the United States and Italian Colonies. Macmillan Press Ltd, 2000.

Kohn, Hans. The Idea of Nationalism: A Study in its Origins and Background. New York: the Macmillan Company, 1956.

Krais, Jakob. "Shakib Arslan's Libyan Dilemma: Pro-Fascism through Anti-Colonialism in La Nation Arabe"? Orient-Institut Studies 1 (2012).

Ibn Kathir, Albidaya wa Nihaya, volume 2 (Arabic)

Laitin, David D and Samatar, Said S. Somalia: Nation in Search of a State. Westview Press: 1987.

Laitin, David. The war in the Ogaden: implications for Siyaad's role in Somali history. Journal of Modern African Studies 17(1), 1979, 95-115.

Laitin, David D. Politics, Language, and Thought: The Somali Experience. University of Chicago Press: 1977.

Le Bon, Gustave. The world of Islamic civilization. Tudor Publication Co., 1974.

Lefebvre, Jeffery. "The US Military in Somalia: A hidden Agenda?" Middle Eastern Policy, 1:2, 1993.

Lefebvre, Jeffery. Arms for the Horn: US Security Policy in Ethiopia and Somalia 1953-1991. Pittsburgh: University of Pittsburgh Press, 1991.

Levtzion, Nahemia and Pouwels, Randall. The History of Islam in Africa. Ohio University Press, 2000.

Lewis, "The Ogaden and the Fragility of Somali segmentary Nationalism", Horn of Africa, 1&2, 1990.

Lewis, I.M. A Modern History of Somalia: Nation and State in the Horn of Africa. London: Longmans, 1980.

Lewis, I. M. "The Somali Conquest of the Horn of Africa," Journal of African History 5, no.1 (1964): 213-229.

Lewis, I. M. Saints and Somalis: Popular Islam in a Clan-Based Society. Red Sea Press,1998.

Lewis (ed.), I.M. Islam in tropical Africa (London, Oxford University Press, 1966.

Lewis, I.M. A Modern History of the Somali: Nation and State in the Horn of Africa. Ohio University Press, 2003.

Lewis, I.M. Saints and Somalis: Popular Islam in a Clan-Based Society. Sea Press,1998.

Lewis, Herbert. "The Origins of Galla and Somali." The Journal of African History, vol.7. No.1 1966.

Lewis, I.M. Blood and Bone: The Call of Kinship in Somali Society (Lawrenceville, Nj: Red Sea Pres, 1994), 233.

Lings, Martin. Muhammad: His Life based on the Earliest Sources. Inner Traditions, 2006.

Lockyer, Adam. Opposing Foreign Intervention's Impact on the Course of Civil Wars: The Ethiopian-Ogaden Civil War 1976-1980. A paper presented to the Australian Political Science Association Conference, September, 2006.

Luling, Virginia. "Come back Somalia? Questioning a Collapsed State" Third World Quarterly, 18:2 (1997), 287-302.

Luling, Virginia. The Somali Sultanate: Geledi city-state over 150 years. Transaction Publishers, 1990.

Lyons, Terrence. "Crises on Multiple Levels: Somalia and the Horn of Africa" in Ahmed Samatar (ed.), The Somali Challenge: From Catastrophe to Renewal? Lynne Rienner Publishers, 1994.

Lyons, Terrence and Samatar, Ahmed. Somalia: State Collapse, Multilateral intervention, and Strategies for Political Reconstruction. Washington: The Brooking Institution Occasional Paper, 1995.

Makki, Hassan. Al-Siyasat al-Thaqafiya fi al-Somali al-Kabir (18871986). Al-Markaz al-Islami li al-Buhuth wa al-Nashri, 1990.

Mansur, Abdalla Omar. "Contrary to a Nation: The Cancer of the Somali State," in Jumale (ed.), The Invention of Somalia. Lawrenceville: The Red Sea Press, 1995, 106-116.

Manning, Patrick. "African and World Historiography." The Journal of African History / Volume 54 / Issue 03 / November 2013, 319 – 330.

Marion, Francesco. Military Operations in the Italian East Africa, 1935-1941: Conquest and Defeat. MA thesis submitted to Marine Corps University Quantico VA school of Advanced War-fighting, 2009.

Martin, Bradford G. "Shaykh Zayla'i and the nineteenth-century Somali Qadiriya", in: Said S. Samatar (ed.), In the Shadows of Conquest. Islam in Colonial Northeast Africa. Trenton, NJ: The Red Sea Press, 1992.

Martin, Bradford G. "Shaykh Uways bin Muhammad al-Barawi, a Traditional Somali Sufi", in: G. M. Smith and Carl Ernst (eds.), Manifestations of Sainthood in Islam. Istanbul, 1993, 225-37.

Maxamad, Maxamad Ibrahin"Liiq-liiqato." Taariikhda Somaaliya: Dalkii Filka Weynaa ee Punt. Mogadishu: 2000.

Mayell, Hillary. "Oldest Human Fossils Identified". National Geographic news, February 16, 2005.

McGowan; Pat and Johnson, Thomas H. "African Military Coups d'état and Underdevelopment: A Quantitative Historical Analysis. The Journal of Modern African Studies, Vol. 22, No. 4. (Dec., 1984), 633-666.

McNeill, William H. Mythistory, or Truth, Myth, History and Historians. Available from https://www2.southeastern.edu/Academics/Faculty/jbell/mcneill.pdf.

Mehran, Kamrava, Understanding Comparative Politics: A Framework for Analysis. Routledge, 1996.

Menkhaus, Ken. "US Foreign Assistance Somalia: Phoenix from the Ashes?" Middle Eastern Policy, l:5, 1997.

Menkhaus, Ken and Prendergast, John. "Governance and Economic Survival in Post-intervention Somalia" in CSIS Africa Note, No.172 (May 1995).

Mesfin, Berouk, Situation Report, Institute for Security Studies, 2011. Available from http://dspace.africaportal.org/jspui/bitstream/123456789/32288/1/15Apr11Djibouti.pdf?1

Metaferia, Getachew. Ethiopia and United States, History, Diplomacy and Analysis. Algora Publishing, 2009.

Metz, Helen Chapin (ed.). *Somalia: A Country Study*. Washington: GPO for the Library of Congress, 1992.

Migdal, Joel. Strong Societies and Weak States: State-Society Relations and State Capabilities in the Third World. Princeton University Press, 1988.

Mire,Sada. "Mapping the Archaeology of Somaliland: Religion, Art, Script, Time, Urbanism, Trade, and Empire" (2015) 32:111–136.

Millman, Brock. British Somaliland: An Administrative History, 1920-1960. Routledge, 2014.

Mitchell, W. Journal of the Royal United Service Institution. Whitehall Yard, Volume 57, Issue 2, 997.

Mohamed, Hamdi. Gender and the Politics of Nation Building: (Re)Constructing Somali Women's History. Lambert Academic Publishing, 2014.

Mohamud, Mohamed Sharif. 'Abdirizaq Haji Hussein, Rais Wasara al-Somali (1964-1967), 2009." Availablefromhttp://arabic. alshahid.net / columnists/6110.

Moḥamud, Moḥamed Sharif. "al-Ra'is Ādan Abdulle Osman Awal Raīs li al Ja mhūriyah al-Somāliyah," 2009, available from See http://arabic.alshahid.net/columnists/1 458.

M-Shidad, Said. "The Ancient Kingdom of Punt and its Factor in Egyptian History", 2014.

Mukhtar, Ismael. "Milestones in the History of Islam in Eritrea." A paper delivered at the Eritrean Muslim Council's 6th annual convention held in Washington D.C. in July 2008.

Mukhtar, Mohamed. "Islam in Somali History.: Fact and fictions" in the edited book by Ali Jumale titled The Invention of Somalia. Lawrenceville: The Red Sea Press, 1995.

Mukhtar, Mohamed. Historical Dictionary of Somalia, New Edition. The scarecrow Press, 2003.

Mukhtar, Mohamed Haji. "Ajuran Sultanate." The Encyclopedia of Empire, 2016. Available from http://onlinelibrary.wiley.com/doi/10.1002/9781118455074.w beoe146/abstract.

Nakayama, Shigeru. "The Chinese "Cyclic" View of History versus Japanese "Progress." In Mittelstrass, Jurgen; Peter McLaughlin, Peter; Burgen, Arnold (ed.). *The Idea of Progress*. Berlin: Walter de Gruyter & Co., 1977, 65-76.

Nicole, David. The Italian Invasion of Abyssinia 1935–1936. Westminster, Maryland: Osprey, 1997.

Nkaisserry, Joseph K. "The Ogaden War: An Analysis of its Cause and its Impact on Regional Peace on the Horn of Africa." A thesis submitted to U.S. Army War College, Carlisle Barracks, Pennsylvania, 1997.

Njoku, Raphael C. The History of Somalia. Santa Barbara, CA: Greenwood, 2013.

Noor, Abdirahman Ahmed. "Arabic Language and Script in Somalia: History, attitudes and prospects." PhD diss., Georgetown University, 1999.

Ogot, Bathwel A. "African Historiography: From Colonial Historiography to UNISCO's General History of Africa."

Okoth, Assa. A History of Africa: African nationalism and the de-colonisation process. East African Publishers, 2006.

Oliver, Roland Anthony. History of East Africa, Volume 2. Clarendon Press, 1976.

Osterhammel, Jurgen. Colonialism: A Theoretical Overview. M. Wiener, 1997.

Otunnu,Ogenga. "Factors Affecting the Treatment of Kenyan-Somalis and Somali Refugees in Kenya: A Historical Overview. Available from ile:///C:/Users/Abdurahman/Downloads/21678-22090-1-PB.pdf.

Omar, Mohamed Osman. The Road to Zero: Somalia's Self destruction. HAAN Associates, 1992.

Omar, Mohamed Osman. The Scramble in the Horn of Africa: History of Somalia (1827-1977). Mogadishu: Somali Publications,2001.

Omar, Mohamed Osman. Somalia: Past and Present. Publications Pvt. Ltd, 2006.

Owens, Travis J. Beleaguered Muslim Fortress and Ethiopian Imperial Expansion from the 13th to the 16th century. A MA Thesis in Security Studies submitted to Naval Postgraduate school, 2008.

Pankhurst, Sylvia. Ex-Italian Somaliland. London: Watts, 1951.

Parker,Charles H. & Bentley, Jerry H. (ed.). Between the Middle Ages and modernity: Individual and community in the early Modern World. Rowman & Littlefield Publishers Inc., 2007.

Pastaloza, Luigi. The Somali Revolution. Bari: Edition Afrique Asie Amerique Latine, 1973.

Patman, Robert. The Soviet Union in the Horn of Africa: The Diplomacy of Intervention and Disengagement. Cambridge: Cambridge University Press, 1990.

Qasim, Maryan Arif.Clan versus Nation. Sharjah: UAE, 2002.

Rawson, Divid. "Dealing with Disintegration: US Assistance and Somali State' in The Somali Challenge: From Catastrophe to Renewal? Edited by Ahmed Samatar. London: Lyne Rienner Publisher, 19994, 147-178.

Reese, Scott S. "Patricians of the Banadir: Islamic Learning, Commerce and Somali Urban Identity in the 19thcentury.", A PhD Dissertation submitted to the University of Pennsylvania, 1996.

Roberts, Alice. The Incredible Human Journey. Bloomsbury Paperbacks, 2010.

Rotberg, Robert I. State Failure and State Weakness in a Time of Terror. The World Peace Foundation: Brooking Institution Press, 2003.

Rotberg, Robert I. Nation-state failure: A recurrence Phenomenon? (www.cia.gov/nic/PDF_GIF_2020_Support/ 2003_11_06_papers/panel2_nov6.pdf), 3-5

Rotberg, Robert I. "The Failure and Collapse of Nation-States: Breakdown, Prevention, and Repair," in Robert I. Rotberg (ed.), Why States Fail: Causes and Consequences. Princeton, 2004, 1-45.

Saeed, Abdallah. Islamic Thought: An Introduction. London: Routledge, 2006.

Sadler, Jr., Rodney "Put". In Katharine Sakenfeld. The New Interpreter's Dictionary of the Bible. Nashville: Abingdon Press, 2009.

Samatar, Abdi. The State and Rural Transformation in Northern Somalia, 1884-1986. University of Wisconsin Press, 1989.

Samatar, Ahmed. Socialist Somalia: Rhetoric and Reality. London: Zed Books, 1988.

Samatar, Ahmed. "The Curse of Allah: Civic Disembowelment and the Collapse of the State in Somalia" in Ahmed Samatar (ed), The Somali Challenge: From Catastrophe to Renewal? Lynne Rienner, 1994.

Samatar, Ahmed (ed.). The Somali Challenge: From Catastrophe to Renewal? (Lynne Rienner Publishers, 1994.

212

Samatar, Abdi Ismail. Africa's First Democrats: Somalia's Aden A. Osman and Abdirizak H. Hussen. Indiana University Press, 2016.

Samatar, Abdi I. "Destruction of State and Society in Somalia: Beyond the Tribal Convention,"The Journal of the Modern AfricanStudies30 (1992): 625-641.

Samatar, Ahmed. "The Curse of Allah: Civic Disembowelment and the collapse of the State in Somalia" in in Ahmed Samatar (ed.), The Somali Challenge: From Catastrophe to Renewal? Lynne Rienner Publishers, 1994, 117.

Samatar, Said. Oral Poetry and Somali Nationalism: The Case of Sayid Mohamed Abdulle Hassan. Cambridge: Cambridge University Press, 1982.

Samatar, Said. "Sheikh Uways Muhammad of Baraawe, 1847-1909. Mystic and Reformer in East Africa", in: Said S. Samatar (ed.). In the Shadows of Conquest. Islam in Colonial Northeast Africa. Trenton, NJ: The Red Sea Press, 1992, 48-74.

Samatar, Said. "Unhappy masses and the challenge of political Islam in the Horn of Africa." Available from http://www.ethiomedia.com/newpress/political_islam.html.

Samatar, Abdi Ismail. The state and rural transformation in Northern Somalia, 1884–1986. Madison: University of Wisconsin Press, 1989.

Savory, Roger. Introduction to Islamic Civilization. Cambridge University Press,1976.

Schoff, Wilfred H. The Periplus of the Erythraean Sea. London, 1912.

Schraeder, Peter. "From Irredentism to Secession: Decline of Pan-Somali Nationalism", In After Independence: Making and Protecting the Nation in Postcolonial and Post-Communist States edited by Lowell W. Barrington. The University of Michigan Press, 2006, 124-25.

Sharma, S. Politics of Tribalism in Africa. Delhi: Kay Printers, 1973.

Sharma, Tej Ram. Historiography: A History of Historical Writing. Concept Publishing Company, 2005.

Shelley, Fred M. Nation Shapes: The Story behind the World's Borders. ABC-CLIO., 2013.

Shiin, David and Ofcansky, Thomass. Historical dictionary of Ethiopia. The Scarecrow Press, 2004.

Shillington, Kevin (ed.), Encyclopedia of African History. Fitzory Dearborn Tylor and Farancis Group, 2005.

Shillington, Kevin. Encyclopedia of African history. CRC Press: 2005.

Strandes, Justus. The Portuguese period in East Africa. Kenya Literature Bureau, 1989.

St John, Ronald Bruce. Libya and the United States, Two Centuries of Strife. University of Pennsylvania Press, 2002.

Sutherland, Jonathan and Canwell, Diane. Vichy Air Force at War: The French Air Force that Fought the Allies in World. Pen and Sword Aviation, 2011.

Szanajda, Andrew. Making Sense in History: Historical Writing in Practice. Bitngduck Press LLC, 2007.

Terdman, Moshe. Somalia at War – Between Radical Islam and Tribal Politics, The S. Daniel Abraham Centerfor International and Regional Studies, Tel Aviv University, Research Paper No. 2, 2008, 27.

The Organization of African Unity, "Resolutions adopted by the first ordinary session of the assembly of the heads of the state and government," Cairo, UAR, from 17 to 21 July, 1964.

The World Bank, "Conflict in Somalia: Drivers and dynamics", January, 2005, 15. Available from http://siteresources.worldbank.org/INTSOMALIA/Resources/conflictinsomalia.pdf.

Galaydh, Ali Kkalif. "Notes on the State of the Somali State." Horn of Africa 13: 1 & 2, 1990.

Thompson, Vincent Bakpetu. Conflict in the Horn of Africa: The Kenya-Somalia Border Problem 1941–2014. UPA, 2015.

Touval, Saadia. Somali Nationalism: International Politics and the Drive for Unity in the Horn of Africa. Cambridge: Cambridge University Press, 1963.

Touval, Saadia "The organization of African Unity and Borders," International Organization 21, no. 1 (1967): 102-127.

Tracy Kup erus, Frameworks of State Society Relations, available fromhttp://www.acdis.uiuc.edu/Research/S&Ps/1994Su/S&P_VIII4/state_society_relations.html.

Trimingham, J. Spencer. "The Expansion of Islam," In Islam in Africa, edited by James Kritzeck, and William H. Lewis. New York: Van Nostrand-Reinhold Company, 1969.

Tripodi, Poalo. The Colonial Legacy in Somalia: Rome and Mogadishu: from Colonial Administration to Operation Restore Hope. Macmillan Press Limited, 1999.

UNDP-Somalia, Somalia's Missing Million; The Somali Diaspora and Its Role in Development. UNDP-Somalia, 2009.

Van De Mieroop, Marc. A History of Ancient Egypt. Wily-Blackwell, 2010.

Velho, Joao de Sa Alvaro. A Journal of the First Voyage of Vasco Da Gama, 1497-1499. Hakluyt Society, 1898.

Walker, R. When we ruled: The ancient and medieval history of Black civilisations. London, U.K: Every Generation Media, 2006.

Wanambisi, Tom. "The Somali Dispute: Kenya Beware". Marine Corps Command and Staff College, 1984.

Warmington, Eric Herbert. The Commerce Between the Roman Empire and India. The University Press, 1928.

Watterson, Barbara. The Egyptians. Wiley-BlackWell, 1997.

Wells, H.G. The World Set Free: A Story of Mankind. Macmillan and Co. Ltd, 1914.

Welsh, Sidney. Portuguese rule and Spanish crown in South Africa, 1581-1640. Junta, 1950.

Wilson, John. The Culture of Ancient Egypt. The University of Chicago Press, 1956. Whiteway, R.S. The Portuguese Expedition to Abyssinia in 1441-1543, 1902. Nendeln, Liechtenstein: Kraus Reprint, 1967.

Wolf, Eric and Eriksen, Thomas. Europe and the People without History. Berkeley: University of California Press, 2010.

Woodward, Peter.The Horn of Africa: Politics and International Relations. London: I.B. Tauris & Co. Ltd., 2003.

Yohannes, Okbazghi. The United States and the Horn of Africa: An Analytical Study of Pattern and Process. Westview Press, 1997.

Yunus, Muhammad Ahdul-Mun'im. AI-Somal: Wadanan wa Sha'ban. AI-Qahira: Dar al-Nahda al-'Arahiyyah, 1962.

Zeno, Muhammad Bin Jamil. The Pillars of Islam & Iman. Darussalam, 1966.

INDEX

CPSIA information can be obtained
at www.ICGtesting.com
Printed in the USA
BVHW040500050821
613445BV00003B/178